ALLEGHENY INTERMEDIATE UNIT
SUNRISE SCHOOL
550 AURA DRIVE
MONROEVILLE, PA 15146

MYSTERIES OF THE RAIN FOREST

THE EARTH, ITS WONDERS, ITS SECRETS

MYSTERIES OF THE RAIN FOREST

Reader's
Digest

PUBLISHED BY

THE READER'S DIGEST ASSOCIATION LIMITED

LONDON NEW YORK MONTREAL SYDNEY CAPE TOWN

MYSTERIES OF THE RAIN FOREST
Edited and designed by Toucan Books, Limited
with Bradbury and Williams
Written by Linda Gamlin and Anuschka de Rohan

The photo credits that appear on page 160 are hereby made a
part of this copyright page.

First English Edition Copyright © 1996
The Reader's Digest Association, Limited

Copyright © 1998 The Reader's Digest Association, Inc.
Copyright © 1998 The Reader's Digest (Canada), Inc.
Copyright © 1998 Reader's Digest Association Far East Limited
Philippine Copyright © 1998 Reader's Digest Association Far East
Limited

All rights reserved. Unauthorized reproduction, in any manner, is
prohibited

Reader's Digest, The Digest, and the Pegasus logo are registered
trademarks of The Reader's Digest Association, Inc. of
Pleasantville, New York, USA

Printed in the United States of America
1998

Address any comments to U.S. Editor, General Books,
260 Madison Ave., New York, NY 10016

Library of Congress Cataloging-in-Publication Data
Mysteries of the rain forest.
        p.   cm.– (The earth, its wonders, its secrets)
    Includes index.
    ISBN 0-7621-0110-5
    1. Rain forests. 2. Rain forest ecology. I. Reader's Digest
Association II. Series.
QH86.M97 1998
578.734 – dc21   98-21012
                          CIP

Front Cover   Tree trunks disappear into the canopy in the
Venezuelan rain forest. Inset: A diminutive squirrel monkey peers
out across a Central American rain forest.

Page 3   A golden eyelash viper searches for prey in a thicket of
Heliconia plants in an American rain forest.

CONTENTS

FOREST RICHES OF THE TROPICS

Hot and humid lowlands, cloud-draped mountain slopes and waterlogged flood plains are some of the varied terrains in the tropical rain forests. Even more striking is the variety of plant and animal life that scientists are only beginning to explore.

A thunderous roar signals the start of the storm. High above the forest floor, branches are whipped into movement by the wind, and pliant leaves tug at their stems, drawn by the gusting air.

At the base of the tree trunks, all is curiously still, almost as though the forest were holding its breath in anticipation. But as the first swollen raindrops beat down on the umbrella of leaves, there is no corresponding deluge on the forest floor, no cascade of water to reflect the torrent hammering down on the canopy, the unremitting curtains of water sweeping the tree tops.

Instead, there is a delay. Then, slowly, the water begins to percolate through the spaces in the foliage. It dribbles and drips its way down successive layers of the leafy maze, trickling down the trunks and oozing along stems. Insidiously, water creeps along the forest floor, soaking the leaf litter and saturating the soil.

As the storm passes, stillness and silence descend on the forest, broken only by the gentle tapping of water droplets rolling over the smooth, shiny surfaces of the leaves above and plopping downwards on their hampered journey to the ground. As the sun returns overhead, many of the raindrops evaporate before they reach the ground. Everywhere are vaporous mists rising from the leaves and hanging in the clearings. Gradually, insects resume their humming, whirring, chirruping backdrop of noise.

Water is the lifeblood of rain forests everywhere. It comes almost daily, drenching the trees, and feeding the streams and rivers that permeate the forest. More than 1 in (2.5 cm) of rain can fall in just 30 minutes. Some seasons are wetter than others, swelling the waterways and flooding low-lying areas of forest, but there is no dry season – the rain falls relentlessly all year round.

THE VITALISING RAIN

Much of the rain never reaches the ground at all. It is caught on the forest canopy and held there in mid-air by the multitudes of leaves, while the tropical heat that succeeds the storm turns it into steam. Rising above the forest again, as water vapour, it eventually reaches the cooler air high above the forest, and once more condenses into cloud.

STORMS OF WATER *Dark storm clouds unleash a downpour of torrential rain across the Amazon Basin (below). Forest streams become torrents during the rainy season (right).*

HANGING RAIN *The air of a tropical rain forest, such as this upland forest in Amazonia, is always humid. Water falls as rain and rises again as steamy vapour.*

Soon afterwards, the same water molecules may fall again as rain.

In effect, the thick canopy of the forest and the atmosphere above bounce the moisture back and forth between them, in an age-old rhythm of rainfall and evaporation which keeps the forests permanently damp, and the sky above a mass of cloud for much of the time. That cloud shields large tracts of the tropics from remorseless day-long sunlight, which would otherwise parch the ground and – by altering patterns of cloud formation and rainfall, winds and ocean currents – transport the climatic effects beyond the tropics, raising the temperature of the entire planet. Thus the surviving rain forests have far-reaching effects on the climate of the tropics as a whole, and that of regions far beyond.

RAIN-FOREST TYPES

Rain forests now cover 3.3 million sq miles (8.5 million km²), 6 per cent of the Earth's land surface. The main tropical rain forests are in Africa, South and Central America, South-east Asia, Australia and New Guinea.

The archetypal tropical rain forest is the tall, mature forest of the lowlands. It grows wherever rainfall exceeds 80 in (200 cm) a year, and where no month has less than 4 in (10 cm). Assuming the forest has never been cleared by human hands, this is known as primary lowland rain forest. Except on infertile sandy soils, such forest grows to impressive heights, with the largest trees standing 150-180 ft (46-55 m) tall.

These lofty columns seem to rise up against a veil of greenness. Each soaring trunk is draped with the twisted cables and ropes of vines and lianas, hung with curtains of mosses, and festooned with drooping leaves that sprout from the precarious tree-top outgrowths of orchids and ferns. At their base, many of the giant trees are supported by prop roots, like massive splayed legs, or by buttress roots – great triangular flanges, twice the height of a man, resembling the buttresses of medieval cathedrals.

TREE-TOP VIEW *Lofty tree trunks (left) rise like towering giants above the leafy undergrowth in an Amazonian rain forest. In Central Africa, chimpanzees such as this one (right) inhabit some areas of rain forest, hooting noisily from the canopy.*

In conditions that are as steamy and oppressive as in a hothouse, plants grow at an astonishing rate. Most keep their leaves all year round, replacing aging ones piecemeal, so there is a continuous dense cloak of greenery over the forest. The trees are like so many ornate minarets, each echoing to the eerie cries of unseen animals. The overriding smell is of composting leaves, an aroma of decay, freshened by the rain. Wafts of a heady, spicy scent catch the wind, the perfume of blossoms far above in the forest canopy luring insects to pollinate them.

Photographs alone do not convey the 'feel' of the rain forest, the myriad odours and sounds, the sweat and dirt, the chafing of damp clothing, the stifling, oppressive heat or the terror of disorientation in a sea of vertical tree trunks. The waymarks and signs are decipherable only by those people and animals who are intimate with the language of the rain forest.

At first, forest animals do not seem to be much in evidence, apart from their distant cries. At night, there are the repetitive chattering or droning sounds of crickets and cicadas, the incessant croaking of tree frogs, and the occasional scream or hoot of an owl. At dawn, the Amazonian forests reverberate to the roar of the howler monkeys, while the drier parts of the African rain forests are awakened by the maniacal yells and hoots of chimpanzees, followed by the croaking rattle of the colobus monkeys. But all these creatures are hidden, either camouflaged underfoot, or concealed, high above, by the crown of canopy leaves.

Many animals, such as the flying mice and the golden pottos of the African rain forests, or the flying lemurs of the Philippines, emerge only at night. Others, such as the sloth of the South American forests, the okapi of the Congo, or the chameleons of Madagascar, are such masters of stealth and camouflage that they can go unnoticed even when close at hand. In the African rain forests, the only warning of the proximity of a little red forest buffalo may be a low warning moo, scarcely audible.

To the uninitiated visitor, the rain forest gives an impression of immense, emerald stillness with ghostly inhabitants. To see most of its animal inhabitants requires patience and skill, although there are flashes of

GREEN CAMOUFLAGE *The mottled patterns on an eyelash viper's skin blend into the background, a palm leaf encrusted with lichens.*

eye-catching colour as a morpho butterfly streaks past, or as a hornbill, a trogon or a toucan flies overhead.

MONTANE FOREST

Where the lowland forests meet the foothills of mountains, the character of the rain forest changes, only subtly at first, and then much more obviously. The air, which is still moist with vapour, becomes more chilly. The humidity frequently condenses into mist, blocking the path of the sun's rays to the light-hungry foliage. There is less warmth and light to power plant growth, resulting in smaller trees, about 50-110ft (15-33m) in height.

This is montane forest, which begins at altitudes of between 3000 ft (900 m) and 6000 ft (1800 m) depending on the size of

A FLASH OF BLUE *A morpho butterfly's iridescent wings shimmer in a shaft of sunlight as it feeds on a juicy papaya in an American rain forest.*

the mountain or mountain range. The trees, being shorter, have no need of huge buttress or prop roots, although a few do have small buttresses. The thick-stemmed woody lianas of lowland rain forest are not in evidence, but there are other climbing plants. Epiphytes – plants that perch on tree branches, such as mosses, lichens, ferns, orchids and bromeliads – are abundant, favoured by the misty air which supplies them with a reliable source of moisture.

Lower temperatures slow down the rate of decomposition, and a thick mat of half-rotted leaves tends to form on the forest floor, in contrast to the sparse leaf litter of lowland rain forests. Nutrients remain locked up in these discarded leaves, and this too hinders tree growth.

UP IN THE CLOUDS

Rising higher still, the characteristic features of montane forest become more extreme. The wispy mist turns into thick cloud and is an almost constant feature. Hot damp air, rising from the lowlands, is the source of this cloud. The ascending air eventually reaches a point where it is so cooled by its altitude that the moisture condenses out into tiny airborne droplets. Seen from the lowlands, this appears as a flat-bottomed layer of cloud brooding over the mountain slopes from mid-morning until late afternoon. From within the forest, all that can be seen is an enveloping greyish-white curtain of fog. Such forests are known as 'cloud forest'.

They are gloomy and damp places, the tree trunks clothed in thick, ferny garments, their branches dripping with mosses and lichens. Disorientation is even more of a problem here than in the vast luminous greenness of a lowland rain forest. Tree ferns – which resemble palm trees but have lacy fern-like fronds – become increasingly important parts of the vegetation in some cloud forests, as do dense clumps of bamboo.

Animal life is more sparse than at lower

ON THE EDGE *Trees give way to mountain vegetation at the uppermost limits of the rain forest in Zaire's Ruwenzori Mountains.*

altitudes, and there are few of the noisy, brightly coloured birds that inhabit lowland rain forests. But for certain animals, such as the mountain gorilla of Central Africa, the cloud forests are their permanent home, a place of refuge, where the pace is slower and the battle for life waged largely with the elements rather than with other species.

Above 9800 ft (3000 m), there is elfin forest, a silent world of gnarled trees, hardly taller than a man. These misshapen ancients are constantly bathed in mist, their leaves tiny and as tough as leather, their growth imperceptibly slow. Lichens dominate here; the mosses, ferns and other epiphytes have given up the battle. This is rain forest at the edge of its territory, the last expression of its existence before it gives way to the sparser alpine vegetation of the mountain tops.

HEATH FOREST

On sandy soils, a special type of rain forest grows, called *keranga* in Borneo, *caatinga* or *campina* in Amazonia. These distinctive areas have differences in appearance and tree species, but enough similarities to warrant a common name: 'heath forest'. The trees are shorter than in normal lowland rain forest, and in the *kerangas* they have very slender trunks. Their lives are hard, for it is difficult

to extract nutrients from the sandy soil, especially if it is also acidic. Tree growth is slow, and leaves are precious, protected from insect attack with chemicals that encourage insects to look elsewhere for food.

Plants that have special means of supplementing the meagre supply of soil nutrients can flourish in heath forests, outstripping the competition. The trees often have a mass of small roots on the surface forming a 'root mat' that scavenges nutrients from dead leaves. At ground level, smaller plants include those that can trap and digest insects, such as the pitcher plants. These highly specialised carnivores drown insects in a pool of liquid contained within a slippery-sided pitcher. The dead insects yield up vital mineral nutrients such as nitrogen and potassium, which allow the pitcher plants to thrive in the inhospitable *kerangas*. Plants whose bulbous stems house ants' nests, and that gain nutrients from the ants' droppings, are also abundant in some heath forests.

SWAMP FOREST

Large areas of swamp forest occur in most of the world's tropical rain forests. Some are seasonally flooded, as in the *várzea* and *igapó* forests of Amazonia. Others, such as areas bordering large lakes, are simply low-lying zones that are waterlogged all year round. In the seasonally flooded forests in particular, trees endure conditions of extraordinary hardship. As saplings, they may have their topmost leaves out in the sunlight, above the floodwater, for only a few weeks of the year. As mature trees, they find their roots starved of life-giving oxygen by the water and silt. Through the process of natural selection, some trees have adapted, even to these seemingly intolerable conditions.

Palm trees are particularly successful in the flooded forests of Amazonia. The silk-cotton tree, source of the kapok once used to stuff children's toys, is also a species of the swamp forest. It has adapted to the rhythm of the flood by producing its lightweight, plumed seeds during the high-water season. The seeds are blown onto the water, then carried by meandering currents to distant parts of the forest, being stranded on damp fertile soil when the waters finally fall.

Yet another form of waterlogged forest is peat forest, where decomposition is slow because of unusual local conditions. The fallen leaves and other dead plant materials do not rot down, so a layer of rich brown peat, consisting of half-decomposed plant matter, builds up. As the peat accumulates, it raises the soil of the forest above the floodwater, so that the upper surface is no longer waterlogged.

MANGROVES – BETWEEN SEA AND LAND

At certain places along the coast, where rain forests meet the tropical ocean, mangrove trees venture out into the sea, creating a tract of dense inundated forest which, when seen from the air, blurs the edge of land and sea into a smudgy blue-green band. Known as a mangrove swamp, this is a strange place indeed, full of mosquitoes, tangled and impassable prop roots, and black stinking mud, a place where mudskipper fish come out on land to catch insects, monkeys come down to the shoreline to feed on crabs, tigers may hunt for young crocodiles and small spotted fishing cats descend from the tree tops to catch fish in the shallows.

The roots of the mangroves stand in briny water, and their trunks are inundated with every high tide. Clinging to the shifting mud at the edge of the land, the mangroves are among nature's specialists, growing in conditions that no other trees are able to tolerate. Stinging salt, choking mud, and the ebb and flow of the tides – all these challenges combine to try the mangroves to their biological limit. Yet still they survive, as long as their load is not increased by pollutants and oil spills.

NOSY BUSINESS *The strange drooping nose of the male proboscis monkey (below) straightens out when he makes his loud, distinctive honking call. Arrow-poison frogs (overleaf) are capable of producing lethal toxins from their skin, and so have few predators to hide from.*

Mangrove swamps provide protection against erosion for the tropical coastline, and are a vital refuge for many young fish, thus helping to maintain fish stocks. To a naturalist they are fascinating places, where rare animals such as the proboscis monkey, with its strange pendulous nose and its remarkable appetite for the tough toxic mangrove leaves, are found.

EXTRAVAGANT LIFE

The primary lowland rain forests are the magnificent towering cathedrals of life where the full potential of the rain forest is realised. The species richness is greatest here, with an undiscovered wealth of different life forms in every tree. Plant food is abundant, especially fruit and nectar, and insect food equally so, shown by the dense columns of army ants flushing out their insect prey as they march across the forest floor in thousand-strong raiding parties. The richness of plant and insect food creates a great variety of opportunities for other animals, from lizards and frogs to birds and mammals. Small and medium-sized animals are diverse and numerous.

Many are also colourful or extravagantly patterned, and spectacular courtship displays are seen in the rain forests, most notably among the birds of paradise which stage magnificent shows of colour, sound and movement. The vivid outsized beaks of the toucans and the extraordinarily long tail of the metallic-green quetzal bird are among the many other exuberant manifestations of rain-forest life. All this is an outcome of the largesse of the rain forests, which provide in such plenty for certain inhabitants – particularly the fruit-eaters – that they can afford, in evolutionary terms, to squander energy on lavish, colourful bodies and elaborate courtship.

Vibrant colour is also seen in many of the insects, and in the tiny jewel-like tree frogs. For the flower mantis, a type of praying mantis that resembles a large and pretty flower, the purpose is to entice insect prey, but for most small creatures bright colour is defensive, a warning of powerful toxins stored in the body, intended to deter potential predators. Life here is often fast and competitive, and the pressure from predators and

NO ESCAPE *Front legs, formidably armed with double rows of spikes, entrap a praying mantis's victim in a tight and lethal grasp.*

other enemies is intense. Everything is well defended, including the wood of the trees, which is laced with poisonous compounds.

The ferment of life in a tropical rain forest is one of the greatest natural wonders of the world. Much about the forests remains mysterious, for large tracts have never been studied in any detail. Yet those mysteries and wonders are being destroyed forever, and at an alarming speed.

When an acre (0.4 ha) of forest goes, thousands of unnamed and undiscovered species vanish with it into oblivion – and much else disappears as well. For the forest protects the soil beneath, shading it from the sun and shielding it from the direct power of the pounding rain, so reducing the chances of landslides and erosion.

Where the forest is removed wholesale – as a result of land clearance, for example – the soil is often rapidly lost, too. The rain that was formerly intercepted by the forest canopy and evaporated back to the atmosphere – accounting for as much as 75 per cent of the total amount of rain falling – now descends to the ground unimpeded. Floods occur downstream of the denuded area and streams are choked with silt, often killing the fish in them. Out at sea, coral reefs may be choked to death by the eroded soil from the forest floor. The rain forests are vital, and the Earth as a whole suffers from their destruction.

HIGH-LEVEL FEASTS *With an abundant food supply in the canopy, squirrel monkeys in the American rain forests rarely need to descend to the ground.*

FERTILE FORESTS

1

To the Light *Giant trees rise from lush undergrowth in the rain forests of Borneo.*

AN ABUNDANCE OF LUSH VEGETATION FLOURISHES IN THE WET AND WARM CONDITIONS OF THE WORLD'S TROPICAL RAIN FORESTS. GROUND-HUGGING HERBS AND SPROUTING SHRUBS ARE OVERSHADOWED BY THE NARROW CROWNS OF SPINDLY SAPLINGS. HIGHER STILL, STURDY TREES CATCH THE FULL POWER OF THE TROPICAL SUN.

TOWERING TO HEIGHTS OF WELL OVER 100 FT (30 M), THESE TREES CREATE A CEILING TO THE GREEN LABYRINTH OF THE RAIN FOREST. YEAR-ROUND LUXURIANT PLANT GROWTH PROVIDES THE CREATURES OF THE FOREST — FROM JAGUARS TO EXOTIC

Pool in a Plant *The rain forest is full of visual delights.*

BUTTERFLIES, ORANG-UTANS TO FLYING FROGS — WITH A TEMPTING RANGE OF FOOD SOURCES AND A MULTITUDE OF PLACES IN WHICH THEY CAN HIDE.

LIFE IN ABUNDANCE

The world's tropical rain forests support a huge diversity of life. The constant recycling of nutrients, together with year-round warmth and moisture, allows the lowland rain forests to rank as some of the richest environments on Earth.

One night in 1848, as he lay aboard a boat moored on a remote part of the Upper Amazon, the English naturalist Henry Bates was awakened by a sound 'resembling the roar of artillery'. Bates, a pioneer of rain-forest studies, was certain that the tremendous noise could not be man-made. 'The first explanation which occurred to me', he wrote later, 'was that it was an earthquake; for, although the night was breathlessly calm, the broad river was much agitated and the vessel rolled heavily. Soon after, another loud explosion took place, apparently much nearer than the former one; then followed others. The thundering peal rolled backwards and forwards, now seeming close at hand, now far off; the sudden crashes being often succeeded by a pause, or a long-continued dull rumbling. At the second explosion, the boatman awoke and told me it was a *terra cahida* or landslip, but I could scarcely believe him. The day dawned after the uproar had lasted about an hour, and we then saw the work of destruction going forward on the other side of the river, about 3 miles [4.8 km] off. Large masses of forest, including trees of colossal size, were rocking to and fro and falling headlong one after another into the water. After each avalanche, the wave which it caused returned on the crumbly bank with tremendous force, and caused the fall of other masses by undermining them . . . It was a grand sight; each downfall created a cloud of spray; the concussion in one place causing other masses to give way a long distance from it, and thus the crashes continued, swaying to and fro, with little prospect of a termination.'

These landslips, which occur from time to time on the steeper banks of the Amazon, dramatically illustrate the complex relationship between water and the rain forest. The incessant, drenching rain, combined with year-round heat and sunlight, creates almost ideal conditions for plant growth, producing a riotous proliferation of vegetable life that translates, over the centuries, into the towering magnificence of the rain forest. But the rain can also be an agent of destruction, threatening always to wash away the thin soil unless the trees cling tenaciously to it. It causes landslips on vulnerable slopes, swells the rivers into erosive torrents and, when accompanied by violent

FOREST RIVER *Rain forest grows thickly beside the Segama river in the Danum Valley conservation area of the Malaysian state, Sabah.*

SUNLIT VIEW *Warmed by the sun's rays, mist rises and escapes through a gap in the canopy of this Venezuelan cloud forest.*

sun's rays. The air is less still and less humid in the clearing. A new era has begun for this small part of the tropical rain forest.

ROOM AT THE TOP

Within days the unaccustomed sunlight has generated new plant life, as seedlings sprout from seeds long dormant in the soil. Spindly young saplings, waiting in suspended animation for just such an opportunity, suddenly surge into growth towards the light. There is an opening, a vacancy in the much-contested canopy above, and the race to fill it will go to the sturdiest, fastest-growing tree, the one that can also fend off insect attack and sustain the burden of creepers and vines that afflicts most trees.

It is not, however, a straightforward race. Initially there will be a short-term contest between the forest sprinters, the opportunists that can grow like smoke but that economise on resources by producing lightweight brittle wood, and so lack the strength or stamina to get beyond a certain height. They may be as tall as full-grown alders or birches in temperate climates, but in the context of the tropical rain forest they are Lilliputians. Nor could they survive anywhere else, for their roots and trunk are too insubstantial. They need the tall canopy trees around them to absorb the shock waves of the storms and create a protected, placid world.

These are short-lived colonists that achieve their full size within a few decades, flower and fruit, then die back as the more sturdy, slower-growing trees take over. The fact that they have not reached the top does

storm winds, topples the tallest and least stable of the forest giants. In some tropical regions, cyclones may fell whole swathes of forest at once, knocking down the massive trees like bowling pins.

Such spectacular mass destruction as Bates witnessed is unusual, but the destabilisation of a single mammoth tree during a storm is quite common. Its fall often brings down smaller neighbouring trees as well, or other giants that have become lashed to it by a mass of vines and creepers.

Their downfall leaves a gap in the forest canopy, and when the storm is over and the clouds have dispersed, the sun's rays penetrate to the forest floor, a rare and brilliant spotlight into this dim green world. Previously, little sunshine reached the ground through the interlocking leaves above – an intricate emerald jigsaw created by the canopy trees, and the smaller trees beneath them. Under this thick, unbroken covering of leaves, the water-sodden air hung heavy, dark and sultry. But now the searing brilliance of the tropical sun burns through the forest's deep green gloom.

Steam rises from the earth, as pearly white wisps of meandering vapour in the

PATIENT GROWTH *If a natural gap opens in the canopy, the Brazil-nut tree of the Amazon rain forest may grow up to 130 ft (40 m) or more.*

not matter: they have seeded and reproduced themselves, and that is enough.

In the shade of these opportunists, the sturdier saplings, species such as mahogany and teak, have been steadily building up their trunks and roots, preparing themselves for the long, hard haul towards the canopy, which may be 100 ft (30 m) from the forest floor. By the time the opportunists are dying back, these new contenders are ready to dominate the clearing: the sprinters have completed their race and the marathon runners take over.

Some of these aspiring giants did not germinate until the gap in the canopy opened, their seeds stirred into life by the novelty of bright light from above. Others had germinated years before, and grown several feet high, nourished mainly by the food reserves in the seed. The Brazil-nut tree favours this strategy, each of its huge nuts being packed with nutrients that give the offspring a good start in life. Once all the food in the nut has

been used up, the sapling scarcely grows at all but simply waits, holding its ground in the dank twilight of the forest basement, until a chance to develop arises.

IMPENETRABLE JUNGLE

Each of these arboreal power struggles – the sprint and the marathon – takes place in the midst of a more general skirmish, involving short undergrowth plants that suddenly flourish with the influx of sunlight. Adding further to the profusion are a variety of vines, creepers and other weak-stemmed climbing plants already rooted in the ground nearby. They now put out new growth – tender, twining young shoots and exploratory tendrils, all encouraged by the extra light to seek out fresh vertical

FOREST FLOOR *A break in the canopy has allowed dense undergrowth to spring up in this part of the Monteverde Reserve in Costa Rica.*

trunks and stems they can use to clamber upwards. These new outgrowths cling to most saplings and large plants (except those with defences against them) and smother the trunks of the fallen trees, compounding the clearing's mad confusion of vegetable life.

Within a few years there is true 'jungle' in this small area of the forest, an impenetrable mass of vegetation that deters intruders with dense, tangled thickets, rapier-like thorns, prickly foliage and chemical irritants. Such dense jungle clumps are recognisable inside the forest many years afterwards, showing where trees have toppled. Outside these areas, the forest floor is relatively open and easy to walk through – there is only a little plant growth at ground level because so much light is absorbed by the canopy. But jungle recurs wherever the canopy is broken – along the banks of rivers and at the edges of roads and man-made clearings – giving the impression of impenetrable forest to those who pass by.

This was the only impression gained by many early, river-borne explorers, some of whom were so thoroughly deterred by the riverside thickets that they made no inroads into the forest beyond. Thus the idea grew up that tropical rain forest was all 'jungle' that could be explored only by wielding a machete at every step. To some extent, this

---

VANISHING FORESTS

One in every five species of flowering plant is a tropical rain-forest tree. It will take at least another 450 years to identify and describe the remaining tropical species. If the current rates of forest clearance continue, most of these plants will be destroyed before they can be identified.

---

false view of the rain forest persists, kept alive by film-makers and comic-strip writers, for whom hacking-a-path-through-the-jungle has become an indispensable cliché.

THE POWER OF THE SUN

Fundamental to virtually all life on Earth is the fact that plants can make their own food. Remarkably, they do so from nothing but sunlight, water, mineral nutrients and carbon dioxide, the invisible gas that is part of the atmosphere everywhere. Sunlight provides the power for making food, hence the name of the process: photosynthesis, meaning literally 'creating with light'.

The intensity of the sun is greatest at the Equator, and rain, the second essential ingredient for photosynthesis, is available in superabundance in the tropical rain forest. Combined with ample carbon dioxide, and abetted by the tropics' steady warmth which puts no seasonal checks on growth, the plants of the tropical rain forest can grow at phenomenal speed, making these forests the vegetable powerhouses of our planet, with far-reaching effects on climate and atmosphere worldwide.

In the forest itself, growth is so fast that you can almost see it. Young *Cecropia* trees, opportunists that are the first to fill gaps in the Amazonian forest, grow as much as 8 ft (2.4 m) a year. Everywhere, just beyond the detection of the human eye, leaves are spreading, buds are swelling and unfolding, stems are thickening and fruits bulging. Eager tentacles of greenery climb upwards towards the light, expanding to fill gaps, capitalising on every chink of light in a frantic contest of vegetable life and death.

But the sheer opulence, the extravagance of it all, is in some ways deceptive. Steady inputs of sunlight and rain mean there is no check on plant growth, especially tree growth. In temperate zones, winter checks plant growth. In areas with a dry season, such as monsoon forest, the dryness halts all the plants for several months. In tropical rain forest, everything can just keep growing and growing. Growth requires mineral nutrients, so these tend to get used up, especially by the trees that 'lock up' a lot of nutrients in their massive woody trunks and branches. These nutrients are taken out of circulation for the lifetime of the tree.

The constant rain makes matters worse by leaching nutrients from the soil. Deep down in the subsoil, the weathering of rock (its breakdown into softer, penetrable subsoil) occurs at higher rates than in temperate regions. But the useful minerals released in this process do not easily reach the surface, as they would in most parts of the world. In

---

EXTRACTING NITROGEN

Rain-forest trees require 13 different mineral nutrients for growth, and those that are most often in short supply are phosphorus, potassium and magnesium. The rain, as well as leaching nutrients from the soil, tends to wash valuable minerals from the leaves themselves, especially potassium.

Nitrogen, which is scarce in many environments, is more readily available in most rain forests because there are so many thunderstorms. The electrical energy released during a flash of lightning helps along a reaction between nitrogen gas and oxygen, both of which are found in the atmosphere. The nitrogen oxide that results is washed into the soil with the rain

and can be taken up by bacteria and then by plants.

Nitrogen in the air is useless to most plants because it is in its simple, unoxidised state. However, some chemically skilled bacteria can take nitrogen directly from the air and turn it into useful nitrogen compounds that plants are able to absorb. This bacterial achievement is called 'nitrogen fixation' – the same term used for the effect of lightning on nitrogen.

Certain plants house these valuable bacteria in their roots, so taking maximum advantage of their nitrogen-fixing abilities. The pea family is noted for this, and there are many trees belonging to the pea family in tropical rain forests: they dominate the rain forests of

Amazonia. In Malaysia, some rain-forest trees even have nitrogen-fixing bacteria living in their leaves.

LIGHTNING NITRATES *A flash of lightning converts nitrogen into more usable compounds.*

any climate with a dry season, tree roots draw up water from the subsoil during the parched months, and this lifts up newly released minerals, dissolved in the water. Such upward movement replenishes minerals lost by leaching at other times of the year and eventually enriches the topsoil. In the tropical rain forest, the constant downward flow of water prevents this from happening, so there is far less input of minerals from the weathering of rock. The only other external source of nutrients is dust blown in from distant regions and dropped with the rain. Studies of Costa Rican rain forests have shown that nutrients are brought in on the wind from the shore of the Pacific Ocean, more than 50 miles (80 km) away.

Constrained by the shortage of nutrients, most rain forests run on a tight budget of careful use and re-use. Soil is ransacked by tree roots for every available nutrient molecule. In the forests that grow on the least fertile soils, branching roots and rootlets are so numerous that they form a thick 'root mat' on the surface, catching the nutrient bounty released from fallen leaves and other debris before it can even enter the soil. Such forests grow on the white sandy soils of Amazonia, which retain little nutrient matter because of their texture, and on the crests of ridges in Sarawak, Borneo, where nutrient leaching is maximised by the steep gradients.

In these rain forests with root mats, the total weight of roots per acre is almost ten

times greater than in rain forests growing on much richer soil. The weight of the plant matter above ground has to be reduced to allow for this extraordinary proliferation of the roots, but only by about 20 per cent. However, leaves are shed and replaced less often to economise on resources.

FRUGAL LIVING

After the fall of a tree, or the death of any other living thing, the nutrient hunger of the other forest life-forms – including fungi, termites and beetles – leads them to invade the decaying remains and extract the nutrients in them before these can be washed away by the rain. This self-interested scramble after resources creates a superefficient recycling process, in which the forest, taken as a whole, guards its nutrients with the utmost zeal.

Biologists in Venezuela investigated the fate of nutrient molecules by sprinkling small

ROOT MAT *A dense network of roots scavenges the leaf litter lying on the infertile soil of a Malaysian forest in a hunt for any available nutrients.*

BIZARRE INSECT *A giraffe-necked weevil, with its strange elongated head, feeds among the leaf litter of a Madagascan rain forest.*

amounts of calcium salts and phosphorous salts, both essential plant nutrients, over the root mat of an area of tropical rain forest. The calcium and phosphorus were in their radioactive forms, which are harmless in small amounts but make useful experimental tools because they can be detected using specialised instruments. By catching the water that percolated through the root mat, and assessing it with the instruments, the biologists could show how much of the calcium and phosphorus had been retained by the root mat, and how much had escaped.

They thought beforehand that the amount retained would be high, because the forest in question grew from extremely poor soil, but they were astonished at their results: only 1 per cent of the added nutrients had leached out with the rain. The tree roots had managed to seize 99 per cent, soaking it up from the passing liquid before it was washed away. Experiments in other forests have shown that this extremely high retention rate is not always achieved. More generally the rate is 60-90 per cent, but this is still high compared to forests in other parts of the world.

Fallen leaves do not rest for long on the floor of a tropical rain forest, unlike in temperate forests where they can take up to four years to disappear. In temperate forests, they form a deep layer of leaf litter which grades into a dark semi-rotted 'leaf mould' beneath. Tropical rain-forest leaves, by contrast, are rapidly broken down and re-cycled, surviving as short a period as four months, so there is never more than a sparse covering of leaf litter on the floor of a lowland rain forest. (Decomposition is slower in the cooler montane forests.) Where there is a root mat, the fine tentacle-like rootlets of a rain-forest tree may spread over and around an individual leaf, clutching it in a needy embrace to extract its nutrients directly.

In a matter of weeks or months, the dead things of the rain forest become part of the living once again. Whereas in a temperate forest many usable nutrients are contained in the leaf litter, leaf mould or rich crumbly soil, in some tropical rain forests almost all the nutrient wealth is contained in the forest's living organisms.

Paradoxically, the richest environments on Earth subsist on some of the most infertile soils. This explains the poor results when tropical rain forests are razed to make land for agriculture: in most areas, the pasture or crop yields are disappointing because the soil is so thin and infertile.

A FAIR EXCHANGE

When the slender roots of a tree grow around a leaf to soak up its nutrients they are generally not alone. In those tropical rain forests that grow on highly infertile soils, almost all tree roots have a microscopic accomplice, a fungus that lives its entire life in close companionship with the roots of that tree.

The fungus is made up of slim hairlike strands called 'hyphae'. In some cases these extend into the root and spread outside it as well, branching to form large bushy outgrowths. In other cases, the hyphae are matted together on the surface of the rootlet to form a socklike cover. Together the root and the fungus are known as a 'mycorrhiza', which literally means 'fungus root'.

However arranged, the function of the hyphae is the same. They massively increase the effective surface area of the root, allowing it to absorb far more nutrients from the surrounding leaf litter or soil. In particular, they boost supplies of phosphorus, usually the scarcest element for trees of the tropical rain forest. The fungus passes the nutrients into the tree root and the tree reciprocates by supplying the fungus with food, the simple sugary food produced by photosynthesis in the leaves and carried down the trunk to the roots. It is an excellent partnership. The tree leaves are harvesting the sun's rays at the roof of the forest, while the fungus is gathering the minerals at ground level, and each exchanges some of its harvested wealth for what the other can provide.

Other fungi, loners that do not need the shelter of tree roots, live in the soil or among the leaf litter. These have the power to break down dead plant matter into its constituent parts, something the tree roots and their intimate fungal partners cannot do. Until that breakdown has occurred the nutrients within are locked away as far as the mycorrhizae are concerned. They need their nutrients to be released into a liquid form, which they can soak up, rather like a sponge absorbing broth.

ROOTS EVERYWHERE

Even with these assiduous helpers in the soil, the trees are still hungry for mineral nutrients, and they have evolved some extraordinary adaptations for supplementing

FOREST FUNGUS *The fruiting bodies, or 'toadstools', are only part of a fungus. Extending far into the wood below is a network of unseen hyphae.*

their supply. Some rain-forest trees develop hollow trunks in old age, just as oak trees in temperate climates do. What is unusual is that rootlets may spring from the outer layer beneath the bark and grow inwards, penetrating the dying heart of the trunk, to absorb whatever nutrients are available there. Some of these minerals come from the decaying wood of the tree itself, released by the activity of termites and fungi. Other nutrients may be brought in by animals such as bats, using the hollow tree for shelter. Their droppings are a valuable fertiliser for the tree.

Roots sprouting from the branches of trees, more than 50 ft (15 m) above ground, may seem even more bizarre, but there are mineral nutrients here as well. In certain tropical rain forests, notably the cloud forests (the fog-shrouded rain forests of mountain regions), many small plants grow on the branches of trees high up in the canopy. These plants, known as epiphytes, do not draw nourishment from the tree, relying on it only for an aerial perch. They scavenge their own nutrients

ATLANTIC RAIN FOREST The Bracogrande river tumbles over rapids in one of Brazil's coastal – as opposed to Amazonian – rain forests. In a Costa Rican forest, even a fallen tree manages to sprout fresh roots in a bid to survive.

from dust settling on the branches with the rain. Many have a dense tangle of roots that act as a basket to retain the dust particles.

Over time, the epiphyte community has created its own layer of soil on the high branches, a mixture of living roots, dead and rotting roots, dust collected from the rain and other debris. In some forests, they

have built up a soil layer that is 6 in (15 cm) thick in the most favoured sites, such as the fork between two branches.

The roots that develop from tree branches penetrate this soil and tap into its mineral wealth. The largest of these roots may be 1 in (2.5 cm) in diameter and they branch into hundreds of tiny rootlets that

ATTRACTIVE SCENTS *Fragrant oils are extracted from orchids by male euglossine (or orchid) bees and then stored in pockets on their hind legs.*

are often associated, like those on the forest floor, with a fungus to form a mycorrhiza.

In some cloud forests, the trees shun the epiphyte soil and simply produce roots that hang from the branches into the space below the canopy. That such roots do not dry out is a testimony to the perpetual dampness of the air in the cloud forests. The fact that they are worth producing at all shows how valuable the wind-borne dust is to these nutrient-starved trees.

LIVING PARTNERSHIPS

The tree and the fungus that make up a mycorrhiza are separate species, creatures of a very different kind. Yet their survival and well-being are permanently entangled. One cannot survive without the other. Such relationships between plant roots and fungi are found the world over, but they assume a particular importance in the tropical rain forests where nutrient shortage is such a powerful check on plant growth.

Coalitions like this, between two distinct species that both benefit from the interaction, are known as 'mutualism'. The name symbiosis is sometimes wrongly used, but this is an umbrella term covering relationships of all kinds between species: from mutualism through commensalism (where creatures feed together but usually to the benefit of one partner only) to parasitism (where one gets all the benefits and lives on or in the other, sometimes to its detriment). These relationships grade into each other and there are no clearcut boundaries between them in nature. What is a mutualistic relationship today may become parasitism tomorrow, following a change in the conditions of life.

Mutualism is common enough in nature. Birds eat fruit and so disperse seeds, insects take nectar and so pollinate flowers. Established relationships of this kind form part of the network of living communities throughout the world, but in the tropical

rain forests they are far more common and achieve an extraordinary complexity. Some species are involved in two, three or even more mutualistic relationships.

The Brazil-nut tree is part of a web of relationships that involve dozens of other species in major roles. It is pollinated by female euglossine bees, also called orchid bees. These large insects are the only bees strong enough to open the heavy hood of the yellow Brazil-nut flower and search for nectar within, at the same time inadvertently collecting pollen and carrying it to the flowers of another tree.

The Brazil-nut tree could not set (produce) seed without the euglossine bees, but the bees themselves could not breed if it were not for orchids. The male euglossine bees visit a number of species of orchid, collecting fragrant oils from the flowers which they use to attract female bees. The bees mate communally, a swarm of up to 50 males gathering in a clearing and buzzing in the sunlight to

NEW WORLD RODENT *The dog-sized agouti belongs to a family of rodents that is unique to South and Central America.*

reinforce the signal given off by the warm, scented oil. In collecting the perfume, the bees pollinate the orchids. Thus there is a strong interdependence between these two.

All orchids have mycorrhizal roots, so the various species of fungus involved in these partnerships are also crucial to the Brazil-nut tree, albeit indirectly. The tree itself is dependent on various fungi, as most trees are, to obtain sufficient nutrients.

In order to disperse its seeds, the tree also depends upon the agouti, a very large, long-legged rodent, whose strong teeth

POLLEN CARRIERS *The euglossine bee at the top of this picture has visited a rain-forest orchid, and is now laden with a yellow packet of pollen, called a pollinium.*

enable it to gnaw through the armoured globular seed case that surrounds a ball of 12-24 Brazil nuts. The nuts within each ball have their own, relatively sturdy seed cases, which the germinating Brazil nut can crack open. But the seedlings cannot break through the outer case, which imprisons them and prevents them from growing into new trees – unless the agouti intervenes.

Although the agouti eats some of the seeds within each case, it buries others for future use. Some are inevitably forgotten and these can germinate and grow.

All these relationships involving the Brazil-nut tree – with agoutis, euglossine (or orchid) bees and so on – have evolved over long periods of time, probably several million years, with the partner species adapting to each other slowly over the passing generations, step by gradual step. It is a process known as coevolution.

The relationship may pass through various stages before reaching its present form, as is true of the agouti and the nuts. At one time, the Brazil nuts were probably enclosed in a relatively thin case and were accessible to a variety of forest animals that ate some seeds and, sated by the huge crop, cached (hid) others under ground. Among these animals were the ancestors of the agouti. As the trees evolved larger and more nutritious seeds, for stronger sapling growth, the incentive for animals to break into those seeds became greater and the Brazil-nut tree lost more and more of its seeds, with fewer being buried. However,

some trees happened to have thicker outer cases, which eliminated some small nibbling animals from the list of diners, and as these trees had more surviving seeds they left more offspring for the next generation.

In this way, thick outer seed cases evolved, but animals, including the ancestors of the agouti, were not completely excluded, and in time they evolved more powerful jaws, making the solid shells less troublesome. The trees in turn developed a thicker shell for the nuts, becoming more and more effective at keeping out seed-thieves. The evolving agoutis kept pace, and eventually became specialists in eating Brazil nuts.

As this 'arms race' continued, there came a point where the agouti was almost the only animal that was able to crack open the Brazil-nut case. The case, meanwhile, had become so thick and durable that it remained steely strong even after months in wet soil, and the seedlings could no longer break through for themselves. In order to germinate at all, the Brazil nut was reliant on the agouti – once its enemy, now its ally.

READY-MADE NESTS

Some partnerships are astonishing for the extent to which one partner (or sometimes both) has shaped its whole being and way of life to that of the other. The most noticeable thing about the *Myrmecodia* plant, found hanging from trunks or branches in the tropical rain forest of New Guinea, lies at the bottom of its stem – a massive bulbous base that dwarfs the leafy part of the plant. This 'tuber' is a warty, misshapen green ball with small reddish-brown ants scurrying about over its bristly surface. The ants appear from nowhere, travel short distances, then disappear down small holes that seem to lead into the plant tuber.

If this tuber is cut open, it is apparent that the small holes are entrances to hollow chambers within, some sheltering the eggs of the ants, others containing piles of ant droppings and debris. All the chambers are frantically alive with activity. The tuber is a ready-made nest, relieving the insects of the need to build their own accommodation. As if the plant had not already made things easy enough, it encourages the ants to move in by regularly providing little droplets of sugar higher up the stem of the plant.

The benefit of this relationship to the plant was not immediately obvious, but research by Dr Camilla Huxley of Oxford University proved conclusively that the plants were benefiting from nutrients in the ants' droppings and food debris. These are left in distinct 'latrine' chambers with an irregular, warty inner surface. This is specialised for the absorption of nutrients from the detritus that accumulates on the floors of the chambers. By growing the plants in controlled conditions, with or without the ants, Dr Huxley showed that growth is better when the ants are in residence.

Other plants and animals have moved in on the *Myrmecodia* plants and taken advantage of their resources. One plant, *Dischidia gaudichaudii*, that often lives alongside the *Myrmecodia*, on the same branch or tree trunk, audaciously extends its roots into the ant latrine chambers inside the tuber to tap the nutrient supplies there. Tiny round worms often live in the latrine chambers, along with beetles and fly maggots. In at least one area of the New Guinea forest, a small lizard of the type known as a skink lives inside the tubers. It raises its young there and feeds them on the ant larvae.

Most of these animals could live elsewhere, and so can the ant species typically found in *Myrmecodia* plants. Clearly, it is the plant that has made all of the effort in this relationship, as if it had deliberately set out to attract the ants and other creatures – proof of how hard it is for plants to gather mineral nutrients in tropical rain forests.

Other plants that shelter ants do so for protection against leaf-eaters or climbing plants. The ants can bite leaf-eaters or repel them with foul-smelling acid. The ants prevent climbing plants from securing a hold: they chew off any tendrils or stems that attempt to twine about their host plant.

The ants are, in effect, an insect Mafia, warding off potential threats but exacting a price for doing so. The plant provides them with living space and, usually, with some type of food. This may be droplets of nectar or more solid nutritious particles produced especially for the ants and pushed out from the flowers, stems or leaves of the plant.

The advantage of an ant, from a plant's point of view, is that it has a ferocious bite, often backed up by a chemical armoury, and it will fight to the death in defence of its colony. If that pugnacious instinct can be harnessed by the plant – which provides the ants with a nest and so becomes their territory to defend – the plant can be free of a great many leaf-eaters, particularly monkeys and other large grazers.

FAST LIVING

The African monarch butterfly (*Danaus chrysippus*) is inappropriately named; its range stretches beyond the African forests, to New Guinea, Fiji and Australia, and as far north as Japan. It is a deep brownish-orange

ANT PLANT *In return for protection against leaf-eaters, some acacias offer ants nest holes and food in the form of nectar (above) and protein-rich nodules, here being taken to the nest (left).*

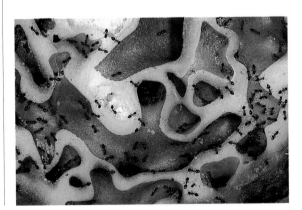

IDEAL HOME FOR ANTS
A slice through this Myrmecodia *plant reveals a colony of ants living in its hollow chambers.*

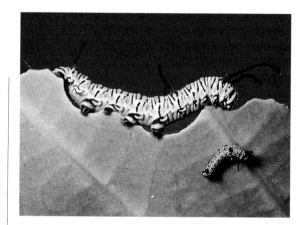

BAD TASTE *By feeding on toxic plants, caterpillars of the African monarch butterfly aquire the toxins and so gain protection from predators.*

in colour, with black edges to its wings and a row of snow-white spots across the black forewing tips. The presence of some powerful toxins in its body means that predators avoid it, and this helps to account for its impressive geographical range.

Studies of the African monarch butterfly have revealed that when it breeds in cool climates, as in Japan, it may sometimes need a whole year to complete its life cycle – a caterpillar that hatches in the spring takes 12 months to mature, change to its winged adult form, mate, lay eggs and produce young caterpillars of its own. In the rain forests of South-east Asia, however, the African monarch can, in the same time-span, complete 12 full generations. In the most favourable of conditions it may race through its life cycle in just 23 days.

This frenetic pace is possible because there is so much food for the taking, and because the high temperatures that speed up plant metabolism do the same for 'cold-blooded' animals such as insects. In fact, the term 'cold-blooded' is misleading and biologists prefer 'ectothermic', meaning that the temperature (*therm-*) of the animal is determined by external conditions (*ecto-*). In this, ectotherms differ from mammals and birds, which have internal bodily processes that enable them to maintain a steady temperature. In the tropics, an insect is quite as hot-blooded as a tiger or even hotter, and in chemical terms, warmer bodies mean faster

THE MEAT-EATERS: CARNIVOROUS PLANTS

While man-eating plants remain firmly in the realms of science fiction, plants that trap and consume insects do exist and they are particularly common in some tropical rain forests. In the rain forests of Asia, pitcher plants (*Nepenthes* species) are the dominant vegetable carnivores. They typically inhabit swampy peat forests, heath forests and mountainous ridge-crests with impoverished soil.

In all these sites, the soils are excessively leached or acidic, and are short of most nutrients, including even nitrates (the form of nitrogen most easily taken up by plants). Pitcher plants can survive here because they have evolved specially modified leaf traps which capture and digest insect prey – a rich, alternative source of nitrogen.

Some pitcher plants nestle on the forest floor, but others climb, lashing onto supports by means of tendrils at the tips of their new leaves. It is these same tendrils which later develop into the vertical, vase-like 'pitchers' that give the plants their name, each capped by a raised

lid to keep out excess rain. Insects are attracted to the pitchers by a pungent odour, or by the bright colours that frequently mottle their surface.

For an insect, the prime goal is the sweet nectar located just within the rim of a pitcher. But as it sets foot on the slippery neck of the vessel, the unwary insect is likely to tumble in, landing in a pool of liquid. Wet, struggling insects are usually unable to climb back up the smooth, waxy walls of their prison. Some species of pitcher also have backward-pointing hairs around their inner surfaces to ensure that insect traffic is one-way only.

Eventually, the doomed insect drowns. The liquid inside the pitcher contains enzymes which digest its body, and make available any nitrogen that was contained in the insect proteins. Other useful minerals, such as phosphorus and potassium, are also extracted. Complete digestion of a large fly can take about two days, and many bodies may accumulate in the base of the pitcher.

The collection of bodies attracts other creatures which feed on carrion and detritus. Occasionally, an inquisitive larger animal may fall to its death: *Nepenthes rafflesiana* has pitchers of 12 in (30 cm) in length, which sometimes trap and drown lizards or small mammals.

Remarkably, some creatures have adapted to survive and breed inside pitchers, evolving resistance to the corrosive enzymes. As many as 27 insect species were found thriving in a single type of pitcher from Penang in Malaysia, including aquatic mosquito larvae, and several of their predators.

DEATHLY TRAP *The gaping mouths of pitcher-plant traps wait for insects. Where the soil is poor, pitcher plants often thrive, immune from the nutrient shortage.*

HONEYMOON FLIGHT *After they have joined together, the male monarch butterfly carries off the female on a post-nuptial flight.*

chemical reactions, thus quicker growth and earlier adulthood.

All this speeds up the pace of evolution in the tropical rain forests. Evolution depends on natural selection, whereby some individuals produce more off-spring than others and increase their genetic contribution to the next generation. Useful genes tend to increase in the population.

Sexual reproduction mixes up the genes from different individuals and sometimes pro-duces winning combinations that give a boost to the evolu-tionary process. For any species that reproduces sexually, going through 12 generations in a year rather than one gives it far more chance of coming up with such combinations. Sometimes a genetic development of this kind allows an insect to exploit a new food source and this may, eventually, lead to the evolution of a new species.

THE SPICE OF LIFE

If variety is the spice of life, then tropical rain forests are, without doubt, the spiciest habitats on Earth. A temperate woodland usually has between 10 and 30 different tree species in an acre (0.4 ha), and the northern coniferous forests may have only two or three species in the same area. But the number in an acre of tropical rain forest will often be over 100 and sometimes 200 species. A single large tree in a tropical rain forest may house more than 50 species of ants and 500 species of other insects.

The range of plant and insect species fosters similar diversity in neighbouring populations of birds, reptiles, amphibians and mammals. In one area of the Peruvian Amazon, 90 species of frogs and toads all coexist in a few square miles – more than are found in the whole of the United States. The number of flowering plants that live in the whole of the British Isles is matched by the number found in about a square mile (260 ha) of tropical rain forest in Ecuador.

In fact, the exact number of species in the tropical rain forest is still hotly debated. It is a debate that engages all biologists be-cause it concerns the species richness of the whole planet. Before 1982, the total number of species on Earth was assumed to be about 2 million – 1.5 million were known to science; the remaining half million were an estimate of the undiscovered species. But that figure has been revised upwards, and dramatically so. Today, the estimate for the Earth's living species is anything up to 30 million. This expansion is entirely due to new information about rain-forest inhabi-tants: the insects, spiders and other small creatures without backbones (invertebrates) that live in the forest canopy.

The revised figures result from work on the insects of Panamanian rain forests, con-ducted by Dr Terry Erwin of the Smithsonian Institute. He devised a method for collect-ing all the insects in a particular tree, by fumigating it with an insecticide, then retrieving everything that had fallen to the ground. The insecticide is biodegradable, so it has no lasting effect on the surrounding forest, and the tree itself is not damaged.

Dr Erwin chose 19 trees belonging to the species *Luehea seemannii* and repeatedly re-turned to them over a period of three years, collecting all the insects each time. Looking at beetles alone, the number of species col-lected was staggeringly high: 1200 different kinds. Some of these – about 162 species – were probably unique to that species of tree; others were more versatile. By a complex series of calculations, guesses and extrapolations, Erwin arrived at an estimate of 30 million for the total number of tropical rainforest insects and spiders. This is obviously a 'round figure', and it so thoroughly dwarfs the 1.5 million known species that 30 million has become the official estimate, among those who agree with Dr Erwin's reasoning, for the total number of species on the planet.

Not everyone does agree, however. Some argue that the tree he studied came from a particularly large and common species, and that many other rain-forest trees would not yield as many unique insect species. But no one would now revert to the old estimate of 2 million species worldwide.

REASONS FOR DIVERSITY

An explanation for the tropical rain forests' richness of species is not difficult to find. In human societies, wherever there is wealth there is variety: in a rich country there may be 20 or more television channels, in a poor country only one. The same rule-of-thumb applies in nature, so that a richly productive, fast-growth habitat sports an extraordinary diversity of life.

From an evolutionary perspective, this diversity comes about in a number of different ways. The relationship between trees and leaf-eating insects – to take just one example – illustrates how diversity arises. Year-round tropical warmth not only favours insect reproduction but also means that there is no winter season to knock back numbers. Leaf-eating insects thrive and would readily strip the rain-forest trees bare of their leaves unless those leaves were well defended. Chemical defences have become very important and different plant families have specialised in particular types of chemical poisons. One family relies mainly on cyanides, for example, another on quinoline and quinazoline alkaloids. In addition, most have a cocktail of minor chemicals to back up the major poison.

Few such defences are invincible, however. Insects have evolved along with the trees, another example of coevolution, and they have, in the course of time, developed ways of overcoming a particular toxin. They overcome it, in most cases, by breaking it

down, using sets of specialised enzymes – chemical demolition teams that shatter the toxic molecule and render it harmless.

The enzymes that break down one type of toxin are, however, of no use against another kind. Each toxin requires its own specific enzymes. In a particular group of leaf-eating insects, such as moth caterpillars, any one species of moth cannot afford to evolve defences against more than one cocktail of poisons, and so it specialises in eating the leaves of a particular tree. Another species of moth will specialise in attacking another type of tree, and so individual species evolve from a single parent species, each with finicky eating habits and a highly specialised way of life.

Although a similar process happens in temperate woodlands, it does not produce

as much species diversity because the competitive struggle between tree and insect is not so intense, the climate being less benign to insect life.

A species of tree may, in the course of beating off these pests with novel chemical defences, itself evolve into two, three or more new species, each with a somewhat different mix of toxins. When this process of mutual diversity and specialisation is repeated for millions of years, the species count of both trees and leaf-eating insects inevitably increases.

DISTANT RELATIVES

The more diverse the trees in a forest become, the more distance there is between two trees of the same species. The 19th-century British naturalist Alfred Russel

PLANT MULTITUDE *The huge species diversity among rain-forest plants is not always obvious. Many of the numerous species in this Peruvian forest look similar.*

Wallace, describing the rain forests of South-east Asia, wrote:

'If the traveller notices a particular species and wishes to find more like it, he may often turn his eyes in vain in every direction. Trees of varied forms, dimensions and colours are all around him, but he rarely sees any one of them repeated. Time after time he goes towards a tree which looks like the one he seeks, but a closer examination proves it to be distinct. He may at length, perhaps, meet with a second specimen half a mile [0.8 km] off, or may fail altogether, till on another occasion he stumbles on one by accident.'

There are a few exceptions to this pattern, notably in the Congo, where large areas of rain forest are made up of a single species, the golden-barked *Gilbertiodendron*
dewevrei. Smaller areas where a single species dominates are found in parts of the Australian rain forest and in Uganda, Borneo and Guyana. But these are exceptions to the rule, and in most tropical rain forests each tree is likely to be surrounded by a crowd of alien species, and one of its own kind may be some distance away.

This arrangement is a side effect of species richness, but it also happens to be favourable to the tree because it prevents the numbers of a particular leaf-eating insect from reaching plague proportions. The caterpillars and other non-flying insects are marooned on a particular tree with nothing else in the vicinity that is (from their specialised point of view) edible. The flying insects may be able to move on, but they face the challenge of locating

the nearest tree of the same species, and not all will survive the journey. Small population explosions of leaf-eaters may occur, but they soon exhaust their host tree and fizzle out.

This side effect of species diversity helps in turn to maintain species diversity. This is well illustrated by the occasional clumps of a single tree species found in Malaysian forests, clumps that have been stripped bare of their leaves by a burgeoning insect pest. Sometimes such depredations kill the trees outright. Clearly, if one tree species evolves some particular adaptation that gives it a special advantage, and begins to outdo all other trees and dominate an area of forest, it will often be stopped in its tracks by the ravages of its insect enemies.

THE RICHES OF TIME

Coevolution is a slow process but one that constantly feeds upon itself, with each change in one species producing further changes in other interacting species. As some core areas of the tropical rain forests have probably survived, relatively unchanged in climate, for more than 100 million years, the opportunity for steady, cumulative coevolution has been enormous.

Variation and diversity have gradually built up over these aeons. The huge number of tree species in a tropical rain forest, which the insects themselves have helped to engender, in time creates an even larger variety of opportunities for insect species – not just those that feed on the leaves, but those that prey on the leaf-eaters or parasitise them, as well as those that pollinate the flowers or shelter under the bark, bore into the seeds or feed on the overripe fruit.

The diversity of plants did not produce the diversity of insects, nor vice versa. Together they produced each other. And they are only one small part of the complex web of coevolution that has created the tropical rain forests of today.

SIGNALS IN THE RAIN FOREST

Piercing the dark of the rain-forest night, fireflies send out their luminous messages in a private code, decipherable only by others of the same species. By day, parrots flash their brilliantly coloured wings, and shriek raucously to one another. For all rain-forest animals, from ants to elephants, the ability to communicate with others of the same kind is an essential part of life.

Animals communicate for a number of reasons: to maintain social contact with other members of their group, to broadcast the presence of food, to warn others of danger, to advertise territorial boundaries, or to make a threat. Most importantly of all, they communicate to attract a mate, and to

DANGER SIGNAL *The vivid colour of the strawberry poison-arrow frog wards off any potential predators.*

PROMINENT BEAK *A toucan's bill is useful for reaching fruit. The beaks also serve to identify one species from another.*

make absolutely sure that their potential partner comes from the same species.

Animals normally make their presence known by emitting sound, by putting on a show of colour, or by releasing potent chemical signals. But the tropical rain forest is dense and wet: scents are diluted, vision is restricted, and sounds are muffled by the thick foliage. To advertise their identity effectively, rain-forest creatures tend to be noisier or gaudier than their equivalents elsewhere. But along with such bold strategies comes the risk of attracting a predator. Sometimes, signals must be kept subtle – a compromise between

the need to be noticed, and the dangers that come with advertisement.

In the well-lit canopy, the use of colour and visual display is highly effective. Plants advertise to potential pollinators and dispersers by producing flowers and fruits of intense hues. In the rain forests of South and Central America, toucans (*Ramphastos*

LAST DEFENCE *If its leaf disguise fails, this katydid grasshopper flashes the eyespots on its hind wings to scare off predators.*

species) flaunt their enormous, flamboyant, multicoloured bills that are almost as large as their bodies. The beaks, like prominent identifying badges, clearly distinguish each toucan from the members of other toucan species, and make it recognisable from afar. More brutally, toucans also use their gaudy beaks to frighten smaller birds off their nests; they wave the bills around until terrified parent birds flee, then they gobble up the chicks. Toucans in the same flock wrestle and 'fence' with each other using their bills; this seems to be a form of play (toucans are very playful birds), with no aggression involved.

Identification, meanwhile, seems to be important in the colours of the uakari monkeys (*Cacajao calvus*) of Amazonia's swamp forests. They have hairless, scarlet faces that stand out boldly against their ginger fur, and may identify them to one another as they clamber through the tree tops.

Poisonous animals normally wear a permanent blaze of contrasting colours to warn potential predators that they contain toxins and should be avoided. The yellow and black patterns of wasps and bees are typical warning patterns, as are the vivid colours of the arrow-poison frogs of South America, and the beautiful markings of the heliconid butterflies. Wherever warning colours are found, harmless, edible creatures evolve accurate copies of the poisonous animals' coloration, thus gaining protection from predators by mimicry.

For some animals, particularly those in the dim lower reaches of the canopy, or those that operate by night, bright colours are not a worthwhile investment. Instead, they take on a typically brown or green camouflage, and rely upon sounds or scents for communication.

While the human nose is bombarded by the most obvious rain-forest odours, it is not usually sensitive enough to notice the subtle territorial scents that stake out boundaries. Ant colonies coat trees with their characteristic chemicals, while mammals might use urine, faeces or oily secretions to define their patch. Some of the smallest animals have the most sensitive odour-detection systems. Male moths can pick up the scent of pheromones (sex hormones) produced by a female several miles away. Few other animals can detect scents at this distance. For most it is a local means of communication.

Sound has some advantages over colour and scent, in that it generally travels over longer distances and can be turned off at once, should danger threaten. It is used by all kinds of creatures. Tiny cicadas produce an incessant shrill song, and tree frogs throw forth throbbing chirrups and bleeps from the balloon-like resonating chambers in their throats. Birds twitter and whistle,

PUFFED UP *A male red-eyed tree frog signals its presence deep in the rain forests of Australia.*

while monkeys shout, whoop and chatter. Orang-utans have learned the clever trick of pushing over dead trees: the crash, which carries much farther than their voice, probably attracts widespread attention to the bout of calling that follows.

The most famous of the rain-forest vocalists, however, is the howler monkey (*Allouata* species) of Central and South America. At dawn, howler monkeys produce a ferocious roar that reverberates through the forest and can be heard more than a mile away. This roar has been likened to that of a ferocious big cat. Its purpose is territorial: by broadcasting their presence in this way to other groups, the monkeys avoid any direct, aggressive confrontation with them.

FROM FOREST FLOOR TO TREE TOP

From the rotting leaf litter lying on the shaded forest floor to the sunlit leaves sprouting from towering tree tops, layers of light and intermingled vegetation provide an array of different niches in the rain forests where life can flourish.

A walk through a tropical rain forest reveals many curious sights. One of the more bizarre of these is a tree trunk, standing out strikingly from the others round it, because its bark is decorated with bunches of large and very beautiful white flowers. They are arranged here and there in drooping clusters, up to the level of the first branches. The flowers, springing from the dull, hard surface of the bark, seem incongruous, almost magical, as if picked from another plant and fixed to the tree.

When the first Europeans set eyes upon such a curiosity in 1752, they decided that the flowers must belong to a completely separate species, a leafless parasitic herb that they imagined was rooted inside the tree trunk and only protruded from its host to flower. They were wrong. A number of trees from the tropical rain forests bear their own flowers, and subsequently their fruits, on the trunk. The habit is known to biologists as 'cauliflory' – from the Latin *caulis*, 'stem', and *flos*, 'flower'.

The explanation for this odd positioning of the flowers only becomes obvious after darkness falls. As the light fades, and thousands of unseen tree frogs strike up their chirruping evening chorus, a strange smell begins to emanate from the flowers. The smell by no means matches their beautiful appearance. It is a powerful, musky aroma, combining the odour of sweaty feet with that of sour milk. This peculiar smell, distasteful and repellent to humans, is irresistible to certain bats. They are drawn from far and wide, swooping through natural passageways between the tree trunks to locate its source.

The flowers' scent resembles the musky fragrance of the bats' own bodies, so it has an inbuilt charm for these sociable mammals. But the bats also know that this smell promises large quantities of sweet, sticky nectar on which they can feed. While lapping up the nectar from one tree after another, they are unwittingly transferring pollen, carried on their fur from flower to flower.

HOVERING BAT *A bat feeds on the nectar of mucuna flowers. The flowers dangle below the canopy on long stems, allowing easy access for the bats.*

A great many cauliflorous trees are pollinated by nectar-sipping bats, and they often have their seeds dispersed by fruit-eating bats as well. With wingspans of 1-6 ft (0.3-1.8 m), bats need ample flying space to avoid damaging their membranous wings. They have difficulty manoeuvring safely through the tangle of twigs and leaves in the canopy, where most trees bloom. Flowers presented to them on tree trunks are in a more spacious zone of the forest, surrounded by negotiable air corridors.

Some bats are able to hover in front of their chosen flower, while others must cling to the trunk. Typical trunk-borne bat flowers are large, pale and trumpet-shaped. The hungry bat plunges its head deep into the flower to reach the nectar, becoming dusted with pollen as it feeds.

Certain other bat-pollinated trees produce flowers like shaving brushes that sprout from the lower branches on long flexible stalks and dangle downwards, clear of the foliage. Bats can reach these through aerial tunnels beneath the main crowns of the trees – passageways that are invisible from the ground.

THE THREE-DIMENSIONAL FOREST

Bats flying between the tree trunks in their search for nectar or fruit are moving horizontally through one layer of a complex, multilayered forest. A tropical rain forest can often seem like a disordered maze – a directionless labyrinth of column-like trunks, fallen branches, splaying roots and looping vines, capped by a confused mass of vegetation. But when the rain forest is analysed with an expert eye, and considered as a three-dimensional space, a remarkably well-balanced, if complicated, order emerges.

The most luxuriant of the lowland tropical rain forests have as many as five different layers of plants: ground-hugging herbs, shrubs, small 'understorey' trees, canopy-forming trees and the gigantic gangling 'emergent' trees that protrude above the canopy. Added to this are the soil and leaf litter, and the spaces between vegetation layers, such as the leafless zone through which the nectar-seeking bats travel. Not all the vegetation layers are

separated by 'empty' zones in this way: often the foliage of one layer grades imperceptibly into that of the next.

Sometimes, where a new road has been cut, or where the banks of a river have subsided and exposed to view a fresh cross-section, the strata of a tropical rain forest may be clear. But in general, mapping the structure is difficult, especially if the leaves of the different vegetation layers overlap. Complicating the issue further are the creepers and lianas, which traverse several layers, and the young trees which move up through the lower layers on their way to a final place in the canopy.

The canopy itself, since it is made up of such a large number of different species, is never completely even. It undulates greatly, causing the various layers that lie beneath it to be irregular in both their thickness and their distance from the ground.

FOREST LAYERS Vegetation in a tropical rain forest is divided into layers. The patchy upper layers contain the emergent crowns of mature trees. The densely packed middle layers shade the forest floor.

TAKE YOUR PICK Easily accessible, a trunk laden with figs offers a tempting feast to fruit-eating bats.

In all, this complex, layered forest offers a whole series of different living spaces, each of which presents its own opportunites and restrictions. There are shady layers and brightly lit stretches, tranquil sanctuaries and exposed windy tree tops, clear flyways and impassable thickets.

Layering is not unique to tropical rain forests, of course, but it reaches its greatest complexity here. Thanks to the unusual height that results from year-round warmth and moisture, tropical rain forests have room for additional plant strata beneath

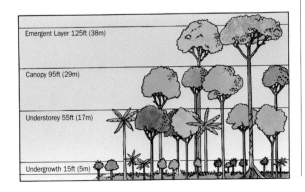

Emergent Layer 125ft (38m)

Canopy 95ft (29m)

Understorey 55ft (17m)

Undergrowth 15ft (5m)

LIFE IN THE CANOPY

A jaguar, frogs, monkeys and birds hover or perch in the middle layers of a South American rain forest. New rain-forest plants and animals are being discovered all the time.

1 Brazilian amethyst hummingbird
2 Salvin's Amazon parrot
3 Black spider monkey
4 Jaguar
5 Common squirrel monkey
6 Toucan
7 Gold and blue macaw
8 Black-headed squirrel monkey
9 Green tree python
10 Red-eyed tree frog
11 Postman butterfly
12 Topaz hummingbird
13 Arrow-poison frog
14 Bromeliad
15 Cotton-top tamarin
16 Cymbidium orchid

their tallest trees. They develop far more tiers of vegetation than in temperate or coniferous forests, and more than in the seasonal tropical forests. It is these extra layers of vegetation, each filtering out yet more of the sunlight, that make the lowest reaches of the tropical rain forest so dark and gloomy.

The most complex layered forests occur in the lowlands, and mainly on more fertile soils. In areas of declining productivity, the number of layers in tropical rain forests declines, and the montane (mountain) forests have fewer than lowland rain forests,

SPREADING THE LOAD *In areas where the soil is very shallow, buttress roots help to stabilise large trees by spreading their weight over a wider area.*

usually just two or three vegetation layers. Mangroves are even simpler in structure; they are often forests of a single vegetation layer, the mangrove trees themselves, which are uniquely capable of surviving in the sticky mud and fluctuating salty water.

LAYERS AND LIGHT

Light is the driving force behind the layering of the rain forest. All plants, except for totally parasitic ones, need light in order to make food, and the plants of the canopy and emergent zone, in particular, are involved in a never-ending struggle to reach the sun, competing with their neighbours for the best position. In the shaded world of the rain-forest interior, meanwhile, plants have evolved a vital ability to make do with less light that allows them to inhabit these lower storeys. Their different

light requirements are keyed to the different levels at which they grow.

Darkest of all is the forest floor, the bottom deck in the stratified rain forest. It is here that the trees send out their roots – most impressively, flared buttress roots that form curving flanks rising more than 6 ft (1.8 m) from the floor up into the shrub layer and beyond. They spread the weight of the tree over a wide area and thus help to stabilise its base. Although not all trees have buttress roots, for some species they are a vital aid to stability. Other species rely on stilt roots for added support; these are curved projections from the main trunk that arch down to the ground and embed themselves in the soil.

Warm, humid and protected from the wind, conditions for plant growth would be excellent here on the forest floor, were it

TREE ANCHOR *A scaffold of prop roots project from the trunk of this species of palm, giving the tree added support in wet areas.*

not for the dismal light levels – as little as one hundredth of the light striking the tree tops makes its way down to the forest floor. Not surprisingly, very few plants can tolerate this green twilight. Those that can are mostly small herbs with large, flat leaves.

The advantage of this existence is that there are fewer competing plants at such levels. However, even here life is not entirely without danger. If a gap forms in the canopy through the death of a large tree, the normally resilient undergrowth plants may die. They are so thoroughly committed to their shady way of life, so well adapted to it in their leaf construction and internal processes, that they are actually killed by too much light.

Beneath fallen logs, behind peeling bark and under the shelter of rotting leaves, the forest floor teems with life: ants, termites, beetles, millipedes, spiders, scorpions, worms and woodlice.

HIDDEN GROUND DWELLERS *A seething mass of centipedes are exposed by the removal of the covering layer of leaf litter from the forest floor.*

Fungi sprout as delicate cups and umbrellas of brown, pink, yellow or grey. These creatures, along with the invisible hordes of bacteria, underpin the cycle of rain-forest life, shredding and decomposing all that falls to the ground from the layers above, until it crumbles into its constituent elements to be recycled once again.

Some trees in the Malaysian rain forests produce their flowers, and later their fruits, at ground level, sprouting on long slender stems from the base of the trunk and drooping onto the forest floor. Exactly which species pollinate these trees and which spread their seeds is still unknown, although the flowers are probably visited by various ground-dwelling insects such as beetles.

Why the trees find it an advantage to flower and fruit at ground level is also still a mystery – as with much else in the rain forests.

ENCOUNTERS WITH UNDERGROWTH

Above the forest floor is a second vegetation layer made up of shrubs: woody plants with many stems sprouting from their base, rather than the single trunk that is typical of a tree. Among the shrubs, there may also be juvenile trees that have just started their ascent towards the canopy.

Many of the larger forest animals do not climb, but seek their food in the shrub layer and on the forest floor, browsing leaves, picking up fallen fruit and nuts, foraging for insects, or hunting other ground-dwellers. Since escape into the tree

tops is often impossible for them, many have evolved stealth, speed or camouflage as their protection from predators. Others emerge from hiding only under the cover of darkness.

In Africa, bush pigs, giant forest hogs and a variety of antelopes are typically found among the herbs and shrubs, browsing on their leaves or, in the case of the pigs and hogs, rooting for nuts and other food to be found in the soil. African forest elephants (*Loxodonta africana cyclotis*) and the rare

RING-TAILED COATI *This relative of the raccoon uses its long, sensitive nose and powerful forepaws to search the undergrowth for food.*

pygmy hippopotamus (*Choeropsis liberiensis*) are also occasionally seen. Both are significantly smaller than their savannah counterparts, probably an adaptation to moving through the denser forest vegetation.

Asia has no antelopes to browse the leaves of the shrubs, but their place is taken by deer and wild cattle. Bearded pigs, moonrats (relatives of the hedgehog) and tapirs roam the forest floor, avoiding the clouded leopards that stalk through the undergrowth. The Amazonian rain forest also has tapirs and several distinctive inhabitants unique to the New World, including long-nosed coatis and the pacas, capybaras and agoutis – three large, long-legged animals belonging to an unusual South American rodent group. Also found here are peccaries, American relatives of pigs that feed mainly on nuts. Any of these forest-floor animals may fall prey to the prowling jaguar.

DIMINUTIVE TREES

Overshadowing the shrub layer is the understorey, made up of spindly trees with long, narrow crowns. They receive only dappled sunlight, the rays that filter through the canopy, but they still thrive and grow, being far more tolerant of shady conditions than most trees.

Their branches interlock with one another, allowing animals to step from one tree to the next without returning to the ground. But the outer branches of understorey trees are not strong enough to support heavy climbing creatures, so large animals tend to avoid this layer. An exception is the

FISHING JAGUAR *At a forest stream in the Belize rain forest, a stealthy jaguar waits patiently before pouncing on its prey.*

orang-utan, a large ape of Sumatra and Borneo, which uses its great weight to sway the flexible understorey trees back and forth, employing them as moving bridges to catapult it into a neighbouring crown.

A gap exists between the top of the understorey trees and the towering canopy above. The trees stop suddenly, as if there were some good reason for not growing any higher. Studies of light in tropical forests show that this is indeed the case. Trees growing too close to those above would receive very patchy light, with parts of their crown being in constant shadow. By staying lower, they receive more evenly spread illumination and can make better use of the same quantity of light. The result is a relatively clear 'flying space' under the canopy – interrupted only by the occasional young tree, passing through, but destined for a higher plane.

THE RAIN FOREST'S ROOF

The canopy itself is a dense thicket of foliage that begins where the large trees start to branch, extending upwards from about 65 ft (20 m). Most canopy trees

average 100 ft (30 m) in height, but some canopies are even higher, attaining a maximum stature of about 150 ft (45 m). The canopy is the roof of the rain forest, made up of the broad, mushroom-shaped crowns of large trees and the branches that support them. For the bats it might be an impassable, interlocking web of snares, but for many rain-forest animals the canopy is home. It is the powerhouse, the most active, productive part of the forest because it is exposed to the full sun, and so most photosynthesis occurs here.

To maximise productivity, each canopy tree has an enormous photosynthetic surface – the leaf area of a mature tree may amount to ten times the area of the ground beneath it. Every leaf, twig, branch and tree crown is positioned to receive the maximum light. Since each leaf casts a shadow on the one beneath, they are spaced to minimise overlap. A leaf can be manoeuvred fractionally on its adjustable stem to slot between the others and glean a share of the rays piercing the rain-forest roof, as the sun moves on its daily path across the sky.

WATER DEFENCE *The leaves of many rain-forest species have a 'drip tip' (above) so that water does not collect on their surface. In the canopy (right), leaves are spread out to catch the sun's rays.*

Although canopy trees appear to be packed tightly together when viewed from above, there are actually significant spaces, sometimes several feet wide, between neighbouring crowns. The cause of this phenomenon, known as 'crown shyness', could well be abrasion by adjacent branches when these are whipped against each other during storms. Its effect is to isolate the tree tops from one another by a series of crevasses. These allow shafts of sunlight to pass through to the understorey, but also make travel between trees much more difficult for animals.

Despite the rich variety of species in the tropical rain forest, the leaves of the trees are all much the same shape. About 80 per cent of species have leaves that are elongated ovals, tapering to a long point known as a 'drip tip'. This tip is angled downwards and channels rainwater quickly from a leaf's shiny surface, ensuring that it stays relatively dry. This is important because a wet leaf loses precious nutrients through its saturated surface, nutrients that dissolve in the accumulated rainwater and then drain away. A puddle on the leaf surface may also encourage the filmy growth of mosses, fungi and microscopic algae, which block out the sunlight. These little plants that colonise a leaf are known as epiphylls, and they tend to become a particular burden for trees in mountain cloud forests, where the air is so permanently loaded with moisture that the leaves are constantly damp.

As leaves grow old, tattered by the wind or chewed by insects, they need to be replaced. In deciduous forests, such as those of the temperate zones, this happens every year in one massive, seasonal leaf fall, but in the evergreen rain forest it is less obvious. On any one tree, leaves may be lost and regrown singly in a continuous process, or discarded and replaced wholesale in sudden flushes of new growth on one or two branches. Some trees shed all their leaves in a sudden denudation, only to sprout a new set within days. Where many young leaves emerge at once they are particularly vulnerable to the ravages of leaf-eating insects while still in their tender early stages, and they may also be damaged by the withering glare of the tropical

TO THE TOP *The gecko (left) has specially adapted feet (above) that allow it to grip almost any surface, whether vertical trunks or the underside of branches.*

sun. The new leaves often emerge in lurid shades of red, yellow, pink or purple; these pigments screen out the harmful ultraviolet rays of the sun. The leaves are also bitter in taste, and as a result deter insects. The pigments in them may act as a fungicide as well.

The combined effect of the different patterns of leaf replacement is that the forest canopy retains its bright green, summery cloak all year round. This is interspersed only by the occasional stark, bare tree frame, where a member of the canopy has died or shed all its leaves, and by bright splashes of colour from young leaves, flowers or fruit. From the air, the canopy looks like an undulating carpet of intense green.

THE EMERGENT LAYER

Towering above the canopy are scattered 'emergent' trees – giants that overshadow the others, and are subject to the combined and furious powers of the searing sun, howling storm winds and pounding torrential rain. Their leaves are thicker than those of the canopy trees, and seldom have drip tips, because the moisture does not cling for long in such exposed conditions.

Emergent trees are among those that tend to drop all their leaves at once, often just before they burst into a brief but extravagantly prolific period of flowering. High above the forest, they are like beacons for their pollinators, whether bats, birds or insects. Losing their leaves just before they flower may make access easier for large pollinators such as bats.

Emergents are often enormous, spreading trees. In one tropical rain forest in Peru, the emergent crown of a single tree may cover ¼ acre (0.1 ha). Each emergent tree partially shades more than 100 smaller trees that grow beneath its sprawling branches.

AN AERIAL MENAGERIE

Animals gravitate to the foliage, flowers and fruits of the canopy. Its bounty attracts all kinds and sizes of creature, from the tiniest ants, beetles and spiders to lizards, frogs, squirrels, and much larger creatures that need the strength of the immense branches to support their weight

COMMON IGUANAS *These agile climbers of the South and Central American rain forests are mostly herbivorous, unlike other lizards. They can grow up to 3 ft (roughly 1 m) long.*

– the cats, monkeys, lemurs, porcupines, anteaters and sloths.

For those that cannot fly, reaching the canopy from the ground requires climbing skill. Some of the largest animals rely upon brute force, shinning up a trunk with their hind legs as they encircle it with their arms. Smaller animals scurry up the vertical stretches by fastening onto the rough bark with their sharp, curved claws.

Gecko lizards have a particularly ingenious adaptation for climbing: textured pads on their feet with many parallel furrows and ridges, the ridges being equipped with millions of microscopic bristles. These combine the force of suction with the grasping qualities of a plant burr, adhering to any surface, either smooth or rough, with surprising strength. As well as being able to glide effortlessly up vertical trunks, some can even travel along the underside of large branches, defying gravity with the power of suction. Tree frogs have evolved a similar adaptation in the form of enlarged discs at the tip of each toe, each one acting as a suction pad on any damp surface.

In order to make the most of the forest canopy's offerings, which are usually spread

ACROSS THE VOID *A squirrel monkey leaps between two tree crowns. These brightly coloured monkeys of the Americas are notable rain-forest acrobats.*

over a wide area, animals need to move around within the precarious world of the tree tops. All of them face hurdles and barriers in their daily movements, irrespective of the scale on which they operate. For a non-flying insect, the hurdle may be a small gap between leaves or twigs. For a large mammal, it may be gaping chasms between tree crowns in the canopy, created by the phenomenon of 'crown shyness'.

Routes connecting trees are rare, and those that exist become well worn. Animals memorise the best footpaths, remembering convenient gangways and underpasses, short cuts and launchpads. Should danger threaten, whole families of monkeys hurtle along the same path, leaping one after another from the same branch. The surfaces of the most popular branches quickly become rubbed free of moss and other clinging plants by the constant traffic of feet – from the scuttling of tiny shrews and mice to the heavier tread of iguanas or catlike civets.

BRIDGING CHASMS IN THE CANOPY

Moving across gaps at great height is a challenge met in several ways. Some animals can simply stretch across the void, making a bridge of their body. Snakes entwine their tail around a small branch and extend the front length of their body, rigid and locked, across to the next branch. A monkey with young may stretch across an aerial ravine

and hold still, allowing the baby to clamber along her back to safety. Weaver ants form a bridge of many bodies, those that make up the bridge staying in position, firmly gripping each other with their legs, while hundreds of their kin clamber across the abyss on this living walkway.

For animals of medium size, meanwhile, there is the option of leaping. Leapers include squirrels, lemurs and many monkeys, which characteristically have powerful hind legs, supple joints and grasping feet. They launch themselves into the air and land, sometimes on a small branch but more often sprawled across a mass of fine twigs and leaves on the outskirts of the next tree crown.

Jumping at such great height always carries risks, but falling seems to be part of everyday life for many animals. The smaller ones regularly plummet downwards, landing unharmed because they weigh so little, so that their impact on hitting the ground is fairly small. Some tiny creatures such as mice, upon whom gravity is least punishing, may even fall from a tree deliberately to escape a predator in pursuit.

Monkeys generally move along branches on all fours, gripping tightly and using their

TIME FOR A REST *Few forest animals can match the speed of gibbons who travel through the forest canopy by swinging swiftly from arm to arm.*

tails for balance. A completely different approach to travel has evolved among the apes, most spectacularly among the gibbons of tropical Asia and siamangs of Sumatra and Malaysia. They hang by their arms beneath the branches and, with apparent abandon, fling their bodies from one thin branch to another, catching first with the long right arm, and then with the left, often at death-defying speeds. Their highly flexible shoulder joints allow an enormous range of movement, and their long fingers provide a strong grip, unencumbered by the thumb, which has become shortened over evolutionary time. Their graceful, swinging mode of travel is known as 'brachiation' – from the Latin *brachium*, 'arm'.

Howler monkeys, woolly monkeys and spider monkeys have evolved something similar, although their shoulder joints are not quite so well adapted for this form of

HUMBOLT'S WOOLLY MONKEY *This American monkey hangs by its tail while using its hands to gather food. On the forest floor, it is capable of walking upright on its hind legs.*

movement. By way of compensation, they have grasping, prehensile tails, which are strong enough to take all of their bodyweight as they dangle, leaving their hands free to gather the food they need. The tail is so long that a spider monkey can hang by arms and tail simultaneously, yet have its body almost vertical.

There are some creatures for which leaping or swinging is simply too dangerous. Despite the extra effort involved, many of these prefer to return to the floor to reach another tree. Orang utans are the largest creatures to live permanently in the trees. Anything much larger, such as a gorilla, is obliged to simply make short visits there. All the largest climbers are highly

cautious, treading slowly and deliberately. To fall from a height for a creature this size would mean death, or terrible injury.

At the other end of the scale, some of the smallest animals are equally unlikely to attempt long-distance leaps. For them the reason is lack of power and speed. Small bodies have proportionately more surface area than large ones of the same shape. In the air, this means that they encounter more friction than larger ones, which slows them down.

Friction of this kind can be turned to good use. Some canopy animals maximise their surface area, and thus their air resistance, to enable them to glide gracefully between the trees, landing softly at their

journey's end. By making their bodies as flat as possible in the air animals can become living parachutes. They are gliders, rather than active flyers, although the names commonly used for them – flying squirrel, flying lemur, flying snake – mistakenly suggest otherwise.

SCRAMBLERS AND TWINERS

Trees are the structural framework of the forest and they are exploited as scaffolding by all manner of other plants. Climbers scramble up the natural trellises provided by the interlocking branches of the understorey in their quest for the sunlit layers of the canopy. In doing so, they save on the enormous energy expenditure required to

---

THE SECRET LIFE OF A HOUSE PLANT

The Swiss cheese plant (*Monstera*), found in homes and offices everywhere, has a much more adventurous existence in its native rain forest. There, it never remains still for long, but clambers from layer to layer, changing guise as it travels. A spindly *Monstera* seedling, bursting forth from its large seed, heads not for the light as almost any other plant would do, but for the nearest patch of darkness. This leafless shoot, extending some 6½ ft (1.9 m) from its seed, thereby usually encounters the dark base of a tree. From there, the plant begins to climb towards the

light, clawing its way up the tree trunk, and putting out roots to tap the soil for water and nutrients.

Its first leaves are small, about 1 in (2.5 cm) across, and arranged in a herringbone pattern, plastered flat against the bark, and overlapping at the base. In this way, the plant progresses through the layers of the forest, first freeing itself from the ground and its deep shadow, then elevating itself to the level of shrubs and small trees. Then, wherever the plant breaks through into patches of sunshine, its foliage undergoes a radical transformation. The leaves, previously small and heart-shaped, expand into enormous drooping leathery blades, held out on stems to soak up the sunlight. In the sunniest places, these can be 6 ft (1.8 m) long.

Monstera grows onward, snaking through the boughs, always seeking a better place to catch the sun.

SUPPORTED GROWTH *Sticky hairs help climbing plants of the Araceae family, which includes the* **Monstera,** *to grip onto their host trees.*

As a mature plant, it may cast off its ground-tapping roots and survive alone in the tree tops as an epiphyte, a plant that grows on another without using it for food. If water becomes scarce, the plant can send down new roots. At any time, *Monstera* is

SWISS CHEESE PLANT *The large leaves of the* **Monstera** *spread out to seek the sun.*

capable of returning to the ground to seek out another tree, reverting to an almost leafless stem as it descends.

IN SEARCH OF THE LIGHT
Stranglers and twisted lianas
surround a sturdy tree as
they wind their way up
towards the forest canopy.

produce a strong, woody trunk, and can invest more resources in leafy growth. The tropical rain forest is heaven for climbing plants; 90 per cent of all the Earth's species of climber originate here.

There are many different kinds of climber. The green-stemmed, short-lived varieties – such as the passion flower, various cucumber-like species and the morning glory – are collectively called vines, while the woody, longer lived climbers are known as lianas. But neither vines nor lianas represent a group of closely related plants. They come from all kinds of different families: there are climbing ferns, palms, pandans (palm-like trees and shrubs that come from South-east Asia), bamboos and a strange relative of the pines and spruces – a botanical oddity called the *Gnetum*, whose thick hooped stem twines loosely about the trunks of trees.

Climbing plants employ all kinds of methods in their ascent. Adhesive hairs may sprout from clinging aerial roots, while the stems of some species bear hooks, spines, bristles, adhesive studs or suckers. Some climbers simply lean clumsily on their neighbours, latching loosely onto any twigs and branches in their path. Some put out tendrils from their stem, which grope blindly for a slender twig and then spiral tightly around it, mooring the climber to its supportive pole. Others coil their entire stem around another plant, circling and firmly hugging its trunk.

Sometimes, their embrace is so tight that they become like a spiralling tourniquet, the supporting tree bulging outwards through the gaps so that it is eventually shaped into a barley-twist form.

Growth is extremely fast: some lianas extend their shoots at a rate of 6 in (15 cm) a day. Their strong, flexible stems come in many forms: looping cables, flattened ribbons or braided threads, and they function as climbing ropes for animals that are unable to clamber up the bark or hug the broader tree trunks. All climbing stems come with excellent plumbing. Wide vessels channel water from the ground to the canopy and store such a quantity of water that a cut length can often be used to quench human thirst.

Once they have reached the ultimate goal of the brightly lit canopy, lianas sprout a mass of foliage, spreading exploratory shoots in all directions over the tree crown, and smothering it with unwanted shade. Some shoots drop over the edge into the abyss that separates one tree from the next, while others, after persistent efforts, manage to bridge the gap. One enormous climber discovered in Panama had draped itself over no fewer than 64 canopy trees.

STARTING AT THE TOP

For many plants, the climb to the canopy is a slow struggle, and keeping contact with the ground is essential. But there is another option – to relinquish the ground altogether, surrendering its steady supply of nutrients and water for a more precarious life which begins and ends in the canopy.

Perched in the tree tops are whole gardens of smaller plants that have adopted this strategy: ferns and orchids, bromeliads, mosses, lichens, cacti, fungi and countless others. They are known as epiphytes. Unlike parasites, which sap supplies of food and water from their host tree, epiphytes simply use their tree for support, gaining the advantages of a seat near the sun without the need to invest in massive stem growth. Indeed, most never encounter the ground at all until the day when they finally topple to their death.

Reaching a suitable tree top in which to germinate is the first problem for an epiphyte. Not just any site will do. The fertile seed must land on a moist branch in the tree tops, not on a dry leaf, for instance, or in the dark of the forest floor. This is often achieved with the help of tiny, light and powdery wind-blown seeds that the plant produces in astronomical numbers. A single orchid seed pod can contain an astounding 3 million seeds. Chance ensures that at least some will land in an appropriate spot.

TREE HOUSES *Bromeliads –*
relatives of the pineapple – make
their home among the branches
of the sunlit canopy but take no
food from their host tree.

Orchid seeds are so tiny that they have no food reserves for the developing seedling. Instead, they make immediate use of the fungi that form mycorrhizae, partnerships of roots and fungi that, among other things, allow roots to absorb more nutrients

EXOTIC BEAUTIES *Orchids are among the most successful of the rain forests' epiphytes – plants that use trees for support but not for food.*

from the soil while the fungus obtains carbohydrates from the plant. Thus fungus and orchid root form a mutually beneficial relationship that scavenges nutrients from the surrounding area.

Epiphytes may be inconspicuous, flat sheets of green, forming a living veneer against the bark, or ostentatious clumps of spiky green and red leaves. There are drooping ferny tassels, small bushy shrubs, broad leafy baskets and enchantingly shaped orchids. Their luxuriant growth and sheer diversity give the impression that epiphytic life is an easy option.

In fact, the reverse is true. Conditions in the canopy are harsh and wildly fluctuating,

PARASITIC PLANTS — LIVING OFF OTHERS

Some plants are parasitic on other plants, using them not only as a means of physical support, but also as a source of food and water. They sap their host's vital supplies, and give nothing in return – much as a

FLOWERING MISTLETOE *Many mistletoe species grow as parasites in the rain forests.*

mosquito sucks the blood of a human or, on a more permanent basis, as a tapeworm remains entrenched in the gut of its host animal.

Some parasites grow in the canopy. These are collectively called mistletoes, although they come from a range of quite unrelated plant groups. Mistletoe seeds are deposited on branches in bird droppings, where they germinate very quickly, sometimes within hours. After growing there for a time as epiphytes, they penetrate the bark, tapping in to the tree's plumbing and stealing a consignment of the water and mineral nutrients destined for the branch on which they grow. The tree inadvertently acts as a substitute root system for the parasite, which manages to combine the advantages of an epiphytic lifestyle with the security of a constant supply of water and nutrition. However, mistletoes still do some of their own work – they have green leaves and can use the energy of sunlight to manufacture their own food, in the process known as photosynthesis.

Parasitic plants that live in the constant gloom of the forest floor do not attempt to make any food for themselves. Instead, they hijack sugar already made by the leaves of their host as it is transported down to

FLOWER POWER *Rafflesia, the world's largest flower, can grow to about 3 ft (1 m) across.*

the roots. Because they have no need to trap light, these parasites have forsaken the green pigment, chlorophyll, that colours most other plants; instead, they are either a blanched ivory or red in colour. Among them is the enormous *Rafflesia arnoldii* of Sumatra, which parasitises the roots of lianas.

particularly in the lowland rain forests. Temperatures may reach 32°C (90°F) when the sun shines, while humidity often falls below 60 per cent, which is perilously low by rain-forest standards.

Except in the cloud forest, where a perpetual fog hugs the foliage, water is surprisingly scarce for those in the upper canopy because the rain drains away from their roots so rapidly. Ironically, the epiphytic rain-forest plants, living as they do in an area of perpetual rainfall, suffer from some of the hardships that afflict plants growing in a desert. Many show similar adaptations with thick waxy leaves to reduce water loss by evaporation.

Apart from the general shortage, water supply is unpredictable in time and in space: the irregular, bumpy surface of the canopy can cause a 'rain-shadow' effect, whereby a large tree intercepts the moisture brought in by the prevailing winds, with the result that smaller trees immediately downwind receive far less rainfall. This can deprive the epiphytes on one tree of water, while others, only a short distance away on the rain-drenched side of a large tree, may be well supplied.

In addition to suffering from water shortage, epiphytes also have problems in finding sufficient nutrients, although they

WATER TANKS *Bromeliads colonise the branches of rain-forest trees (above). There, they accumulate water, creating small aerial ponds that prove valuable to the red-eyed tree frog (right) and other creatures of the canopy.*

have, over the centuries, accumulated their own layer of soil on the branches.

To overcome the first of these problems, epiphytes trap and store rainwater as it falls. Orchids store water in their plump leaves and bulbous stems, but can also extract droplets from the damp air that swirls about their roots.

Other plants create special funnels and tanks from their leaves. Staghorn ferns, for example, produce two different kinds of leaves. The first are broad with frilled margins, and are arranged in consecutive, overlapping whorls, rather like a cabbage or a lettuce, except that they form an open, funnel

FIT FERN An elkhorn fern, growing on a rain-forest tree trunk, captures water and nutrients with its bucket-like inner leaves.

shape instead of a closed ball. The other leaves are darker green and narrow, and they fulfil the normal functions of fern leaves: photosynthesis and spore production. The broad, frilly leaves exist simply to catch water within the funnel. They also trap some organic debris which provides the fern with extra nutrients. When the central leaves of the funnel die, they rot down, so providing recycled nutrients for new growth.

FUNNELS LIKE PINEAPPLES

Bromeliads, plants that are related to the pineapple, are major epiphytes of the American rain forests. They also form a natural funnel, but their leaves are arranged in a tight whorl of upright spikes. The pool that collects at the base of the leaves may hold as much as 2 gallons (10 litres) of water.

This is a miniature pond in the sky that teems with animal life, providing a welcome source of drinking water for thirsty lizards, birds and monkeys.

A bromeliad pond also traps leaf litter and other debris which decays and releases nutrients for the plant. Water and nutrients are soaked up by tiny hairs on the leaf bases. The roots, which would normally perform this task, are simple adhesive clamps, encircling the branch and maintaining a firm grasp.

Bromeliad roots and those of other epiphytes entwine and interweave, until the bark of the canopy branches becomes girdled by a second living coat, a turf made up of roots, plants and particles of decaying compost, where earthworms burrow and hundreds of other soil-living animals thrive.

Although the nutritional advantage to the tree of this epiphyte soil is significant, in other ways epiphytes are more of a burden to their arboreal host, encumbering its boughs with an additional weight that can amount to several tons. Eventually, the overladen branches may weaken and break, plummeting to the forest floor with their load of doomed epiphytes. Many

SMOTHERED TO DEATH
Roots of the strangler fig
encase its host tree (below)
and eventually kill it, leaving
the fig to stand alone (right).

trees, especially the more fast-growing species, continually shed their flaky bark, probably to rid themselves of troublesome epiphytes and clinging vines.

STRANGLING FOR A LIVING

A bird, replete from a banquet of figs, alights in the top of a nearby tree to preen and roost. As it perches, the bird defecates, producing a gluey package of tiny, gritty fig seeds that plummets downward. Some of the sticky seeds catch in the fork of a branch. There they lodge, nestled in the epiphyte garden. Through this garden crawl ants, beetles, centipedes and mites. Some of the seeds fall prey to their scavenging jaws, but one or two, soaked by the rain and warmed by the sun, push out a minute rootlet into the compost, and a tiny shoot that turns up towards the sun.

In its elevated seedbed, one of the tiny fig plants escapes the attentions of leaf-eating insects, grows larger and slowly becomes established, putting forth one leaf after another and drawing nutrients from its aerial supply of soil.

Eventually, it becomes a small bush, cramped in its natural container and rapidly using up the limited supply of nutrients and water found there. With enough foliage now to generate plentiful food and thus to fuel new growth, the juvenile fig sends searching roots out over its branch in the tree top. They are slender roots, but tough ones, that cling to the trunk and grow rapidly towards the ground.

As the first roots contact the soil, they tap into a supply of water and, in the more fertile forests, some nutrients. The new contact with the ground enables the fig

TREE-LIKE FUNGI *Fungi and other decomposers play an important role in forest life.*

DEADMAN'S FINGERS *Many fungi flourish in the rain forest. They grow on fallen tree trunks and fallen leaves and even some living leaves.*

plant to rapidly expand, growing leaves to overshadow those of its neighbouring epiphytes and the tree upon which it sits. More roots course down the trunk, wrapping and wreathing, swelling and encircling, until they completely enclose the tree trunk in an intricate web.

Initially, the fig is no more than a minor hindrance to its supporting tree, but gradually the fig overwhelms it. Spreading foliage prevents sunlight from reaching the tree's leaves, and the long descending fig roots sap water and nutrients from the ground around the tree's own roots, supplies upon which the tree was dependent. As the tree trunk expands in girth, it encounters the restraint of the fig's cylindrical mesh of roots. They slowly become a stranglehold upon the tree, crushing vital conducting vessels in the outer layers of the trunk, and so depriving the roots of food and the leaves of water.

It is a very slow death that may take several years. Once the tree has died, it decomposes in the grip of its usurper, falling

SMELLY FLOWER *Animals and plants have found many ways of surviving in the rain forest. Here, the odour of rotting meat given off by the* **Rafflesia** *attracts visitors, such as this tree shrew, to its flower.*

prey to termites, bacteria and fungi. The fig is thus left standing, now forming a tall, hollow 'tree', moulded around its predecessor. It has obtained a prime site in the rain forest without ever needing to struggle for light in the gloom of the forest floor.

PYRAMIDS OF LIFE

In a realm where plants strangle other plants, lizards glide and earthworms live in the tree tops, the unexpected can always be found. To survive in the crowded, multi-layered rain forest, plants and animals have adopted the unlikeliest lifestyles and the most improbable dwelling places, slotting into empty niches, and grasping at opportunities that have not yet been exploited by any other creatures.

Life is packed into every tiny space in the rain-forest tiers. Within every layer there are further sublayers. Everywhere, large ecosystems contain smaller ones in a pyramid of life. Trees carry epiphytes, which in turn bear on the surface of their leaves miniature epiphylls – plants that specialise in colonising leaves. In these diminutive gardens live tiny insects, each of which carries bacteria and other microorganisms on its surface or inside its body.

The rain forest is like a nest of boxes, or a Russian doll. As one part is studied, or taken apart, it reveals more components within, all fitting precisely together. Its complexity will take years to understand fully.

FINDING FOOD IN THE RAIN FOREST

Juicy fruits, sweet nectar, chewy gum and even wood are

some of the delicacies feasted on by rain-forest creatures.

Vegetation is not the only food source – insects and other

small animals also fall prey to predators lurking in the forest.

Advancing across the forest floor, like a flickering brown river of death, is a fast-moving swarm of ants. It divides into separate columns and then rejoins, fans out into a delta shape and then coalesces again, flowing around tree trunks or over small shrubs, but always moving relentlessly onwards. These are New World army ants (*Eciton burchelli*) in search of food. They seize whatever insects and other small creatures are in their path, piling up the spoils in temporary caches to be taken back to the nest later. The swarm churns up the sparse leaf litter as it goes, generating a powerful smell of decay that fills the air.

There may be 50 000 of the ants, a huge extended family hunting as one. Long-legged scurrying predators, they surge over the ground, race up the long dangling stems of lianas, and ascend tree trunks into the canopy, as menacing to creatures of their own size as a thousand-strong pack of wolves, yet utterly silent in their rapacious advance. In the damp conditions of the forest floor, there is not even the rustle of dead leaves.

The nest, to which the army ants eventually return with their booty, is not an established site as with most ant species, but a temporary bivouac. This may be either under ground or in a hollow tree where the ants hang in a huge seething ball, with the queen, eggs and larval ants at the centre, protected by those on the outside.

Like most ants, there are different castes within the community, including worker ants and soldier ants. The workers are tireless drudges that collect food and raise the young, while the much larger soldier ants are aggressive well-armed guards. It is the soldier ants that form a defensive stinging 'skin' over the ball of ants at the temporary nest site.

WAITING TO STRIKE *The well-camouflaged Brazilian horned toad sits patiently, waiting for any insects to emerge from the leaf litter.*

ON THE MARCH *A mass of army ants scour the undergrowth for prey (left), leaving the queen well guarded at their temporary nest (above).*

Each food-finding swarm travels between 160 and 230 ft (50 and 70 m) from the bivouac and may continue for as long as nine hours. It is so terrifyingly efficient that within two or three weeks the surrounding area will be virtually devoid of insect life. The army ants must be nomadic to ensure their food supply, but they do not simply move on when food runs short, as naturalists once assumed.

Instead, the ants move on at set intervals, driven by an internal rhythm that causes them to stay at one nest site for three weeks, then to spend three weeks roaming the forest, finding a different bivouac site every night, then to establish a fixed bivouac for a further three weeks but in a site distant from the previous one. The rhythm is timed by the reproductive cycle of the colony. During the stationary phase, the queen ant lays her eggs – a staggering 100 000-300 000 of them. These hatch and the helpless, maggot-like larval ants must be cared for and fed by the workers, who are also still caring for the previous brood. As soon as the previous brood mature into adult workers, the next nomadic phase begins, with the larvae of the latest brood being carried by the workers.

The migration of the whole colony always takes place at night, to minimise the risk to the queen ant. Even in the nomadic phase, the queen and her brood stay put at the nest site during the day, while many of the worker and soldier ants are out foraging. The queen must be protected at all costs because she is of paramount importance, the source of all the eggs, and thus of all the workers and soldiers in the colony.

ANT FOLLOWERS

The army ants, in their search for food, unwittingly create opportunities for other forest animals, and they have, over millions of years, come to form part of a more complex pattern involving numerous other creatures. What is remarkable is the enormous number of animals that benefit from their swarm, most commonly the antbirds that pounce on crickets, grasshoppers and spiders escaping from the marauding ants. Indeed, some of these species, such as the white-plumed antbird (*Pithys albifrons*) and the red-throated ant-tanager (*Habia fuscicauda*),

CLOSE BEHIND *The rusty-breasted antpitta is one of the many birds that feast on the rich pickings exposed by swarming army ants.*

are heavily dependent on the army ants for their food. For the white-plumed antbird, in particular, this means that each individual has to inhabit a huge area of rain forest – over 500 acres (200 ha) – to be sure of finding a swarm within its home range. Other antbird species, such as the black-crowned antpitta (*Pittasoma michleri*), the ruddy woodcreeper (*Dendrocincla homochroa*) and the ocellated anthrush (*Phaenostictus mcleanani*) derive about 70 per cent of their food from following ants.

One study in Central America revealed that 44 different species of birds might, at one time or another, follow the army ants. The different species challenged each other for positions directly above or around the swarm, with the central area of the

swarm being the most productive and therefore the most sought-after. There can be up to a dozen or more individual birds in attendance on each foraging swarm.

Then there are the flies that hover overhead. As many as 1000 flies may accompany an ant column, all of them belonging to species whose young are parasitic on other insects. The adult flies land on the larger and more agile insects escaping from the ants, and either lay eggs on them or deposit already-hatched maggots. The fly maggots will thrive as parasites inside these unfortunate escapees, before maturing into adult flies and becoming ant followers themselves.

In addition to the antbirds, flies and other regulars, there are animals that make more occasional appearances, feeding on prey flushed out by the ants. Toads and frogs may be seen feasting alongside the ant columns, as well as iguanas and other types of lizard. It is sometimes said that lizards and frogs can themselves fall prey to the army ants, being torn to shreds in moments by thousands of tiny jaws. In fact, this is a rare event that occurs only if the larger animal is already injured or ill. Any healthy frog or lizard can escape the ants with ease. However, small lizards scavenging on insects around the ant swarm may be killed and eaten not by the ants themselves, but by one of the larger species of antbird, such as the bright-rumped attila (*Attila spadiceus*). In the violent turmoil created by the army ants, even the predators can suddenly become prey.

Researchers in Brazil have recently discovered that marmosets, too, join the ant followers on occasion. These small monkeys perch up to 3 ft (1 m) above the ground, slightly ahead of the advancing swarm, seizing spiders, crickets and cockroaches fleeing the mayhem. They spare the ants themselves, deterred by their painful stings, but will steal prey that has already been captured, shaking it vigorously to remove the ants. Occasionally, they are stung by ants resentful at this theft, but the benefits to the monkeys clearly outweigh any such painful costs. Marmosets are not dependent on the army ants for their survival but when they happen to encounter a raiding party, it provides them

ON THE LOOKOUT *As insect prey are flushed out by army ants, a basilisk lizard lies ready to ambush any that cross its path.*

with a sudden bonanza of high-protein food and they stay with it for up to three hours.

There are yet more beneficiaries of the army-ant columns, less conspicuous to the untrained eye. Some insects and other small animals, rather than falling prey to the ants, benefit by running along with them, sharing their food and acquiring the same protection from larger predators that the ants enjoy. These fellow travellers include rove beetles, wasps, primitive insects known as silverfish and hordes of tiny mites that act as stowaways, riding on the ants themselves.

Some of the wasp and beetle species closely resemble the ants, a remarkable piece of mimicry that may protect them from being identified as aliens and attacked by the ferocious soldier ants. How the silverfish and other species get away with imposing themselves on the ant colony is as yet unknown, but they probably produce scents that placate the ants' aggressive inclinations. Since much ant behaviour is controlled by chemical signals it can readily be manipulated in this way.

PUZZLING BEHAVIOUR

The most enigmatic of all the ant followers is the army-ant butterfly (*Melinaea lilis imitata*) which flutters along above the ant swarm, occasionally alighting on a leaf for a while before moving on. Butterflies are not predatory, so their presence here is strange. Closer inspection shows that the army-ant butterflies are feeding when they rest, sipping at the semi-liquid droppings left by the antbirds that are moving along just ahead of them.

Feeding on bird droppings is not unusual. It is thought to provide army-ant butterflies – and many other butterfly species – with a source of nitrogen and amino acids. Both these raw materials can be used to make proteins, which are as vital to butterflies as to any other living creature. Their staple diet of sugary nectar, while it provides plenty of energy, is generally lacking in protein.

Exactly why these butterflies follow the ant swarms is something of a puzzle. Some biologists have suggested that the odour of decay that accompanies the ant swarm

TASTY SNACK *Insects provide an important source of protein in a squirrel monkey's diet, and are quickly crunched up by sharp, narrow teeth.*

both continents underlines the value it has for birds in tropical rain forests.

It is the particular circumstances of these forests that make ant-following so thoroughly worth while. The vegetation of a tropical rain forest is lush and complex, each small area of forest creating a maze of a million evergreen leaves that provide endless hiding places for insects and other small prey. Finding insects is a constant challenge, and the power of the army ants to flush them out provides a golden opportunity for other insect eaters.

It is not the only opportunity, however. Just as antbirds follow army ants, so other birds follow, for example, squirrel monkeys, energetic gregarious animals that feed mainly on insects and fruit. Even the smallest troops of squirrel monkeys number about a dozen, and others are far larger. Some have almost 100 playful chattering monkeys moving about together – feeding, mating, quarrelling, or simply scampering after each other along the branches. The

attracts these butterflies, because it resembles the aphrodisiac smells released by the males for courtship. This theory is based on the fact that only female butterflies follow the army ants. The flaw in this argument was revealed when a researcher exposed captive army-ant butterflies to the courtship scents of the males. Surprisingly, both sexes responded to the smell, not just the females. If the butterflies were being tricked into following ant columns by the resemblance to the mating scent, then both sexes should be ant followers.

It seems that the butterflies really are following the army ants intentionally, to feed on the bird droppings. In this case, the absence of males may have a nutritional explanation. Because females must lay large numbers of eggs, which contain stores of protein, they have a much greater need for nitrogen than male butterflies. It is constantly being lost from their bodies during egg-laying and must be replaced. So there is more incentive for the females to follow the ant swarms, where they will find a constant supply of fresh, nitrogen-rich droppings.

The butterflies are protected from the antbirds' predatory instincts by distasteful toxins present in their bodies. These toxins

they obtain from the plants they feed on as caterpillars. Their foul taste is advertised by the orange-yellow-and-black stripes on their wings, a typical 'warning coloration'.

FINDING FOOD TOGETHER

The army ants of South and Central America are not alone. They have an intriguing parallel in the African rain forests, where different ant species, known variously as army ants or driver ants, show the same type of marauding behaviour. But, despite the similarities in lifestyle, these ants are products of an entirely separate evolutionary experiment that began with different parent stock. Similar environments often produce similar species in this way in a process known as 'convergent evolution'.

Most striking of all is the parallel behaviour of African ant-following birds, belonging to different bird families, unrelated to the antbirds of the Americas. The fact that ant-following has evolved independently on

MONKEY FOLLOWER
A woodcreeper clings to a tree trunk, ready to catch any insects flushed out by the troop of passing monkeys.

disturbance created by these lively monkeys sends insects fleeing in all directions, and one creature in particular has learned to take advantage of the mayhem to pick up the insects – the double-toothed kite (*Harpagus bidentatus*), waiting on a bare branch just above the monkey troop.

As well as cicadas, crickets and dragonflies, the kite may pick up small lizards, scorpions and even bats disturbed from their tree-top roosts. These are mainly fast-flying prey that have already escaped the squirrel monkeys, so the kites are not robbing the monkeys of food. Nor do they benefit the monkeys by their presence. This type of relationship is known as 'commensalism', which means 'eating at the same table'.

At the same time, as with the huge variety of ant followers, there are other birds, too, that attend the monkey troops, though they have a different approach to feeding. Tawny-winged woodcreepers (*Dendrocincla anabatina*) cling to tree trunks below the monkey troop and fly out on short circular tours to pick up insects that are swooping down out of the danger zone. They tend to capture smaller dragonflies, flies and beetles. Grey-headed tanagers (*Eucometis penicillata*) also work the forest layer just below the monkey troop, perching on small branches and flying upwards to catch escaping insects. Both these birds will also follow army-ant swarms when the opportunity arises.

BIRD WAVES

Sometimes insect-eating birds simply follow each other, producing enormous 'bird waves' that flow through the trees like storm tides, flushing the insect population before them. One species of bird may concentrate on scorpions and large, well-defended

insects, another on small inconspicuous crawling species, a third on the fastest fliers.

In this way, they are not competing too much for food, and the flurry that they create by foraging together exposes far more of their potential prey. There can be as many as 50 different species in these bird waves, moving forward through several different layers of the forest simultaneously, with those below often benefiting from prey ousted by those above – and vice versa.

SIX-LEGGED ANTELOPES

Insects have a pivotal role in the life of the tropical rain forests. Indeed, what antelopes are to the African plains, for example, insects are to the rain forests: the primary harvesters of the plants, and the main type of high-protein food for others to feed on.

By comparison with a savannah or prairie environment, however, the range of food available to larger animals, such as

SHY BROWSER *Stealthy, silent and quick to dive for cover when disturbed, duikers and other small forest antelopes are a rare sight.*

NIGHT STALKER *Enormous eyes and sharp ears help the spectral tarsier of South-east Asia to track down a cricket in the darkness of night.*

mammals and birds, is generally very different in the tropical rain forests. On the savannahs of Africa, 50 per cent of the grass and other plant growth is harvested by herbivores such as zebra and antelope and converted to highly edible flesh that is preyed upon by lions, leopards, cheetahs, hyenas, wild dogs and vultures. In the tropical rain forests the corresponding figure is only about 2.5 per cent – ground-dwelling grazers such as tapirs, antelopes, peccaries and wild pigs are thinly spread through the forest. As a direct consequence, the large predators that feed on them, such as jaguars and tigers, are even more scarce.

Insects, then, are a prime source of animal food in the forest. The trouble is, an insect diet cannot sustain most large mammals. The primates – monkeys and their relatives – illustrate this well. The very smallest species, such as the tarsiers of South-east Asia, rely almost entirely on insects, though

FUSSY EATERS *After feasting on carefully chosen young leaves, the red howler monkey relies on bacteria in its gut to help it to digest them.*

they may also take small snakes and lizards when they get the chance. Slightly larger species such as squirrel monkeys, however, cannot get enough energy by eating insects alone. The problem here is that a larger animal needs more energy in total, but the rate at which it can capture insects is no higher than that of a small primate. To boost their energy supplies, squirrel monkeys therefore eat fruit that is rich in sugar.

This dietary combination – high-protein insects and sugary fruit – is popular for many small and medium-sized primates, that is those weighing less than 2¹/₄lb (1 kg). Above that size, more and more species opt for a mixture of fruit and leaves, with the leaves providing the protein and other nutrients that the fruit lacks. For large animals, the time taken to catch insects is no longer worth while in proportion to the food they supply.

The largest of the monkeys, such as the howler monkeys, rely on leaves for about half their diet. But leaves are not an easy source of food because the toxins that the trees make to keep insect pests at bay are usually just as effective, or even more so, against mammals. The monkeys are particular about the tree species they eat, and they choose the youngest leaves to minimise the poisons present, but their diet is still a chemically challenging one.

Nor are leaves easy to digest. Their main constituent is cellulose which cannot be broken down by mammals – if it could, people trying to lose weight would not be able to eat huge helpings of salad, because these would be as fattening as a slice of bread. As a result, mammals that specialise in eating leaves all enlist the help of bacteria with a talent for digesting cellulose. This is true both inside and outside the tropical

rain forests. Thus, in the case of zebra and horses, the cellulose-digesting bacteria live in a substantial pouch attached to the large intestine, known as the caecum – likewise, in the tropical rain forests, the howler monkeys of the Americas and the gorillas, both primates that rely heavily on leaves for their food. (It is the evolutionary remnant of the caecum that is known, in humans, as the appendix, a reminder of our leaf-eating past.) The bacteria also help to break down many of the toxins in the leaves.

Some leaf-eating mammals, such as cows and deer, keep their bacteria in part of the stomach. The same is true, in the rain forest, of colobus monkeys. This arrangement is far more efficient than hindgut fermentation, since it allows the nutrients released by the bacteria to be absorbed as the food travels on through the intestine. Keeping the bacteria in the hindgut, as gorillas do, has disadvantages in that nutrients are not absorbed

DIVING FOR COVER *The hoatzin's untidy stick nest is built in a tree that overhangs the water, thus offering a quick escape route for its chick.*

most efficiently in this part of the gut. To get the most from the leaves, howler monkeys and gorillas have to keep them in the gut for a long time to maximise the absorption of nutrients.

This mass of food in the gut makes them into heavy, slow-moving animals, not quick and curious like the squirrel monkeys and marmosets. Howlers spend more than half their time just resting and digesting. For a tree-dweller, being heavy and ponderous is far from ideal, and given the unusual toxicity of the leaves as an additional drawback, it is not surprising that the number of specialised leaf-eating mammals is relatively small in a tropical rain forest compared to an environment such as the savannah.

THE STINKBIRD

If a bellyful of leaves being slowly digested is a burden for a monkey, then it might seem an impossibility for a flying animal with the same type of diet and digestive system. In the hoatzin, however, a bird of the South American rain forests, evolution has apparently achieved the impossible.

The hoatzin lives alongside rivers and favours the young leaves of mangroves. The cellulose in these is digested by bacteria that live in two enlarged chambers that are located between the bird's mouth and its stomach. Fresh leaves go into these chambers and are ground up in one of them (the crop), then slowly fermented by the bacteria, before being moved along to the stomach and intestine. It is a system akin to

IN A FLAP *After a large meal, the hoatzins of South America are not the best of fliers. They use their wings chiefly to help their balance when moving from branch to branch.*

that of cows, and the hoatzin reputedly smells of cow dung, hence its alternative name – 'stinkbird'.

The slow processing of the leaves, which may spend up to two days in the bird's digestive system, makes the hoatzin weighty and cumbersome. The crop alone accounts for a third of its body weight. The hoatzin is such a poor flier that it usually does not bother to try, clambering about in the trees and using its wings mainly to balance itself or to prevent a fall. Even perching is a little difficult when its crop is full of leaves, as the bird tends to topple forwards. Hoatzins therefore choose a roost where they can rest their breasts against a neighbouring branch. The front of the breast has a hard callus to resist the abrasion.

Hoatzins live in small flocks of up to 20 birds, which gives them some protection against predators. They make their nests on branches that overhang the water so that the nestlings have a quick escape route should danger threaten: the young birds clamber out of the nest, drop into the water and swim for the bank. They can regain the nest when the danger has passed by clambering slowly up the tree using two small, mobile claws positioned on the front of each wing to grip small twigs, and grasping larger branches with their powerful feet.

The wing claws are an interesting relic of the evolutionary past of the birds, being present on the wing of the ancestral bird *Archaeopteryx*, and derived from the clawed fingers of its reptile forerunner. The claws have survived in the young of only a few bird species, and it is the young hoatzin that seems to put them to best use.

In order to digest leaves, young hoatzins must acquire the same bacteria that their parents possess, a necessity that also faces the howler monkeys, gorillas and most other leaf-eaters. The adult hoatzin is thought to regurgitate leaves that have already been processed in the crop, and are therefore rich in bacteria; it then feeds them to the chick.

TRAILS IN THE FOREST

Immediately after a rain storm, a trail of green confetti may be seen on the forest floor. It consists of neat little fragments cut from leaves, some dark green, some paler, lying about 1-2 in (2-5 cm) apart. The trail can be followed through the forest and leads eventually to a large bare mound of soil, almost 33 ft (10 m) in diameter, that leans against the base of a tree. There are many small openings in the mound, but no sign of life. Tiny, well-worn paths lead from the mound in all directions.

As the forest vegetation dries out, however, the inhabitants of the mound emerge, and once again, it is ants that are showing a remarkable adaptation to rain-forest living.

The mound-dwellers are leaf-cutter ants, tiny insects that set off in a long file to a suitable tree, laboriously cut pieces from leaves using their scissor-like jaws, then carry them back to the communal nest. Each piece takes as much as 10 minutes to cut, but if rain begins falling during the journey, the leaf pieces are promptly abandoned, producing the trails of green confetti on the ground. Despite all the effort they have expended, the ants do not return to claim their damp, muddy leaf discs later, but set out to cut new ones.

This peculiar fussiness can be understood by looking inside the nest, where an extraordinary form of miniature 'gardening' is taking place. The leaf fragments are turned into a compost on which the ants cultivate a particular species of fungus, later harvesting this fungus for food.

The growing conditions for the fungus must be exactly right, which is why clean, dry leaf fragments are essential. Even these fragments need to be processed before the fungus can use them, a job that is done by a

CUT TO PRECISION *Minima workers wait patiently to process crescents carefully carved out from a succulent new leaf by the larger leaf-cutter ants.*

specialist caste known as 'minima workers'. As their name suggests, they are extremely small, only $1/12$ in (2 mm) long, compared to the leaf-collecting workers that measure a more substantial $2/5$ in (10 mm). The minima workers remove any particles from the surface of the leaf and then strip off its outer layer.

These items, which might carry contaminants such as the spores of other fungi, are disposed of outside the nest. Sometimes, the cleaning process begins before the foliage even reaches the nest; minima workers cling to the leaf particles being carried home by the leaf-cutting workers, and remove particles from them while in transit.

Having cleaned the leaf fragment, minima workers then chew it up to produce a sticky mass that is placed on the edge of an existing fungal garden. A few tufts of the fungus are collected from elsewhere and added to the new patch of compost, where they begin to proliferate. Thus the garden grows slowly in size.

The fungus gardens are whitish and spongy, measuring 6-12 in (15-30 cm) across and resembling thin slices of bread. There may be several hundred gardens in a well-established ant colony, each in its own chamber with labyrinthine tunnels connecting the different chambers. It takes about

STARTING AFRESH *Once her nuptial flight is over, a queen leaf-cutter ant sheds her wings and looks around for a suitable site to make a nest.*

four years for a colony to reach this stage, and it may survive another four years thereafter, or even longer in some favourable areas of rain forest.

THE FLIGHT OF THE QUEENS

Given the complex organisation of the mature colony, it is amazing to think that it begins with a single queen ant flying out alone from her parent colony with a small store of the indispensable fungus in a cheek pouch. She swirls upwards into the air to mate, encountering newly emerged winged males during her flight. All the colonies in a particular area of forest release these virgin queens and reproductive males at about the same time, so there is the opportunity to mate with males from other colonies.

Having mated with three or four different males, the queen flutters down to the ground, crawls about until she finds a suitable site for her nest, usually close to a tree trunk, and then starts excavating. Having created a shaft with a small underground chamber at the base, the queen begins her garden, initially using her own eggs and droppings as the compost. Once the fungus is growing well, she lays some eggs in a separate area of the nest so that they can hatch into grubs and then mature into workers.

She neither eats nor drinks during this period, and it takes at least four weeks from

her arrival before there are workers available to bring home leaf fragments, tend the garden and care for the queen. Only one in ten of the queens survive this difficult stage, many succumbing to the attack of other species of fungi, which invade a queen's body and slowly kill her. Once there are workers in the colony, they groom the queen, removing any fungal growth before it can become established.

The fungi that the ants cultivate is not itself a threat, lacking the enzymes it would need to grow on their bodies. Indeed, it has become so enfeebled in the course of its long coexistence with the leaf-cutter ants that it cannot survive outside their nests. Attempts to cultivate it in a laboratory show that, without the help of the ants in predigesting its food, the fungus grows very slowly. Nor can it reproduce itself unaided. It no longer generates spores, as other fungi do; it is spread solely by the ants.

The leaf-cutter ants, meanwhile, are just as dependent on the fungus, for they cannot digest cellulose well enough to thrive on a diet of leaves. Each species is thus locked into its relationship with the other. As a partnership, however, they are stunningly successful. One biologist estimated the weight of leaves cropped by leaf-cutter ants in an area of tropical rain forest in Panama to be 267 lb per acre (300 kg per hectare) each year, as much as all the leaf-eating mammals and lizards put together.

CHEWING GUM

To try to protect their leaves from marauding leaf-eaters, trees use poisons, but they must also defend their trunks from the ravages of insects. A popular method is to produce a sticky 'exudate' whenever the bark is pierced, a glutinous ooze that solidifies on contact with the air, immobilising an insect's tiny mouthparts. This method is used by pine trees and generates lumps of a clear brownish-orange resin. (The same resin,

exuded millions of years ago and hardened by the passage of time, is the beautiful, jewel-like substance known as amber.) Other trees, such as the original rubber tree, a native of the Amazonian rain forests, produce a more fluid exudate that solidifies into a malleable opaque gum rather than a hard, clear resin.

Such resins and gums are employed by various other trees and lianas in the tropical rain forests. But in the forests of South America, it is not necessarily insects that are provoking the flow of gum – nor are the trees benefiting from the exercise. Here, tree gums are exploited as food by various small monkeys, principally the marmosets.

The most enthusiastic gum feeder is the pygmy marmoset, a tiny maned animal weighing only $3^1/2$ oz (100 g) with long clawed toes that make it adept at clinging to tree trunks. About two-thirds of the feeding time of these monkeys is spent on tree exudates, whether eating them or gnawing shallow holes in tree trunks to generate new feeding sites to be exploited during the following days. Fruit and insects make up the rest of the pygmy marmoset's diet.

STICKY DIET *A pygmy marmoset feeds on gum. This strange foodstuff oozes from a hole the tiny monkey gouges in the tree trunk.*

The marmoset's front teeth are adapted for this special diet, with hard, straight edges set level across the front of the mouth, rather like a broad, sharp chisel. Armed with these powerful teeth, the marmosets can gouge out surprisingly large holes from the wood. Once made, the holes can easily be reopened to stimulate more flow, and the marmosets return to the same holes again and again.

These are often in one main feeding tree, with the marmoset family centring its life around this tree, rarely moving far from it and ferociously defending the territory against intruding marmosets. At least once a year, the pygmy marmoset family will change the main feeding tree and move to another area of forest. There are three other species of marmoset that eat tree exudates, but these species prefer insects and fruit, turning to tree gums only when other food is scarce. A variety of other small monkeys eat gums when they come across them, but do not go to the trouble of making feeding holes for themselves. Their teeth are generally unsuited to this purpose, although close study of golden lion tamarins in Brazil has revealed that these small, long-tailed monkeys do bite into liana stems to provoke a flow of exudate that they then lap up.

FORAGING FUNGI

Many rain-forest creatures thus eat the leaves of trees, while monkeys such as pygmy marmosets find a useful part of their diet in exudates produced by trees. The actual wood of the trees, meanwhile, also has its own specialised takers.

Few foods are as defiantly indigestible as wood. Like leaves, it contains cellulose, but wood also possesses a hardening agent called lignin that is even tougher chemically. The living creatures that can digest lignin are rare indeed, but they include many of the fungi that flourish on the dead wood of the rain forest.

A fungus grows from a microscopic spore that settles on the bark. And at first there is nothing to see, for the fungus works away inconspicuously within the dead trunk or branch, suffusing it with long, slender white strands known as hyphae. These flimsy threads of fungal life grow rapidly through crevices and channels in the wood. At the same time, they feed on it, breaking the wood down by producing digestive enzymes, then soaking up the nutrients that are released.

The hyphae of a fungus – known collectively as its mycelium – will permeate a fallen tree, unseen from the outside but spreading great distances within, until the day comes when the mycelium is well-fed and vigorous enough to produce spores. At this point, the mycelium sprouts colourful spore-producing bodies that erupt from the dead wood with astonishing speed. They may have the familiar toadstool shape, or be tall and slender like folded umbrellas, or take a variety of other forms. Some glow in the dark, an eerie spectacle in the rain-forest night. It is these spore-producing bodies that most people think of as the fungus, but in fact they are just the tip of the iceberg.

Fungi are neither plants nor animals, but an entirely separate group with a variety of unique attributes. Their unusual form of growth, whereby they can spread vast distances with little expenditure of energy, combined with their special method of feeding, in which the food is digested externally and then absorbed in liquid form, allows them to exploit all kinds of unlikely food sources, particularly dead material.

TERMITE GARDENERS

Their special talents make fungi into useful accomplices for many rain-forest animals. Just as leaf-cutter ants grow fungus gardens on leaves, so there are termites in Africa that cultivate fungi to help them to digest wood. However, these termites first eat the

A PASSION FOR WOOD *Swarms of workers from a colony of nasute termites travel along the stems of woody vines that hang above their nest.*

wood themselves, extract some nutrients from it, and then use their droppings as compost on which to grow the fungus. Once it is flourishing, the fungus is cropped by the termites and provides an important supplement to their diet.

Not that the termites benefit much from broken-down products of the lignin in the wood. Indeed, some of these products may even be toxic to termites. The value of the fungus is in opening up the fibres of the wood, by fracturing the lignin molecules, so that more of the cellulose in those fibres can be extracted. The fungus simply releases cellulose from its lignin prison.

Although termites are the supreme wood-eating animals of the tropics, even they cannot digest cellulose for themselves. This job is done for them by microscopic creatures, either bacteria or single-celled animals known as protozoa, depending on the species of termite. The cellulose-digesting microbes dwell in the hind part of the termite's gut and their importance can be judged from the huge numbers present. A single drop of gut fluid from a termite will contain 1 million protozoa, and even more of the bacteria.

Outside Africa, termites do not cultivate fungus gardens, but they do benefit from

*SHELTERED LIVES **Termite** **workers are hidden from view as** **they scurry through underground** **tunnels (above) and covered** **walkways, in search of food.***

the activities of free-living fungi that have already infested the dead wood where termites feed. The wood fibres are partially dismembered already and, as a bonus, the termites ingest nutritious mouthfuls of the fungus while eating the wood. Biologists believe that there may be a further benefit. Some of the fungal enzymes that break down cellulose may survive being eaten and continue to act once they reach the termite's stomach. In this way, the termites steal the chemical competence of the fungi.

WORLD OF WOOD

Wood is the staple diet for most termites, but it is everything to the nasute termites of Central American rain forests: their food, their home and their whole way of life. They eat it, chew it up into a pulp to build their tree-nest, and even make covered walkways, all from the same material. The thoroughly masticated wood is mixed with faeces which acts as glue, and the result resembles brown papier mâché. It dries into a cardboard-like material known as 'carton'

*UNDER COVER **Termite colonies** **build magnificent nests,** **composed of droppings or** **chewed-up forest litter, that** **may be up to 7 ft (2 m) tall.***

that is fairly soft at first but becomes progressively harder with time.

A nasute nest is a black or brownish hemisphere stuck to the trunk or large branch of a tree. Within are successive layers of carton, forming various chambers and passageways, with the queen termite safely ensconced in the central chamber. Covered walkways lead from the nest, along the branches and down the trunk of the nest tree, then through the forest to feeding places within dead trees or fallen branches. By running along these constructed passageways, worker termites escape the attention of many insect-eaters and can be more easily defended by the termite soldiers, which rush to any breach in the walkway and attack ferociously. Once the danger has passed, worker termites repair the damaged walkway using fresh supplies of carton.

The nasute soldiers defend their kind in a remarkable way. They have globular heads that taper into a sharp point at the front, this point being a nozzle through which the soldier can squirt a foul-smelling gummy fluid. The odour is caused by chemicals known as monoterpenes, which are also irritants. Various different enemies are seen off by this fluid. Predatory insects become ensnared by the sticky threads, while larger would-be termite eaters are repelled by the chemicals.

Among the larger animals that sometimes do battle with the nasute termites is the tamandua or banded anteater. This long-nosed golden-brown creature is an expert tree-climber, having a prehensile tail that can grip tightly onto branches. Its massive front claws are strong enough to break into the hardest ant or termite nests, yet it usually shuns the nests of the nasute termite, deterred by the soldier's chemical warfare. Instead, the tamandua feeds on concentrations of worker nasute termites while they are gathering wood in rotten logs. There may be a few soldiers present here, but not as many as would assault the tamandua at the nest.

NEST RAIDERS

The only time the tamandua tackles the nest itself is when the termite colony has just produced its young virgin queens and reproductive males – winged forms that are, at this point, about to take flight in the hope of founding new colonies. These

large flying termites are particularly rich in calories and nutrients, making it worth the tamandua's while to endure the hostilities of the nasute soldiers.

Several rain-forest ant and termite species are less repellent to the tamandua, so their nests are raided more often. On the other hand, some species are better defended than the nasute termites, and are therefore avoided by the tamandua altogether. The hard-stinging army ants escape its attentions, as do the leaf-cutter ants which seem to have especially distasteful toxins in their bodies.

Animals such as the tamandua provide exceptions to the rule that insect eaters must be small. Besides the tamandua, there are the armour-plated pangolins of Africa and Asia, which resemble gigantic mobile

pine cones, the giant armadillo of the Americas, which is similarly armoured although unrelated, and the giant anteater of South America, a larger cousin of the tamandua with a massive bushy tail. All these animals specialise in breaking open ant or termite nests and consuming the occupants together with their innumerable eggs and larvae. Here, they have a concentrated mass of insect food that can readily be harvested. Served up in this way, the ants and termites provide enough energy to sustain animals that can reach the size of a large dog, and can weigh as much as 132 lb (60 kg) in the case of the giant armadillo.

It is not, however, a diet for the faint-hearted. Most ants and termites produce soldier castes whose stings, bites and chemical defences are formidable deterrents. Some rain-forest ants are so potent that an attack on a human being will result in severe and incapacitating pain for several days. This level of aggression keeps most animals out, but the armour-plated skin of the armadillos and pangolins protects them from the worst of the onslaughts. Pangolins even have a horny surface to their stomach to protect them internally. Giant anteaters and tamanduas resist the ferocious ants with their dense fur and thick, relatively insensitive, skin.

FOOD FOR FREE

Vegetable foods such as leaves and exudates and animal foods including termites and ants mostly present some kind of deterrent to their would-be eaters. But there are some foods in the tropical rain forest that positively want to be eaten. These are foods that trees and other plants offer up as part of an exchange system with animals – they offer them to animals that pollinate their flowers, spread their seeds, or defend the plant from its enemies.

Sugar is the one food that plants have in abundance. Consequently, their offerings

SCALY PROTECTION *Well protected by its coat of armour, the long-tailed pangolin is almost immune to the attacks of termite soldiers.*

POLLINATION USING BIRDS AND BATS

Pollination by birds and bats is a speciality of the tropics, particularly the tropical rain forests. It is something uniquely possible in a habitat without either a severe dry season or a cold season. At any time of the year, some plants will be in flower in the rain forest, whereas in other climates there are seasons with no flowers. During these, the pollinators have to be able to survive as eggs or go into a state of suspended animation. Both are possible for insects, but not for warm-blooded creatures such as birds and bats.

Insect pollination is undoubtedly the original method of pollination and one which many flowering plants have retained. But some plants have gradually evolved from insect pollination to either bat pollination or bird pollination. Those that attract birds tend to have red or orange flowers, and many are equipped with particularly strong flower stalks to bear the weight of a perching bird. Bat-pollinated flowers are usually white or cream with musky scents.

From the plant's point of view, these large flying animals have advantages as pollinators because they fly farther and can cross-fertilise plants that are widely scattered. But they also need more fuel, and bat-pollinated trees in particular produce huge amounts of nectar. Apparently the advantages are sufficient to make this worth while.

FOREST TREAT *A blossom bat feeds on a banana flower in one of Australia's surviving rain forests in Queensland.*

are frequently sweet – either nectar or fruit pulp. They generally try to conserve other nutrients, so that nectar and fruit are often lacking in minerals and protein, forcing the animals that feed on them to supplement their diet. Some plants are more generous and offer a little protein to tempt favoured animals. Certain plants relying on ants for defence even produce what are known as Beltian bodies. These are small, easily removed nodules at the edges of their leaves that are rich in fat or protein. It seems that these packets of high-quality food lure ants of the most useful species.

One 'fruit' that is particularly rich in fat, vitamins and minerals is the avocado, now cultivated for human consumption, but descended from Central American rain-forest trees and domesticated by the Aztecs some 8000 years ago. Wild avocados are much smaller than the ones we eat, but they still provide a substantial and nutritious meal for a small animal. Among those feeding extensively on wild avocados is the resplendent quetzal bird (*Pharomachrus mocinno*) that swallows them whole and then regurgitates the hard-shelled seed. The seed even of small avocados is fairly large, compared with the size of the bird's head, and the layer of fruit covering it is relatively thin. The richness of this fruit may therefore be a necessary inducement to tempt birds like the quetzal to swallow such an enormous seed.

All these exchange systems have come about through a slow process of coevolution, operating over the millennia. Curiously, a hallmark of such systems is that they are often imperfect, with some animals taking the food and not providing any service to the plant in return – or taking the wrong

food. Many animals are seed-thieves, for example, consuming the more nutritious, protein-packed seed rather than the fruit around it; trees attempt to outdo such enemies by encasing the seed in a hard, uncrackable case. The honeycreepers and the flowerpiercers are birds that steal nectar by piercing flowers at the base. Some hummingbirds will also do this, taking nectar without carrying out pollination.

Even more damaging is a type of ant that steals pollen from the flowers of the orchid *Spathoglossis plicata* and uses it for food; the pollen is more nutritious than the sugary nectar the orchid produces around its buds and flowers as a means of attracting ants for defensive purposes. The pollen-eating ant takes the nectar as well, but does nothing to defend the orchid from leaf-eating animals. Fortunately, there are other species of ant that do 'play the game', taking only the nectar and vigorously defending the plant.

SWALLOWED WHOLE
In exchange for a nutritious meal, the resplendent quetzal offers wild avocado trees a first class seed-dispersal service.

The small, long-tailed tamarin monkeys in the rain forests of eastern and central South America feed on nectar from a variety of flowering trees, and they do so in a particularly destructive fashion, tearing off the whole flower and then licking the nectar from the base of it. This ruins any chance of the flower maturing into a viable seed, even if it has already been pollinated in the usual manner by a nectar-eating insect, bird or bat.

A researcher working in one part of the Amazonian rain forest in Peru found that a small troop of a dozen tamarins destroyed 5000 flowers a day from their favourite species of tree. Many trees have evolved methods to protect their flowers by bearing them on slender branches that dangle from the very edge of the tree canopy – thus positioning them in a void between the tree and its neighbours where the monkeys find it difficult to reach.

FIGHTING FOR FOOD

Inevitably, there is competition among the different animal species for this free food, particularly for fruit. A fruit bat swooping down on fruits of the African fig, for example, is likely to suffer a sharply painful nip on the nose. Although it flies off immediately, the pain continues, and there are further nips to the bat's face and eyelids. Weaver ants have attacked the bat, and a few are still swarming over its face as it flies

GUARDING ASSETS *Ants ward off hungry animals, protecting their 'herd' of leafhopper insects and the branch tips that supply the hoppers with sap.*

away. Their attack represents an attempt to keep the figs for their own kind.

The ants also raise scale insects on the fruits and branches of the fig tree. The scale insects produce a sugary fluid by sucking out tree sap from the branches or juice from the fruit that is then 'milked' by the ants. Herding and milking scale insects in this way is a common strategy for ants, and they normally defend their herd against all hazards.

But in defending it against the fruit bats, they are being particularly unhelpful to the tree, since many of the figs are not eaten as a result, and the seeds are therefore not dispersed. Beneath an African fig tree that houses a weaver ant colony, much of the fruit lies rotting on the ground.

When a rain-forest tree is rich with fruit, animals may gather from far and wide. One type of fruit tree in the rain forests of Panama was found to attract 23 different species of fruit-eating birds and mammals. Inevitably, there are contests for access to the fruit, with aggressive displays, pecking and chasing, as the different species compete for the best feeding sites.

NOURISHING REMAINS *Bird droppings are rich in nitrogen, and supplement an inadequate diet for many butterflies, such as these from Trinidad.*

Parrots are often the victors at fig trees, since they are large, bold and have heavy beaks, but they still take only about half of the fruit, with the rest being shared among other species. Unfortunately for the figs, parrots destroy their tiny seeds rather than dispersing them.

SUPPLEMENTING THE DIET

Many nectar-eaters and fruit-eaters are forced to supplement their diet in some way, to make up for the protein or minerals it otherwise lacks. Nectar-eating birds and bats tend to snap up insects feeding at the same flowers – a simple solution to the problem. For the nectar-feeding insects themselves the difficulty cannot be resolved as easily. The nectar of some flowers visited exclusively by insects contains minerals and amino acids (the building blocks of protein), but not all

SALT OF THE EARTH *In the Amazon*
Basin, brilliantly coloured macaws
gather at a river bank to obtain
vital minerals from the clay.

flowers are able to afford this luxury and
many insects must look elsewhere. Like the
army-ant butterfly, many other butterflies
resort to sipping from bird droppings for

the nitrogen compounds they contain,
essential ingredients for making proteins.
Other butterfly species may drink at putrefy-
ing corpses, urine, dung or rotting seeds in
their search for nitrogen.

Among the fruit-eaters, some take the
occasional insect to improve their diet.
Others have different techniques. Flying
foxes living on islands in South-east Asia

drink sea water to gain important minerals,
while the colourful scarlet macaws of South
America take great beakfuls of rock from
crumbling cliff faces in their search for the
minerals that are lacking in fruit.

Forest elephants also take soil, particularly from termite mounds. The same somewhat curious preference was observed
among populations of red leaf monkeys

Many rain forests experience a constant shortage of mineral nutrients and the dearth that affects the trees and other plants is inevitably passed on to the forest animals. Termites are only able to concentrate mineral nutrients because they process such a huge amount of dead wood. Some of those minerals appear in their droppings, which then enrich the soil of which their nests are made.

Termites also have their own special source of nitrogen which supplements the low protein content of wood. Among the bacteria living in their hind gut are species that can 'fix' atmospheric nitrogen gas, turning it into useful nitrogen compounds. Bacteria such as these generally live in the soil, or inside plants, and the termites are unique in housing them within their bodies. These bacteria make an invaluable contribution to the termites' diet.

MEAT-EATERS OF THE TREE TOPS

There are flesh-eaters in the tropical rain forest, and they pose a threat to many of its inhabitants. For anolis lizards seeking out night-time roosts this threat leads to one important criterion: the roosts must be places that shudder and shake if anything approaches, and there must be one approach route only. The tip of a palm frond is ideal, and the lizard will stretch out along the midrib of the leaf. Alternatively, a slender twig, or a large dangling leaf at the very end of a branch will do.

What the anolis lizard cannot guard against is attack by a hungry blunt-nosed snake, reaching up vertically from a branch way below, like a crane with ravenous jaws. To achieve a stiff vertical body, the snake has evolved unusual adaptations of the vertebrae, the discs that make up its spine. They allow the spine to stay rigid as it reaches upwards, but also to have some limited side-to-side movement so that it can home in on its prey. The blunt-nosed snake can also prey on bats feeding at flowers, using the same hunting strategy.

Snakes are among the most successful of the tree-top carnivores because their climbing abilities and stealth are virtually unmatched. Many species can adapt to prey of widely differing sizes, thanks to their venomous bite and ability to swallow prey as large as their own head.

FEAST OF EGGS *The cat-eyed snake is found in the rain forests of the Americas, where it feeds on little else but tree frogs and their eggs.*

(*Presbytis rubicunda*) in Borneo, which only ever ate lumps of soil that they had broken from termite mounds. The possible reasons for this were investigated and the termite soil analysed for nutrients. It turned out to be far richer than the ordinary forest soil in minerals such as potassium and calcium, minerals that may be lacking from the monkeys' diet of leaves and seeds.

This adaptability is valuable in a habitat where animal life is so effectively cloaked and concealed by the curtains of greenery. Nor do snakes need to feed often. Most eat less than once a week, and a large python may survive for many months without food.

Several species of rain-forest snakes have become highly specialised in particular types of prey, especially small items such as nestling birds. One of the most unusual species is the cat-eyed snake (*Leptodeira septentrionalis*) which feeds almost exclusively on tree frogs and their eggs. Since many tree frogs lay their eggs on the ever-damp leaves of rain-forest trees, these are easily found and consumed by the snake, which sucks in great mouthfuls of the jelly-like eggs.

Many of the mammal predators are themselves rather snake-like with long slender bodies that cling closely to the branches as they climb. Civets, linsangs and genets, all inhabitants of the Old World, are small, sharp-nosed animals with long thickly furred tails and coats that are spotted or striped for concealment in the dappled sunshine of the canopy. The tails are moved to one side or the other to gain extra balance when

SKY PROWLERS *Vultures, such as the black vulture, patrol the skies of New World tropical rain forests, searching for prey in the canopy beneath.*

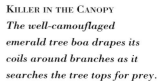

KILLER IN THE CANOPY
The well-camouflaged emerald tree boa drapes its coils around branches as it searches the tree tops for prey.

climbing, although one species, the binturong of South-east Asia has a prehensile tail that can grasp branches and acts like a fifth limb. Most of these small, lithe predators feed on lizards, tree frogs, birds and nestlings, sometimes taking insects as well.

Birds of prey are the other supreme carnivores of the rain forest, hovering above the canopy or perching on the bare branch of an emergent tree, until they spot their prey. The largest of the eagles swoop down on monkeys and other large mammals such as sloths or flying lemurs. Small vultures known as turkey vultures also thrive in the rain forests of South America, locating their carcasses by smell rather than by sight as most vultures do. This is an essential adaptation to the nature of the tropical rain forest, an environment where food is usually abundant but may often be hard to find.

RAIN FORESTS OF THE WORLD

2

FRILLY FEATHERS *This exotically plumed pigeon is found in New Guinea.*

THE WORLD'S TROPICAL RAIN FORESTS ARE SPREAD AROUND THE EQUATOR AND DIVIDED INTO FOUR MAIN REGIONS: THE AMERICAS, AFRICA, ASIA AND AUSTRALASIA. WHILE TROPICAL RAIN FORESTS SHARE MANY SPECIES IN COMMON, LONG PERIODS OF SEPARATION AND ISOLATION HAVE ALSO ALLOWED EACH OF THESE REGIONS TO DEVELOP ITS OWN DISTINCTIVE ARRAY OF PLANT AND ANIMAL SPECIES. AN EXTRAORDINARY COLLECTION OF BEAUTIFUL AND DIVERSE CREATURES — INCLUDING THE COLOURFUL MORPHO BUTTERFLIES OF THE AMERICAS, PYGMY HIPPOS OF AFRICA, HORNBILLS OF ASIA AND TREE KANGAROOS OF AUSTRALASIA — HAS EVOLVED WITHIN ALL THESE UNIQUE HABITATS FILLING EVERY CONCEIVABLE NICHE THAT EXISTS WITHIN THEM.

FIGHTING CATS *Jaguars in the Amazon rain forest.*

THE WEALTH OF
THE AMERICAS

River dolphins swim through flooded forests, hummingbirds

hover beside flowers and sloths hang motionless from trees.

The rain forests of the Americas are home to unique wildlife

and represent more than a third of the world's rain forests.

It is early afternoon in the rain forests of eastern Costa Rica. Overhead, the skies have just cleared, and the leaves of the forest canopy, washed by nearly 24 hours of constant rain, now steam gently in the tropical sunshine. Within the forest itself, hardly any sunlight reaches the ground, and the animals of the forest floor seem indifferent to the change in the weather. But nearby, beyond the dimly lit confusion of the forest's interior, the clearing skies bring about a transformation, as if a million stage lights had suddenly been switched on.

Here, the sun's rays blaze down on a noisy torrent of water that tumbles over ancient volcanic boulders, tugging gently at the aerial roots of trees trailing over its surface. As the light floods down into this green-walled, water-worn corridor, one of the forest's most beautiful spectacles is about to begin.

At first, it seems like some optical illusion – a brief vanishing streak of brilliant blue glimpsed out of the corner of the eye, but never quite seen head-on. Several minutes go by without the event repeating itself, and then suddenly and in silence, it happens again, this time a little bit closer at hand. The azure flashes begin to multiply, and soon the air above the stream is sliced by numerous bursts of metallic colour, each one gliding through the sunshine, and then disappearing once more into the shade. The flight of the morphos, the most exquisite butterflies in the rain forest, is under way.

Morphos are found only in the Americas, and rarely stray far from the forest. Unlike some rainforest butterflies, these jewels of the insect world are mainly fair-weather fliers, taking to the air during breaks in the rain. Instead of flying erratically, in the usual fashion of butterflies, morphos move in a much more purposeful way, propelling themselves along 'flyways', such as streams or forest tracks, with powerful flicks of their long wings. The total wingspan of each butterfly is 4-5 in (10-12.5 cm). Often, more than a dozen of them may be airborne at once, forming a noiseless procession along their private highway through the trees.

In many species of morpho, only the male is blue. And his electric livery is confined to the

A TRICK OF THE LIGHT
Reflecting blue light with maximum intensity, thousands of tiny, precisely arranged scales (left) give the wings of morpho butterflies a dazzling blue sheen (below).

upper surfaces of his wings, while the undersides are brown. This arrangement of colours camouflages the butterfly while it is feeding or resting, because its wings are then held tightly together above the body. But the moment it prepares for takeoff, its full splendour is suddenly revealed.

The extraordinary intensity of the morpho's colour, and its metallic sheen, are produced by the structure of the wings themselves, not by chemical pigments, such as give colour to flower petals, fruits and most butterfly wings. Like all butterflies and moths, morphos are covered with scales – tiny stiff flaps made of a hard material called 'chitin'. Scales cover nearly the whole of a butterfly's body, and those on the wings are arranged in neat rows, like miniature tiles hanging on a roof. The scales are anchored to the wing along a single edge.

In a morpho wing, the scales have an unusual surface structure, a series of microscopic parallel ridges, arranged with mathematical precision. These ridges ensure that the scales absorb most of the colours in sunlight, but reflect blue wavelengths. The rays of blue light reflected by each of the ridges interact with one another after they leave the wing, and the result is a rippling iridescent sheen that subtly changes according to the angle from which it is seen. The colour also disappears entirely when the observer is at a certain angle to the wing, or when the wing is not lit directly by sunlight, which is why a morpho can appear as a brilliant blue flash one moment and apparently vanish the next.

Morphos are not the only forest animals that produce iridescent colours in this way – they can also been seen, for example, in beetles and hummingbirds. However, few other animals use a single colour over such a large surface area, and to such breathtaking effect.

A NEW WORLD

Morpho butterflies are just one of the thousands of animal groups that are found only in the tropical region of the Americas, sometimes called the 'neotropics'. (*Neo* comes from Greek and simply means 'new' – it distinguishes the tropical zones of the New World from tropical areas of the Old World, that is, in Africa and Asia.)

In the neotropics, ancient geographical configurations allowed plants and animals to evolve for a while in relative isolation from the rest of the world. In its living diversity and range of unusual species, the neotropical region is perhaps the richest treasure house of our planet, rivalled only by the rain forests of South-east Asia.

This diversity includes the butterflies and their lifestyles, each of them adapted to different feeding patterns,

weather conditions

and so on. Given the power of tropical rain, the morpho's preference for dry weather, for example, seems like a simple matter of prudence. But in general, tropical butterflies and moths are more robust than their relatives in cooler climes, and not all of them are grounded when the rain sets in. During bad weather, some seek shelter by flying through the forest itself rather than along open 'flyways', but others make headway across clearings and tracks, apparently unaffected by all but the most severe downpours.

The black-and-white heliconid butterfly (*Heliconius cydno*) is a common species in

PASSION AND THE BUTTERFLY
The passionflower deploys a range of defences against heliconid butterflies and their destructive caterpillars. These include ant and wasp allies and phoney eggs on its leaves.

Central America and a member of this band of all-weather aviators. Smaller and a good deal daintier than the morphos, it belongs to a family known as the long-wings, which reaches northwards as far as the southern United States. There are about 50 species, and they can be recognised almost instantly by their elliptical wings which have a narrow, almost spoon-shaped outline. Many species are boldly patterned in orange, yellow and black, making them easy to pick out against their dark background.

Like other heliconids, the black-and-white heliconid feeds only on passionflowers – scrambling vines with grasping tendrils that coil up like springs. It uses their nectar and pollen as food for itself, while the passionflower leaves nourish its caterpillars.

Passionflower plants are often widely scattered, and they can take a little time to find. So, hour after hour, a female black-and-white heliconid will tirelessly investigate the various low-growing plants along the forest edge and in clearings, approaching each one with a characteristic bobbing flight, in the hope that it will prove to be a suitable place for her to lay her eggs.

Even when the female heliconid does manage to locate her target plant, she does not rush into laying. Too many eggs on one plant could spell danger for her offspring, partly because heliconid caterpillars can become cannibals when crowded together, and partly because a single plant can provide only a limited supply of food. She is instinctively cautious and inspects the plant carefully for signs of other eggs before laying any of her own.

Once the eggs have been laid and the caterpillars hatch, they make short work of the leaves on which they find themselves. As the days pass, the caterpillars grow rapidly and march onwards over the passionflower plant, stripping young shoots and leaves with small but ruthless jaws. A major caterpillar infestation can devastate a plant, leaving little more than a wiry stem hanging by its tendrils. But passionflowers are not entirely defenceless victims of these attacks. Over millions of years, the contest between plant and butterfly has produced some extraordinary examples of natural warfare, as the plants struggle to fend off their unwelcome visitors.

ALLIES AND DISGUISES

In nature, as in the human world, there is usually a price to pay for protection received. At the same time, an enemy's enemy frequently becomes a friend. For passionflowers, the payment is sugar-rich nectar, and the protectors are hungry ants and wasps that are equipped with poisonous bites or stings.

As in many plants that rely on ants for protection the nectar-producing glands are widely dispersed along the stems, ensuring that the ants and wasps patrol the whole plant in an agitated search for the sugary liquid. While on patrol, these aggressive insects instantly attack any other animal that dares to intrude on their source of food. Should a butterfly venture a landing, it is immediately chased off, while any caterpillars that manage to hatch are likely to be

POUCHED MAMMALS OF THE AMERICAS

Millions of years ago, South America was part of the great southern supercontinent, Gondwanaland. So too were Africa, Antarctica and Australia. Gondwanaland split up during a crucial phase in the evolution of mammals, and just as Australia inherited the pouched mammals, or marsupials, so too did South America. Neither continent had placental mammals – mammals, including humans, that nourish the developing young in the uterus and then give birth – for millions of years, and so the marsupials could evolve without competition from placentals. In South America, the marsupials diversified to produce a variety of forms, including a doglike pouched predator called *Borhyaena*.

But placental mammals did reach South America in time, arriving in successive waves from North America as the two continents were partially linked by a string of islands, then joined completely by the Central American isthmus. Gradually, most of the pouched mammals died out, unable to compete with placental mammals for food, or to evade placental carnivores.

A few survived, however, and they live on today in the form of the American opossums, 75 species of small shrew-like or mouse-like animals that range in size from just over 2¹/₂ in (6 cm) long to almost 20 in (51 cm) in the most successful and widespread species – the Virginia opossum, which has colonised large areas of North America.

Some opossums live on the forest floor, while others are expert climbers.

They are mostly opportunistic feeders, taking anything from fruit, insects and lizards to carrion, flowers and earthworms.

SAFE WATERS *The woolly opossum is one of the pouched mammals that has survived in South American rain forests.*

killed. For the plant, making extra nectar means using up extra energy – but it is a small price to pay for maintaining such a vigilant garrison.

Heliconid butterflies have unusually large eyes, and some naturalists believe that vision plays a large part in their choice of plants. In response to this, passionflowers seem to have evolved some remarkable visual tricks that help them to escape attack. Typical passionflowers have distinctive leaves with five narrow lobes, making up a shape that resembles a small splayed hand. However, some species have unlobed leaves, either elliptical or oval in shape, while others have a variety of leaf forms. Each type grows at different heights from the ground. If heliconids are guided mainly by sight, rather than smell, this confusing variety of leaf shapes could prove to be an effective defence. Like most butterflies, heliconids are very selective about where they lay their eggs, and any plant they do not recognise is likely to be ignored.

In a few passionflower species – perhaps one in fifty – one of nature's most bizarre visual defences comes into play. These passionflowers have evolved 'eggs' of their own, each one an oval yellow swelling that perfectly mimics the egg of a heliconid butterfly. The eggs not only look right, they are also 'laid' in the right place – usually at the tips of the tendrils. When a visiting female makes her inspection, the counterfeit eggs immediately catch her eye. Faced with this apparent evidence that she has arrived too late, she is likely to move on and search elsewhere.

OUTSIZE RODENTS

The richness and diversity of neotropical species extends well beyond butterflies. Among other special animals found in the tropical rain forests of the Americas are the cavimorph rodents. They include the world's largest rodents, species such as the seed-eating paca, a stripy tailless animal the size of a spaniel, and the even larger capybara, a sturdily built rodent that grows up to 4¹/₂ft (1.3 m) long. The first European naturalists to explore South America mistakenly, but understandably in view of the

SAFE WATERS A female capybara (above) escorts her young along the banks of a Venezuelan riverbed. Right: A capybara's swimming skills.

animals' water-loving habits, named them 'water hogs'. Capybaras can weigh as much as 177 lb (80 kg) and are the largest rodents in the world.

Capybaras can run like horses when danger threatens, but they prefer to resort to water for safety, forming a tight cluster, with the vulnerable young capybaras protected at the centre of the group. With nostrils, eyes and ears located close to the top of the head, capybaras can swim almost totally submerged while still breathing and scanning the river bank for enemies such as jaguars. Their lungs are so well adapted to diving that they can disappear under water for up to five minutes at a time. Webbed toes and powerful back legs make them strong swimmers, in spite of their far-from-sleek, somewhat barrel-shaped bodies.

Grass is the staple food of the capybara – those that inhabit the rain forests mainly crop the short grass of the river bank, but occasionally sample other forest vegetation. Feeding takes place in the late afternoon and early evening, while the heat of noon is usually endured by wallowing in water. Mating also takes place in the shallows of a river or lake, simply for safety from predators.

Like the paca and the agouti (a burrowing creature with brownish or dark grey fur), the capybara is descended from ancient rodents that were able to evolve in isolation during the long interlude when South America was an island. Their ancestors came from North America, arriving between about 35 million and 25 million years ago, at a time when a string of small islands existed between the two continents, formed by the highest peaks of the Central American mountains breaking the ocean surface. These ancestral rodents, relatives of the porcupines, probably rafted southwards on floating vegetation, moving from island to island and finally reaching South America.

Here, they found food sources that were not being fully exploited by the archaic mammals that then roamed South America, the inefficient and uncompetitive products of its long era of utter isolation. Presented with such rich new opportunities, the ancestral rodents rapidly diversified their

FOREST CAT *The beautiful ocelot, widely hunted for its fur, is becoming increasingly rare.*

diet and evolved into a variety of large species, filling the sort of plant-eating niches that are occupied by deer and pigs in other parts of the world. Many have survived to this day, despite the arrival of new immigrants from North America, when the two continents were completely joined within the last 5 million years.

The union with North America brought more advanced plant-eating mammals, such as peccaries and tapirs, southwards, as well as faster and more efficient carnivores, including jaguars (*Panthera onca*) and ocelots (*Felis pardalis*). These new invaders were probably responsible for the demise of some species of giant rodents that we know only from fossils. They included an outsized capybara that was twice as long as its surviving relative and weighed as much as a grizzly bear. Even bulkier was a plant-eating rodent known as *Telicomys*, related to the living pacarana, a shy stripy nocturnal creature of the cloud forests, which subsists on leaves, stems and fruits. *Telicomys* was the size of a small rhinoceros, making it the largest rodent ever to have lived.

KINKAJOUS AND ARMADILLOS

Another legacy of South America's long isolation is the kinkajou, a strange-looking animal related to raccoons. It is the size of a domestic cat, with a long, muscular, thickly furred body, a small round face with a pointed nose, and tiny, rounded ears set at the side of the head. Most remarkable of all is the kinkajou's tail which is prehensile, wrapping itself tightly around branches as the animal climbs through the trees.

THE BENEFITS OF AN EXTRA LEG *The kinkajou anchors itself with its long, muscular tail, thereby leaving its front paws free to pick food from the trees.*

No other member of the raccoon family has such a tail, not even the olingo, a close relative which looks very like the kinkajou and often feeds alongside it in the tree tops. Kinkajous are sweet-toothed animals, using their extremely long tongues to lick out fruit pulp, nectar from flowers and honey from the nests of wild bees. They also take some insects. Olingos likewise eat fruit but are far more carnivorous, taking insects and any other animal they can catch, such as small birds and mammals. Exactly why the two species feed together is a mystery, but the olingos may benefit from the increased number of insects and lizards that are disturbed by the kinkajous.

The kinkajou and olingo evolved at about the same time as the capybara and its relatives, between 35 and 25 million years

BRIGHT-EYED *The olingo rests during the day and then emerges at night to forage in the tree tops for fruit and small prey.*

ago. But there are far more ancient products of South America's isolation, unique inhabitants dating back well beyond 60 million years ago and still alive today in the form of sloths, armadillos and anteaters. These survivors are known collectively as edentates, or toothless ones, although it is only the anteaters that lack teeth entirely, an adaptation to their diet of ants and termites. In all the edentates, however, the teeth are less differentiated and more primitive than in other mammals. There are many other peculiarities of the edentates which suggest that they split off from other placental mammals at a very early stage in their evolution.

A MEETING OF WATERS

The unique wildlife, species richness and exceptional luxuriance of the neotropics have developed over millions of years. As in other rain forests, the constant warmth and abundant rainfall play major roles in fostering diversity and engendering new species. But it is not simply the quantity of rain that gives a rain forest its particular qualities. What happens to the rain as it descends, as

SAN RAFAEL FALLS *On its journey towards the Amazon Basin, the Quiros river gushes through the Andes' eastern foothills in Ecuador.*

well as afterwards, is another crucial factor.

In Central America – the northern part of the neotropics – most of the land consists of a narrow mountainous spine, and rainwater runs quickly down the forest-clad hillsides until it meets the sea. But more than 1000 miles (1600 km) farther south, in the basin of the River Amazon, water follows a journey of a very different kind. In tropical South America, rain is created by damp air that blows in from the Atlantic Ocean, but is intensified by the moisture that evaporates from plants in the steady heat of around 27°C (80°F). Instead of cascading rapidly to the sea, the rainwater flows eastwards across a plain so flat that its opposite horizons differ by the height of a few feet.

The plain is flanked by the mountains of the Guiana and Brazilian Highlands to the north and south, and by the rampart of the Andes to the west. Impounded within these walls is not only the world's largest rain forest, but the greatest volume of moving freshwater on Earth. Seen from space, this colossal river system seems like an outstretched hand reaching into the heart of the South American continent. The fingers of the hand claw at the surrounding mountains, slowly eroding their rocks and carrying them away as sediment. They also gather organic matter on their journey through the forest, and this helps to give each river a characteristic colour and chemical make-up which identifies it as surely as a fingerprint.

The Amazon itself is a whitewater river – a liquid conveyor belt that carries an enormous burden of suspended particles from the distant Andes. In geological terms, the Andes are relative newcomers among the world's mountain chains, and their young rocks fall easy prey to the destructive effects of both frost and rain. They generate a constant supply of mineral particles that make water as opaque as paint, with a colour that varies from bluish whiteness to the darkest chocolate. As the river flows eastwards, the heaviest particles gradually settle on the riverbed, and the water becomes more translucent. But the Amazon is never transparent, and anything lowered beneath its murky surface rapidly becomes invisible.

Near the busy Brazilian port of Manaus – which lies an astonishing 1250 miles (2000 km) inland from the Atlantic – the silty Amazon meets the Rio Negro, a river whose waters resemble strong black tea, dark but clear, like a molten stream of tinted glass. The two kinds of water could not look more different and where they come into contact, they swirl and eddy around each other, preserving a moving but razor-sharp boundary for many miles downstream. Gradually, however, the superior volume of the River Amazon triumphs over its tributary, and the Rio Negro's water is diluted until it seems to disappear altogether. This confluence is one of the most remarkable on Earth.

Although it is the largest blackwater river in the world, the Rio Negro is only one

WHERE WATERS MEET *Even after the mighty whitewater Amazon and the blackwater Rio Negro meet, their waters stay separate for many miles.*

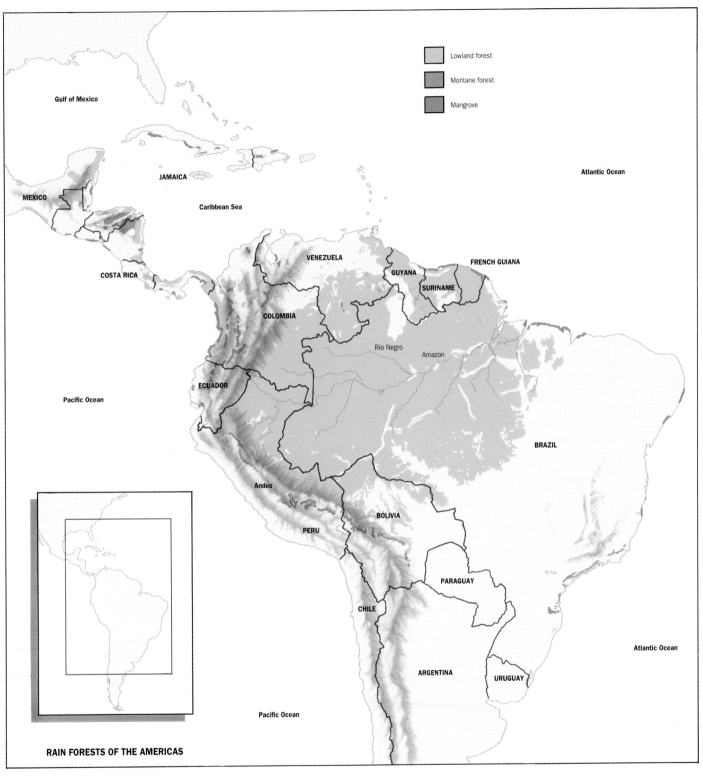

RAIN FORESTS OF THE AMERICAS

FOREST STRONGHOLDS *The world's largest rain forest covers some 2.5 million sq miles (6.5 million km²) in the Amazon Basin. The rain forests of the Americas also include Brazil's coastal forests and the forests of Central America and the Caribbean.*

of a number of such rivers that rise in the Amazon's northern margins, among mountains that are considerably older than the Andes. Here, erosion has had many millions of years to do its work. The original exposed rock has gradually been weathered and turned into sand, before being swept into the lowland plain, where it has built up a layer hundreds of feet deep. The rock that remains in the highlands is extremely hard and extremely durable, so that any water draining off it is not only very pure, but also sparklingly clear.

As this clear highland water flows downstream, it travels through the sand-covered lowlands, and here its complexion darkens.

BLACKWATER RIVERS

The resemblance of blackwater rivers to strong black tea is no coincidence. Tannins colour these waters and it is also tannins that give black tea both its colour and bitterness: these are produced when the leaves of the tea bush are crushed after harvesting.

In the wild, tannins serve as defensive compounds, toxins that protect the tea bush – and millions of other plants – from insects and other leaf-destroyers. Many rain-forest trees produce tannins to protect their leaves, wood and roots from insect pests. These bitter compounds are abundant in both timber and leathery tropical leaves. And where the trees grow on sandy soils, the tannins and other toxins remain intact long after the plants that made them have rotted away.

This legacy of natural chemicals in the blackwater rivers makes them somewhat inimical to life, and they are poor fishing grounds. But they also tend to harbour fewer mosquitoes, so the villages of Amazonian Indians are often sited near them. An ideal village site is

BLACK WATER *Humic acid and other organic substances give the waters of the Rio Negro its clear dark appearance.*

on the banks of a blackwater river, but has a whitewater river flowing nearby, where fish can be obtained.

The sandy soil is very poor in nutrients, and despite its luxuriant vegetation contains relatively little microscopic life. In the absence of an abundant supply of soil bacteria and fungi, resistant chemicals such as tannins are washed into the river by the rainfall, without being first broken down – tannins are produced by plants for protection from insects. Ironically, the trees also produce larger quantities of defensive tannins on these sandy soils than they do in more fertile areas, because replacing the leaves is an expensive process, using up large quantities of nutrients.

LIFE IN WHITE WATER

In the shadowy underwater world of the River Amazon, eyes are of limited use. Anyone diving into its deeper reaches would be surrounded by an impenetrable, silty gloom, with just the faintest illumination filtering down from above. Despite these murky conditions, river animals seem to navigate and find food as easily as if they were moving in broad daylight.

Many Amazonian fish interpret their surroundings by using their sense of smell, and by being able to detect vibrations travelling through the water. Nearly all fish, whether in the sea or in fresh waters, make some use of these two senses, but in the Amazon they have often become the most important senses of all.

The tambaqui (*Colossoma macropomum*), a fruit and seed-eating member of the characin family, is typical of the fish that live in these waters. Its large nostrils can pick up faint scents from floating food, and it detects sound vibrations with the aid of its swimbladder – a gas-filled organ that also controls its buoyancy. Guided by these two senses, tambaquis congregate under wild rubber trees, gulping down their nutritious seeds as soon as it feels them splash into the water. Like most of the fish of the Amazon, the tambaqui does have functional eyes as well, but it uses them only when swimming near the surface.

SEARCHING FOR SEEDS
Highly sensitive to vibrations and smells, tambaqui fish navigate with ease through the murky waters of the Amazon.

The infamous red piranha (*Serrasalmus nattereri*) is a relative of the tambaqui, but this shoal-forming fish uses the senses of smell and waterborne vibration to very different ends. Piranhas are carnivores that attack other animals *en masse*, forming a formidable and ruthless throng armed with razor-sharp teeth. Spurred on by the thrashing movements made by their feeding neighbours, piranhas attack animals that they can smell but can very rarely see. Although red piranhas are little more than 12 in (30 cm) long, their protruding lower jaws can cut through skin and scales with the ease of a meat-slicer, removing neatly wedge-shaped pieces of flesh. Red piranhas have been known to bite humans, and they frequently attack smaller mammals and other fish. From time to time, a larger mammal such as a capybara may be ambushed if it is already ailing, and the carcass stripped in minutes. However, despite their grim reputation, there are no recorded instances of people being killed by piranhas.

Bottom-dwelling fish live in a world that is darker still than that of the tambaqui and piranha. Here, a keen sense of touch is the most reliable way of finding static food. This is the realm of catfishes – large-headed animals able to survive in slow-flowing or stagnant water that contains little oxygen.

One of the largest of all these species is the cuiu-cuiu catfish (*Oxydoras niger*), which searches the riverbed with tentacle-like sensory organs known as barbels that project from its lower jaw. The barbels can be up to about 6 in (15 cm) long, and they probe the sediment like so many restless fingers, feeling for worms and insect larvae. When the fish, measuring about 3 ft (1 m) from tip to tail, senses food, it suddenly opens its large jaws, creating a suction force that brings a mass of animals and silt into its mouth.

Other fish use a sense that is, to human beings, much more remarkable because it

SMALL BUT DEADLY *Red-bellied piranhas hunt in fearsome shoals. They can rip through the flesh of their prey with alarming efficiency.*

lies completely outside our experience. By activating specially adapted sets of muscles, knife-fish and their relatives produce weak electric currents that create an electromagnetic field through the water around them. These fish can sense the electromagnetic field as well, and they are able to detect any distortions in it that are produced by nearby objects. Guided by this remarkable electromagnetic map, they are able to find their way through even the most turbid water with ease.

One relative of the knife-fish has refined the use of electricity and turned it to more devastating ends. Instead of using it just to navigate, the electric eel also uses it to kill. Its body contains rows of modified muscles that act as high-power batteries, and these generate a powerful electric charge of about 500 volts. When the charge is unleashed,

anything close to the fish receives a massive and often fatal shock. The electric eel uses this potent weapon to kill small fish, and also to disable its enemies.

THE PINK DOLPHIN

One of the most exotic Amazonian animals is the boutu or river dolphin, a curious-looking creature, $5^{1}/_{2}$-10 ft (1.7-3 m) long, whose body is largely pink, with a streak of grey along its head and back. Its long, slender jaws resemble the beak of a stork or heron, while above them on the forehead is a curious, slightly misshapen bump. This houses a structure known as the melon, responsible for focusing the beam of high-pitched sounds which dolphins emit so that they can listen to the echoes – a sensory system known as echolocation that operates on the same principles as radar.

RIVER DOLPHINS *A small group of boutus or Amazon river dolphins swim in search of fish, using echolocation to track down their prey.*

All dolphins use echolocation, but none are so heavily dependent on it as the river dolphins, for they inhabit waters of impenetrable murkiness. Fish and shrimps can be detected with this echolocation system, aided by an ultrasensitive snout that probes in the bottom mud. Boutus do not inhabit the blackwater rivers such as the Rio Negro, being uniquely suited to the silty conditions of the Amazon itself. During periods of flooding, the dolphins move into the forest and swim between the inundated tree trunks, using their echolocation technique to avoid obstacles such as buttress roots.

Not surprisingly, the eyes of the boutu are reduced to tiny specks that do little more than distinguish light from dark. It lives in sociable groups usually of about 12-15, though sometimes there may be as many as 20 dolphins together, including the young ones that are entirely blue-grey in colour. Boutu groups occasionally follow giant otters, which likewise feed on fish but can operate in shallower waters than the

dolphins. As the giant otter hunts near the river bank, fish flee towards the deeper waters midstream, only to fall prey to the waiting dolphins.

FORESTS WITHIN FORESTS

To a traveller journeying slowly up the Amazon, the forest along the river banks can sometimes seem even more featureless than the muddy water that slides past them. The river at least has its mud banks and sandbars, shallows and islands, but the forest often looks like a monotonous green rampart, with few memorable landmarks to distinguish one sweep from the next.

In fact, this impression of monotony could hardly be more misleading. Studies have shown that the Amazon rain forest varies enormously from one area to another, both on a large scale, and also much more locally. Taking the Amazon as a whole, scientists have identified over 24 distinct forest types, each with its own particular mixture of trees and other plants, and its unique structure and type of soil. Some of these various formations are known by the Portuguese names used by early European settlers in the region, while others have names originally used by the first inhabitants of the forest.

Terra firme, for example, is 'firm ground' forest, the most widespread formation, found on slightly raised ground that is rarely flooded. There are several types of *terra firme* forest, ranging from forest with a spacious floor where walking is quite easy, to forest so choked with lianas that any kind of progress through it is practically impossible. Where *terra firme* meets open ground – for example along a track or a river bank – the result is true jungle, a mass of tangled plants, all competing for their share of the incoming light.

From June to September, the Amazon experiences the wettest months in its already wet calendar. Over a period of weeks, some of its tributaries may rise by over 50 ft (15 m), as a massive surge of rainwater slowly makes its way towards the Atlantic, spilling out into the surrounding flood plains. From October onwards the waters begin to fall again, exposing land that was inundated for several months. This annual cycle, endlessly repeated, has produced two special kinds of forest where water dominates the landscape.

Várzea is a form of swampy forest found on clay, where muddy 'white' water brings extra sediment during annual flooding. *Igapó* is another type of swampy forest, this

VARZEA FORESTS *These are lowland forests, founded on clay, which are seasonally flooded by the muddy whitewater rivers of the Amazon Basin.*

BLACK AND WET *On the sandy plains of blackwater rivers, expanses of lowland forest, known as* igapó, *are submerged for many months of the year.*

time flooded by silt-free blackwater or clear water. *Igapó* develops on sandy soils, and where it is exposed along the river bank the sand can be as white as that on any coral beach. At the climax of the annual flood, thousands of square miles of *igapó* are inundated, and each tree top becomes a crowded island of life, sometimes just a few yards above the surface.

Most animals can move to avoid the rising water, but plants have no way of escaping this prolonged immersion. All plants need oxygen to survive. Under normal circumstances, they absorb much of it from the air through their leaves, but they also need to soak up some from the soil in order to keep their roots alive. Maintaining healthy roots in soil that is waterlogged for a few months at a time is a taxing business, and no one yet knows exactly how *igapó* trees achieve this.

The dividing line between rain forest and river is blurred indeed in these flooded forests. When the waters recede again, some river species are left behind, including a small catfish, no longer than a thumbnail, which passes the rest of the year in the moist surroundings of the leaf litter. It is bright red in colour and preys on small insects by feeling for them with its sensitive mouth barbels (sensors). Surprisingly, this tiny fish has no visual powers at all, suggesting that it evolved in the darkness of the turbid Amazon riverbed.

Also left behind are freshwater sponges that grow on the trunks of trees in the flooded forest. Astonishingly, the sponges can survive the long months out of water, protected by a thick, leathery skin that develops on the outer surface. They do not feed or grow during this time, but simply wait for the flood waters to rise once more.

A FOREST FLORA

As in all tropical rain forests, the Amazon is a place of bewildering botanical variety. Few people would have any trouble recognising the lofty cannonball tree (*Couroupita*

guianensis), when it is bearing its wooden ball-shaped fruits, or the spreading guayaán (*Tabebuia chrysantha*), when covered in its beautiful waxy flowers. But at any one time, only a fraction of the forest's trees are flowering or fruiting, and the leaves of rain-forest trees are remarkably similar, making plant identification exceptionally difficult.

The members of the melastome family, or Melastomataceae, provide just one example. This family contains about 3000 trees and shrubs, found mostly in the tropics, particularly the Amazon region. Nearly all are low-growing, and have oval leaves arranged in pairs. They have the same pointed tips, the same characteristic rows of parallel veins and the same leathery texture. Most species also have the same gangling growth, and the same slim, smooth trunks. Only the characteristics of their different flowers and fruit allow one species to be distinguished from another.

A few Amazonian trees are, however, instantly recognisable. Among them is the graceful cecropia or umbrella tree (*Cecropia* species), a low-growing inhabitant of tracks and river banks, that is both common and

UNPOPULAR FRUITS *The solid, round fruits of the Amazonian cannonball tree are hardly appetising and find few takers. Often they accumulate in rotting piles below its branches.*

widespread throughout the American tropics. The cecropia's bright green leaves are lobed and fan-shaped, giving no hint that it is actually a relative of the stinging nettles. But instead of having poisonous stings, cecropias are protected by ants that set up home in their hollow stems. Any interference with the plant instantly mobilises the ants, which prepare to fend off leaf-eating intruders.

The cecropia is a typical pioneer plant – a species that survives by making rapid use of temporary spaces that open up in the forest and along river banks. Its seeds are light and spread easily, and they germinate quickly, within a few days. But although cecropias grow extremely rapidly, they never reach any great height, and they are eventually shaded out by taller trees with longer lifespans.

Even the fast-growing cecropia is outpaced by another pioneer that often grows near to it along the river edges. This is the balsa tree (*Ochroma lagopus*), an open tree recognisable by its very large light green leaves. Balsas are famous for having the lightest wood in the world, highly valued for model-making. In the wild, they can reach a height of over 30 ft (9 m) in two years, but later their growth slows and they rarely reach more than about 80 ft (25 m).

Palm trees, although usually pictured in the desert or on tropical beaches, are also important rain-forest trees. Indeed, some forest areas in the lower Amazonian basin are dominated by palms. Elsewhere, smaller palms can be found scattered throughout the rain forest, particularly on damp sandy soil, and in places where the canopy lets enough light filter through to the forest floor. These understorey palms are often covered with epiphylls – small plants such as liverworts and mosses that give their leaves an encrusted and almost dirty appearance. Many of these low-growing palms have to be approached with caution, because they are often armed with hard, black spines, a few inches long, which can puncture the thickest skin.

Palm leaves are distinctive and variable in shape. Some look like giant fans or combs, while others resemble brush-like tufts, or ragged flags that hang limply in the wind. In most palms, the leaves spread out in a circle, but in a few, including the beautiful Caribbean royal palm (*Roystonea regia*), they grow in a single plane, overlapping each other to form a giant hand with dozens of fraying fingers.

Like tree ferns – which are deceptively similar – palms grow taller without the trunk ever becoming any thicker. They lack side buds, so if the top of a palm tree is severed or eaten away, the tree stops growing and dies. Palms produce clusters of hard seeds that are often enclosed in soft flesh, and these provide important food for many birds, mammals, and even fruit-eating fish.

Throughout the rain forests of the Americas, one tree in particular does reach outstanding dimensions and looms over the riverside forest, forming an unmistakable, flat-topped silhouette against the sky. This is the ceiba or kapok tree (*Ceiba pentandra*), whose girth and mass at maturity make it one of the rain forest's most awe-inspiring and magnificent sights.

Propped up by buttresses that can be as high as a house, its battleship-grey trunk rears up through the forest, often rising for over 200 ft (60 m) without a single branch. Then, having emerged from the surrounding canopy, the trunk ends abruptly, fanning out into a wheel of perhaps half a dozen almost horizontal limbs. These branches are massive indeed, each up to 6 ft (1.8 m) in diameter.

The ceiba's creamy-white flowers open at night, and are pollinated by bats that are attracted to them by their syrupy and sickly smelling nectar. After the flowers have withered, they go on to produce pear-sized fruits that look as though they were destined to fall to the forest floor.

But, like the cecropia and balsa trees, the ceiba spreads its seeds using the wind. Its fruits burst open while still on the tree, releasing seeds that float over the forest canopy on a mass of waxy yellowish-white fibres. A variety of this tree is cultivated in South-east Asia, where the fibres are harvested and used for stuffing a number of objects that range from cushions to lifebelts. The Malayan word for these fibres – *kapoq* – gives the tree its alternative name.

UMBRELLA TREE *Housed in a cecropia's hollow branches, Azteca ants (above) patrol the tree's surface. Right: The foliage of a cecropia sapling.*

Surprisingly, wild ceiba trees are also found in tropical West Africa. As all the ceiba's close relatives live in the Americas, it is probable that it is a native of this region. In the distant past, individual ceiba seeds or fruits must have managed to cross the Atlantic, perhaps to be washed up on the muddy banks of a West African estuary. From this beachhead, they slowly began to colonise the Old World.

GARDENS IN THE SKIES

In the windless interior of a rain forest, the floor bears witness to the endless contest being fought between gravity and growth. Decaying trunks mark the demise of trees, but strewn among them are casualties of a different kind – fleshy, cabbage-sized plants that have tumbled out of the canopy above. Some of these plants are in pieces, like the scattered wreckage of crashed planes, but others are largely intact, and look as though they might survive their fall. But even for these, the outlook is bleak. Starved of the bright light in their original habitat in the canopy, they are doomed to a lingering death in a world of shade and shadows.

HANGING CLOUDS *Bunches of seeds, each bearing silky threads, dangle from the sturdy branches of a kapok tree, as they wait to be carried by the wind.*

These intruders from above are bromeliads – spiky-leaved plants that are found almost exclusively in the Americas. Some bromeliad species, such as the cultivated pineapple, grow on the ground, but in rain forests most bromeliads are epiphytic, meaning that they live out their lives perched on the branches of trees. In this way, they exploit trees in the struggle for light, rather than fight against them.

Bromeliad seeds are mostly spread by air currents within the forest, and they germinate to produce tiny plants that look like minute tufts of grass. These tufts can be found on anything wooden in or around the rain forest – not just living trees, but also dead trunks, fence posts, and even the shingles of wooden roofs. As each seedling grows, it produces a mass of stringlike roots that slowly clamp it to its perch.

After several years, a mature bromeliad can measure over 2 ft (61 cm) across and may weigh several pounds. If it has the luck to be growing on a strong support – such as a ceiba branch – its prospects are good. However, if its perch lacks strength, it cannot swap it for another, and life becomes increasingly precarious. Sometimes, individual plants become dislodged as their roots fail to

PRIVATE POOL *Protected by a thin film of moisture, two tadpoles are carried on the back of a reticulated arrow-poison frog.*

anchor the increasing load of leaves. Alternatively, the combined weight of several dozen bromeliads may be enough to snap off their shared branch, sending them all plunging to the ground.

Despite such hazards, bromeliads are tremendously successful plants, especially in the forests of Central America. Here, almost every tree has its share of these uninvited guests, and their green or red foliage can be seen wherever there is enough light to sustain them.

Like all other epiphytes – including orchids and some palms, ferns and cacti – bromeliads take little or no sustenance from their host plants. To grow, they need only four things: sunlight, air, water and a small supply of minerals. Obtaining the first two presents few difficulties, but collecting the last two can be much more problematic.

Seen under a microscope, a bromeliad's leaves are covered with trichomes – tiny hairs that work very much like roots. Using their trichomes, small bromeliads, such as the air plants (*Tillandsia* species), extract all the water and minerals they need from rain and dust. But even in rain forests, rain is intermittent, so large bromeliads risk wilting in the strong sunshine that blazes down

BROMELIAD AND ANIMALS *A bromeliad anchored to a tree trunk is the focus of an entire ecosystem. Frogs and insects with aquatic larvae deposit their eggs in, on and under it; anolis lizards display next to it; butterflies come to drink from it; and a whole range of predators, from spiders to snakes, take advantage of the constant stream of juicy visitors.*

on them between downpours. Many solve this problem by having a private reservoir that can be used as it is needed. Their leaves act as gutters, channelling rainwater into a central tank formed by their overlapping leaf-bases. A really large bromeliad can hold as much as 2 gallons (9 litres) of water, which also contains a useful supply of minerals washed in with each shower.

LIFE IN A BROMELIAD POOL

Clamped to branches high above the forest floor, bromeliads can form miniature worlds of water, each with its own astonishingly complex web of life. Their residents include microscopic water plants and tiny aquatic animals such as flatworms and snails. Some bromeliads harbour crabs and most contain the larvae of mosquitoes and damselflies – insects that spend the first part of their lives in water. Spiders lie in wait for insects flying near the water, and small snakes, such as young eyelash vipers (*Bothrops shlegellii*), often curl among the bromeliad leaves, ready to catch lizards that come to sun themselves near the water's edge. Small birds

known as euphonias may nest among the sword-edged leaves at the side of the plant, away from the water tank. One study found 250 different animal species that lived in the niches provided by bromeliads.

Bromeliad tanks also act as nurseries for arrow-poison frogs – brilliantly coloured amphibians that produce some of the animal world's most powerful toxins. These have long been known and used by some of the native Amazonian Indian peoples to tip their arrows or blow-pipe darts for hunting game, hence the frogs' name.

Many arrow-poison frogs are little bigger than a fingertip, and they usually live among the leaf litter on the forest floor, where they forage for insects and other small animals. For most of the time, they are hidden beneath dead leaves, but when they do briefly emerge into the open, their garish hues warn potential enemies to leave them alone.

The toxin of arrow-poison frogs is exuded by glands in their skin. It acts only when it enters an animal's digestive system or bloodstream, so the frogs are quite safe to pick up. However, arrow-poison frogs are

TIMID LEAF-EATER *Despite a formidable appearance and size, the common iguana is a shy creature that prefers to run away from trouble.*

but not by catching prey for them, as one might expect. Instead, the female lays special, infertile eggs that the tadpoles immediately eat, an extra food supply to see them through their early development.

LIVING ON LEAVES

With a 6 ft (1.8 m) body, hooked claws and jagged crest, the common iguana (*Iguana iguana*) seems to have all the attributes of a powerful predatory reptile. Massive jaws and a long whiplike tail add to this menacing air, as does the steady gaze with which it looks down from its customary vantage point, sprawled out along an overhanging branch high above the river.

But its threatening appearance could hardly be more misleading, because this giant lizard is entirely vegetarian. Although it can use its sharp claws to good effect when cornered, its usual response to trouble – for example, the silhouette of a hunting eagle – is to launch itself into the air, landing with a stupendous flat-bellied crash in the water below. The impact seems not to trouble it, and with the steady strokes of a proficient swimmer, it heads for the river bank and vanishes into the forest.

The majority of the world's lizards are, in fact, meat-eating

TREE-TOP ROAR In the dense canopy of the Belize rain forest, a male black howler monkey announces the presence of his troop.

predators, and they are legendary for their speed and agility. In South America, they include the brilliantly coloured teiids, some of which are fast enough to catch birds, and the extraordinary basilisk (*Basiliscus plumifrons*), a lime-green species that escapes its enemies by running on two legs – sometimes for short distances across the surface of water, its lightness and swiftness preventing it from sinking. Most of these animals are relatively small, so that they can afford to spend energy pursuing individual animals as trifling as beetles or flies.

For the common iguana, however, chasing insects would be an exhausting and unprofitable task. Its body is far too heavy and cumbersome for chasing small prey, and even if each chase were successful, the effort would outweigh the reward. Instead, common iguanas feed on buds, leaves and fruit. This abundant and immobile food supply has allowed them to evolve into a species of impressive size and sluggish lifestyle.

A similar kind of lifestyle can be seen in howler monkeys, which are the largest – up to 28 in (71 cm) long with tails that are roughly as long again – and certainly the noisiest among almost three dozen monkey species found in the Americas. Howlers feed on leaves and fruit, a diet that is only practicable for a large monkey.

There are six species of howler monkey and they live in small family troops of up to

extraordinarily nimble, and they can disappear into leaf litter in the blinking of an eye. In the half-light of the forest floor, catching these fascinating little amphibians is no easy matter.

Arrow-poison frogs usually mate on the ground, and the female then climbs into a tree or shrub to lay a clutch of about six eggs which she fastens to a leaf. As soon as the eggs have hatched, one or both of the parents carry the tadpoles to water, ferrying them in a film of moisture that covers the adults' backs. They then guard the tadpoles for several days. Tadpoles that grow up in bromeliad tanks have fewer predators to contend with than ones that live at ground level. On the other hand, they inhabit a world where food can often be scarce. The females of some species feed their tadpoles,

30 animals. For each troop, by far the most energetic part of the day is at dawn and in the late afternoon, when males from neighbouring troops roar at each other across the tree tops.

This roaring sounds like the prelude to a savage territorial dispute, and it does indeed serve to establish ownership of a particular area of forest, although it is not always followed by any direct physical combat. The roaring undoubtedly reduces the need for actual fighting and is an adaptation to life in dense forest, where visual displays and communication are difficult because leaves are always in the way. The roaring of the red howler monkey can be heard up to 3 miles (5 km) off, and it announces to a troop's various neighbours that a piece of forest has been claimed and is currently occupied.

The value of making this extraordinary din is obviously substantial, because howler monkeys have extensive modifications of their larynx (vocal cords) to boost the decibel level of their voices. The cartilage larynx of the cords (the part which can be seen as the 'Adam's apple' in a human) is hugely enlarged into a saclike structure that hangs

HOWLING CHAMBER *An expanded hyoid bone gives the howler monkey an inbuilt resonating chamber – the secret of its impressive roar. This roar establishes the monkeys' territory: the louder the roar, the larger the territory.*

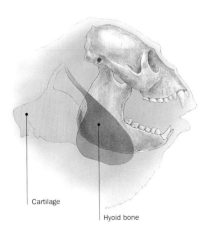

Cartilage

Hyoid bone

behind the monkey's jaw, obscured by a thick furry beard. More remarkable still is the enlargement of the hyoid bone, in humans a modest little bone of about 2-3 in (5-7.5 cm) in length which lies horizontally above the cartilage of the vocal cords, and can be felt just below the jaw.

During the evolution of the howler monkey, this bone has ballooned out into a massive bony chamber that sits within the lower jaw for protection. The hyoid acts as a resonating chamber for the sound that is produced by the vocal cords, amplifying the howler monkey's voice to an impressive lion-like roar.

Howlers spend most of their time high above the ground, visiting it only for water and minerals, which they obtain by eating small amounts of soil. They are placid animals, spending long periods lazing in the tree tops while they slowly digest their food. However, compared to their fellow leaf-eaters, the sloths, howlers lead a life of almost frenzied activity.

A WORLD UPSIDE DOWN

At first sight, sloths provoke both amazement and disappointment in almost equal measure. Amazement comes with the realisation that anything so lumplike and inert can actually be alive, while disappointment sets in when the lump fails to move, or indeed to do anything at all for hours on

SLOWLY, SLOWLY *Using its curved claws as hooks, the three-toed sloth moves cautiously among the branches in search of food.*

end. Sloths are largely nocturnal, but even when darkness has fallen, watching them can still be a tedious business.

There are five species of sloth in the Americas, forming a unique group of leaf-eating mammals that are entirely adapted to life in trees. Each sloth is essentially a leaf-digestion factory suspended, upside down, by strong hook-like claws. Like howler monkeys, sloths rely on bacteria to digest cellulose, the major component of leaves. The bacteria inhabit a large multi-compartment stomach, like that of a cow, and digestion is extremely slow even by the standards of other leaf-eaters. It can sometimes take up to a month for leaves to be dealt with, so there is always a great mass of part-digested leaves inside a sloth, adding to its weight and langour.

Although sloths are surprisingly common – even living in trees in towns and along roads – they are not at all easy to see, and many people fail to spot them when they are just a few yards away. This is partly because of the sloths' daytime immobility and partly because of their excellent camouflage. A sloth's downward-hanging

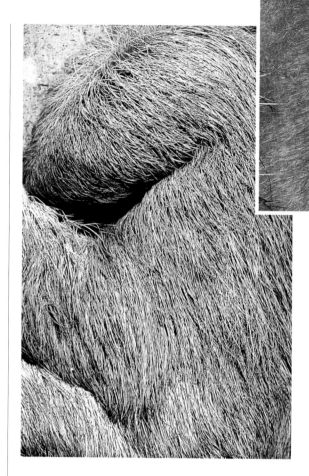

FUR-DWELLERS *The three-toed sloth is camouflaged by microscopic green plants, called algae, that grow in the long grooves of its hairs (left). Also living in the animal's thick coat is the sloth moth (above).*

fur, itself a dull brown colour, harbours algae (microscopic plants) that add a greenish tinge, making the animal blend in well among leaves and branches. Its moon-like face is tucked against its chest when resting, making it even less conspicuous.

The entire life of a sloth is devoted to the process of being frugal with energy. Its body temperature is lower than that of most mammals and varies with the external temperature, rather than being maintained at a constant level. This, combined with the characteristically slow movements, allows the metabolic rate to be about half the usual rate for mammals.

A sloth's muscles make up less of its body weight than in a typical mammal and even hanging uses little energy, because a sloth's claws are so constructed that they automatically lie at right angles to the limb without any muscular contraction. Unlike the fingers of a monkey, they do not need muscle power to provide a secure grip on a branch. This is illustrated in macabre

fashion by sloths that die of age or ill-health, for they remain attached to the branch and decompose where they are.

Trees supply everything a sloth needs – food, shelter, and protection from most of its enemies. But at weekly intervals, the three-toed sloths abandon the security of the tree tops to make a laborious journey to the ground. Here, the sloth scrapes out a depression in the forest floor, fills it with its droppings and urine, covers these with leaves, and then crawls back up into the branches. Sloths climb slowly and can only drag themselves across the ground with great difficulty – as a result, this round trip may take between 30 minutes and an hour. While on the ground or approaching it, they are vulnerable to attack by jaguars and other predators.

Clearly, this strange behaviour, with all its attendant dangers, must bring important benefits, or it would never have evolved. Some biologists have suggested that the sloth's droppings act as fertiliser for a tree that it particularly favours as food, resulting in more leaf growth in the months ahead. But it is difficult to see how natural selection could favour such high-risk behaviour when it may only have fairly small and delayed

benefits. Perhaps the dung does make a substantial difference to the survival of the sloth's preferred trees, but it would take some intensive scientific research to support this theory. The three-toed sloth's behaviour currently remains an enigma.

There are various animals that cohabit with the sloth, including a moth that lives in the thick, damp, mildewy fur. This insect's life is so closely interwoven with that of the sloth that its caterpillars live on the sloth's dung. The moth's breeding cycle is synchronised with the rhythm of the sloth's digestive tract and when the sloth descends to ground level the moths fly out from the fur, land on the fresh droppings and lay their eggs.

They quickly roost in the fur again before the sloth embarks on its slow ascent back into the canopy.

BIRDS OF THE FOREST

When the first European settlers arrived in Central America, over five centuries ago, they encountered a dazzling wealth of bird life quite unknown in the world they had left behind. Their discoveries included such creatures as toucans and aracaris, a family of fruit-eating birds with extraordinary colours

MAGNIFICENT MACAWS *The hyacinth macaws, the largest of all the parrots, are now rare in the wild – thanks to their popularity as pets.*

HUNGRY FOR NECTAR *A saw-billed hermit hummingbird displays perfect control as it approaches a flower in the Atlantic rain forest of south-eastern Brazil.*

and outsize beaks; magnificent macaws that easily eclipsed any parrots then known from Africa or Asia; and crow-sized oropendulas, birds whose flask-shaped nests hung from lofty, isolated trees like strange fibrous fruit. They also encountered giant harpy eagles, which could pluck monkeys and sloths from the tree tops; and the laughing falcon, with its hollow mocking cry, which preys on some of the most venomous snakes of the forest. Deep within the cloud forest, they saw the breathtaking male quetzal birds, whose iridescent green tail feathers are nearly three times the length of their bodies.

But despite these wonders, their greatest amazement was reserved for the hummingbirds, a group of about 320 species found only in the Americas. These jewel-like creatures still astound visitors, partly because of their iridescent colours, but mainly through their stunning agility in the air.

LIFE IN THE FAST LANE

Hummingbirds expend so much energy in flight that they must consume a quantity of nectar equivalent to half of their bodyweight every day. Hummingbirds live life in the fast lane, their heart rates reaching 1260 beats per minute. At night, however, they slow down their metabolism to conserve energy.

Hummingbirds feed mainly on nectar, an energy-rich fluid that they collect from flowers. Nectar is, in fact, the bird equivalent of high-octane gasoline, and hummingbirds burn it off very rapidly, thanks to an extremely fast metabolic rate and a body temperature of up to 42°C (108°F) – one of the highest of all warm-blooded animals. This high temperature allows their muscles to work at an astounding speed, and as a result their power output – measured on a weight-for-weight basis – is unmatched by any other bird.

A hummingbird beats its wings up to 90 times a second, allowing it to hover in one spot with rock-steady precision, or to dart abruptly away from it in any direction. The wing is structured in such a way that hummingbirds can even fly backwards. A typical hummingbird weighs just 1/5 oz (5.5 g), so even at top speed, its momentum is minute. This means that it can start and stop almost instantly, just by changing the angle of its wing beat, while a heavier bird would need much more time and effort to carry out the same manoeuvre.

The two halves of a hummingbird's beak fit together to form a neat tube, while its tongue works as a pump, sucking nectar up along the tube and into its mouth. The shape of the beak varies from one species to another. The ruby-throated hummingbird (*Archilochus colubris*), for instance, which migrates from Central America as far north as Canada, has a long beak with a very slight curve, while the white-tipped sickle-bill (*Eutoxeres aquila*) has a beak that curves through very nearly 90°.

The swordbilled hummingbird (*Ensifera ensifera*), meanwhile, has a 5 in (12.5 cm) straight beak that is considerably longer than its 3 in (7.5 cm) body. It uses this extravagant piece of equipment to collect the nectar from hanging flowers that other species of hummingbird are unable to reach. As in the world of insects, some plants and hummingbirds have evolved so that one species is entirely dependent on another, for pollination in the case of the plant, for food in the case of the bird.

Hummingbirds are among the most important pollinators in the American rain forests. Unlike insects, they are strongly attracted by the colour red, and this is why red flowers are so common in this part of the world. Vivacious, noisy in flight (thanks to the humming of their beating wings), and surprisingly aggressive, these unique and spectacular animals can be seen in almost all forests at all altitudes, from the rain-soaked lowlands of the Atlantic coast to the cool and clammy cloud forests of the Andean foothills.

SURVIVORS IN AUSTRALIA AND NEW GUINEA

Over the course of time an intriguing mixture of species has settled in the rain forests of Australia and New Guinea, including giant, flightless cassowaries, dazzling birds of paradise, pouch-bearing possums and egg-laying mammals.

Dawn breaks over the forest-clad ravines and ridges of the highlands of New Guinea. The early morning mist, hanging in the valleys and swirling about the trees, starts to rise. Birds begin their chatter. On a high horizontal branch, the outline of a large crouched animal is clearly visible, dark against the brightening sky, its long, thickly furred tail hanging downwards. It rests on its haunches, munching at leaves and steadying itself by grasping a forked branch in one of its front paws. It looks like a monkey, but closer inspection reveals something odd. Its hind feet are remarkably long, each soled with a rough pad and bearing a set of large curved claws to grip the bark.

Something about the animal's sturdy body and shuffling movements suggests that it is not totally at ease in the forest canopy. When it begins to descend the tree, this becomes even more obvious. It moves along the branches to the trunk and then backs down clumsily, tail first, slithering groundwards in a rain of debris. A glimpse of its head confirms that this curious tree-dweller is definitely not a monkey. The pointed muzzle and furry triangular ears are almost bear-like. But a bear with a long tail?

On reaching the forest floor, the animal hops away between the trees, clearing moss-covered fallen logs in graceful arc-shaped leaps. It is obviously far more comfortable on the ground than it was in the tree tops. Indeed, its effortless, bounding gait reveals the identity of this mysterious mammal: it is neither a monkey nor a bear, but a kangaroo.

At some point in the distant past, small ground-dwelling forest animals, similar perhaps to today's forest wallabies, ventured into the trees, lured by the abundant supply of leaves and fruit that awaited them there. These were the predecessors of the modern tree kangaroos.

During their precarious forays along the branches of the canopy, tree kangaroos tread

MATSCHIE'S TREE KANGAROO
With no monkeys or apes competing with them for food, tree kangaroos have made a home for themselves in the forest.

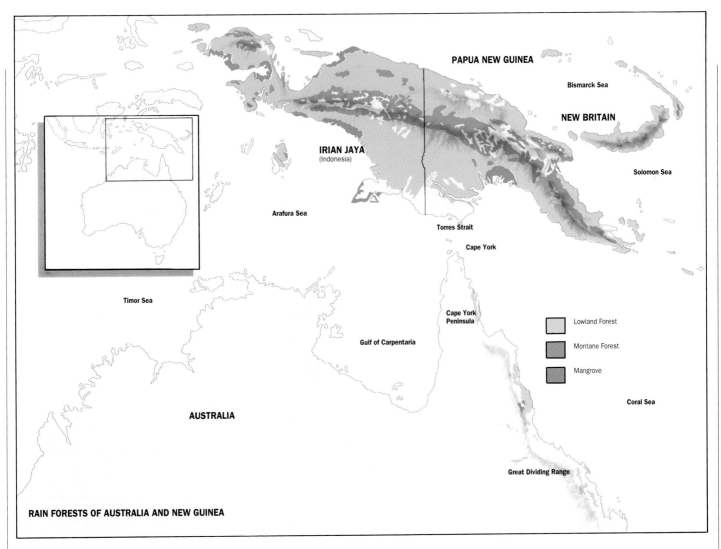

RAIN FORESTS OF AUSTRALIA AND NEW GUINEA

Lowland Forest

Montane Forest

Mangrove

NEAR BUT DIFFERENT *The rain forests of New Guinea and north-eastern Australia are home to species quite different from those of neighbouring Asia.*

carefully, balancing with the help of their long tails, and moving their back legs one after the other – an action that would never normally be seen among ordinary kangaroos. On the ground, however, the tree kangaroos become a lot nimbler, reverting to the swift, springing movements of their plains-dwelling Australian cousins.

BRIDGING THE GAP

Ancestors of the tree kangaroos first arrived in New Guinea from Australia. On several occasions in the past, Australia and New Guinea have been joined by land bridges and during these times many plants and animals were able to pass between the two

land masses. Thus New Guinea inherited much of the wildlife that is characteristic of Australia, and these unusual animals mingled with smaller creatures that had migrated southwards to New Guinea, over the sea from South-east Asia.

Along with the early tree kangaroos came a whole collection of other Australian mammals to populate the rain forests of New Guinea. They included ancestors of the modern-day forest wallabies, wide-eyed possums, scuttling bandicoots and weasel-like quolls, all marsupial (that is, pouched) mammals like the kangaroo.

So far, Australian marsupial mammals have spread not only north to New Guinea, but also to the Solomon Islands farther east, to Timor in the north-west, and to Sulawesi (formerly Celebes) in Indonesia. Their distribution overlaps with that of many placental mammals (that is, mammals, like most of those in the rest of the world, that nourish

their developing young in the uterus and then give birth) which originally came from South-east Asia. But there is a fairly sharp dividing line, particularly when larger animals are considered.

This dividing line between Asian and Australian animals, which runs just to the east of the Philippines, Borneo and Java, was first noticed by the Victorian naturalist Alfred Russel Wallace, who published his observations in 1860. While it holds broadly for animals, 'Wallace's Line' is less distinct for plants, which disperse more easily over large distances, either as floating seeds or mats of vegetation.

THE MISSING MONKEYS

Primates – the apes, monkeys, lemurs, lorises and tarsiers – are the most prominent group of mammals in almost all tropical forests. The primates of the Americas are completely different from those in the

DRIFTING CONTINENTS AND CHANGING CLIMATES

The surface of our planet – the Earth's crust – is made up of several massive plates of rock that are constantly on the move, travelling with extraordinary slowness, separating here, colliding there. Their wanderings cause the phenomenon of 'continental drift'. Over the past 100 million years, the plate that carries Australia has drifted gradually northwards, detaching Australia from the ancient southern supercontinent of Gondwanaland.

Gondwanaland was a place of warm lush forests, benefiting from a much hotter phase in the Earth's history. Australia carried with it the ancient Gondwanan plants and animals, including the ancestors of today's marsupials (pouched mammals) when it broke away from the supercontinent, about 65 million years ago.

For much of its past Australia was hot, wet and covered in rain forest. But during its slow northward journey, the climate changed, due to the continent's movement across the globe, and to changing conditions worldwide. Over the millennia, the tropical rain forests receded into coastal belts, ousted from the interior by drier conditions.

The same crustal plate that forms Australia also carries southern New Guinea. Northern New Guinea is formed of land carried by the Asian plate, while the island's central mountains mark the zone where the two plates meet, pushing against each other with terrifying force. Over millions of years, this impact has forced the land up, buckling it into mountains.

The animals of Australasia are an intriguing mixture of Asian and Australian species. New Guinea, although situated close to Asia and part of it belonging to the same crustal plate, was probably never linked by land bridges to the north, but there were land bridges at several times in the past between New Guinea and Australia. These geological events,

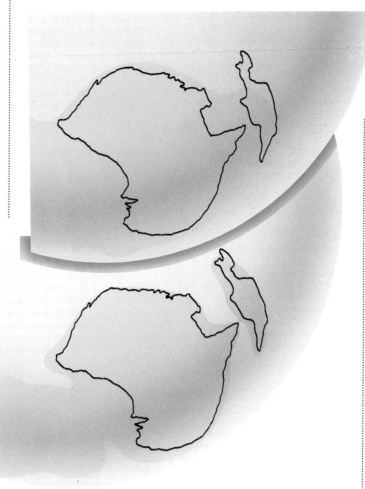

along with changes in climate, have had an important influence on the fauna of both islands.

Despite its isolation, New Guinea received some animals from the north – those that could cross the ocean. First to arrive were probably insects, birds and bats, to whom water presented no obstacle. These animals could move on easily to Australia.

After the flying creatures came the first rodents, which probably arrived sporadically in New Guinea, and later in Australia, carried by floating vegetation. These small placental mammals have been present for a very long time, and have diversified into many local species in both New Guinea and Australia.

Humans arrived in New Guinea from Asia over 50 000 years ago, probably

MOBILE PAST *About 100 million years ago, the landmass that now composes Australia and southern New Guinea (in green, top) was part of the supercontinent Gondwanaland. By the ice ages, Australia and New Guinea (in green, bottom) had mostly separated, but land bridges between the two emerged from time to time as sea levels changed.*

using rafts. But for some of the other large mammals, such as the monkeys and the large hoofed mammals, New Guinea and Australia were permanently out of reach.

The land bridges between Australia and parts of New Guinea occurred at

various times in the past, due to sea levels changing and landmasses tilting.

The most recent links were during the recent ice ages, when much of the world's water was locked up in the ice caps and sea levels fell. The seabed was exposed and animals wandered across the former divide.

At these times, however, the climatic changes of the ice ages produced dry savannah on the land bridges themselves and in the adjacent regions, which meant that rain-forest animals could not easily make the migration. Small ones, in particular, were marooned in their forests, and it is notable that the mice of New Guinean rain forests belong to entirely different species from those of Australian rain forests.

Larger rain-forest animals might perhaps have crossed the savannah areas in search of new living space. Some pouched mammals from Australian savannahs may also have moved north and then adapted to rain-forest habitats once they were established in New Guinea.

Whenever the ice ages pushed back the rain forest, the mountain tops of New Guinea kept their cloak of trees and acted as refuges for the forest animals. Species confined to these refuges had the chance to evolve and diversify in isolation. This produced unusual developments among rain-forest creatures, with a variety of new species evolving from the original colonisers.

Just as animals moved across the land bridges, so did human beings, wandering southwards from New Guinea to reach Australia between about 50 000 and 30 000 years ago. With the arrival of man, and more his fire and axe, the dwindling Australian forests were reduced further still. Today, tropical rain forests remain as tiny pockets clinging to the eastern side of the Great Dividing Range.

African rain forests, and Asia too has some unique species, but they fill a similar set of 'niches' or roles in their distant environments – inhabiting equivalent layers of the forest canopy and having a similar range of feeding habits.

With the exception of humankind, primates failed to reach either the Australian or the New Guinea rain forests. This is why tree kangaroos have evolved to fill the monkey niche, yet they fill it so clumsily and are such inept climbers that they pose a puzzle to evolutionary biologists.

Why is it that tree kangaroos never evolved the agility of monkeys, or the climbing skills of those other tree-top athletes, the squirrels? It could simply be that they have not yet had time to do so, because they evolved from ground-dwellers relatively recently. Another possible answer to this puzzle is that tree kangaroos have never needed to be particularly speedy in the canopy. Safe in the isolation of the rain forests of New Guinea and north-eastern Australia, tree kangaroos had little competition from the

SPOTTED CUSCUS *This large possum is a creature of the night. It is a marsupial that has adapted well to life in the forests of New Guinea.*

large leaf-eating tree-dwellers which dominated so many other rain-forest tree tops.

They virtually had the canopy to themselves. Their only serious competitors were other animals of Australian origin, the smaller possums and cuscuses: slow-moving creatures with dense fur and bulging eyes, which clamber deliberately through the trees by night in search of leaves, fruit and flowers. The cuscuses use their prehensile tails to wrap around twigs and branches as a kind of safety rope. For the most part, there is ample room for cuscuses, possums and tree kangaroos to coexist in the tree tops.

Tree kangaroos also have few predators, other than humans. If danger threatens, they make little attempt to escape through the canopy. Sometimes they simply leap from their tree-top perch to the ground, a distance of 50 ft (15 m) or more, and escape by bounding into the undergrowth.

MEAT-EATING MARSUPIALS

During their evolution, marsupials spread to fill every niche in the rain forests of Australia and New Guinea – colonising the trees and the undergrowth, and adapting to feed on a huge variety of foods. Indeed, until the arrival of humans in Australia during the last 50 000 years, there were marsupial lions and marsupial wolves living

GROUND-LEVEL HUNTERS
Alert to the slightest rustle, a cinnamon antechinus searches the leaf litter on the forest floor for insects and other small prey.

alongside enormous browsing marsupials the size of rhinos, and giant kangaroos standing 10 ft (3 m) tall. Soon after the arrival of humans, however, most of these large mammals vanished, probably wiped out by hunting. A similar process happened in Europe when humans first became skilled hunters, and it was echoed by extinctions in North America, South America and many other regions soon after the first human inhabitants arrived. Our distant ancestors were responsible for dispatching many giants of the animal kingdom.

Today, although the larger marsupial carnivores are extinct, there are still many smaller meat-eaters in the rain forests of Australia and New Guinea. One creature inhabiting the tree tops of both islands is the striped possum (*Dactylopsila trivirgata*). It has a diet of wood-boring insect larvae, supplemented by leaves, fruit, honey and a number of small vertebrates. By night, the little possum taps and sniffs at rotten branches to locate insects deep within, before biting and tearing into the dead wood. The specially elongated fourth finger (a feature shared with its relatives, the squirrel-like trioks) enables the striped possum to prise insects from holes and crevices.

The completely unrelated aye-aye of Madagascar has a similarly elongated finger,

POUCHES V. PLACENTAS — BIRTH FOR MARSUPIALS

Like the kangaroos of the Australian outback, tree kangaroos raise their young in a pouch. Indeed, all the larger forest mammals of Australian origin raise their offspring in this way. They belong to a unique order of mammals known as marsupials.

In contrast to placental mammals (that is, almost all other mammals, including ourselves) marsupials give birth to tiny young ones that are still at a very early stage of development. The baby kangaroo looks rather like a large maggot when born, except for its front limbs which are large enough to allow it to crawl laboriously upwards through its mother's fur and eventually reach the pouch. These apparently helpless scraps of life are somehow able to make this strenuous climb, locate the pouch by purely instinctive means, and attach themselves to a teat inside the pouch.

Although marsupial reproduction was once thought to be rather primitive, it has certain advantages that the placental version lacks. For example, birth is considerably less strenuous and the female kangaroo does not have to face the dangers that attend an antelope giving birth in the same type of open country. Many marsupials are able to stop the development of a new foetus if conditions become harsh or if food is scarce, retaining it in the womb in a dormant state until the situation improves, or evicting it entirely in a real crisis. Why the marsupials are largely confined to Australasia, and why many species tend to decline if faced with competition from placental mammals is far from clear.

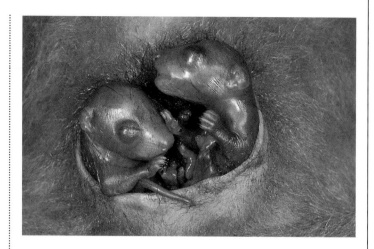

MOBILE NURSERY *Young ring-tailed possums do not leave the protection of their mother's pouch until they are about four months old.*

and the same sort of diet. This is an interesting case of natural selection arriving at a similar solution to the same environmental problem in quite different animal groups: a phenomenon that is known to science as 'convergent evolution'.

Scuttling through the New Guinea rain forest understorey and over the forest floor there are other small hunters, searching for the beetles, cockroaches, ants, centipedes and slugs that lurk under fallen leaves and beneath the peeling bark on rotting logs. They include the active mouse-like dunnarts (*Sminthopsis*), and the shrew-like *Antechinus* species, also found in Australia. Bandicoots (*Peroryctes*), strange-looking animals with long pointed noses, scrabble for soil insects, digging conical holes with their forepaws. They occasionally take fruits, seeds and fungi.

There is also the New Guinea quoll (*Dasyurus albopunctatus*), a hunter of rats, birds, lizards or even larger prey. This beautiful, spotted hunter, weighing about 3 1/3 lb (1.5 kg), is considered by biologists to be the marsupial equivalent of a cat – making it another instance of convergent evolution.

Like possums and cuscuses, the small marsupial hunters are active mainly at night. In the cover of darkness, the rain forest is full of their pattering, scratching and snuffling sounds. Other hunters are active, too, at this time: snakes slither across the leaf litter and over branches in search of sleeping prey, while owls and insect-eating bats patrol the skies.

A SPINY SURVIVOR

Another, quite different, carnivorous mammal inhabits the rain-forest floor in the mountains of New Guinea. Like the marsupials, this creature has a pouch, and shuffles through the leaf litter, probing under rotting logs for its staple food – earthworms. It also prefers the cover of darkness. But unlike the dunnarts and bandicoots, it has short sharp spines beneath its fur, and its head ends in a very long, toothless, tubular snout that curves downwards to contact the ground. Strangest of all, it lays eggs.

This is the rare long-beaked echidna (*Zaglossus bruijni*), an animal that came originally from Australia, but which became

PRICKLY DEFENCE *When disturbed, the short-beaked echidna curls up into a spiky ball or quickly burrows into the ground for safety.*

extinct there more than 10 000 years ago. Mystery surrounds the long-beaked echidna in New Guinea. Some local people believe that echidnas hatch from the eggs of birds, others say that they are a reincarnation of old tree kangaroos – the tail of the kangaroo becoming the elongated echidna beak. In reality, echidnas hatch from eggs laid by the mother echidna, and are then transferred to her pouch where they suckle milk. The echidna is a surviving offshoot of the 'missing link' between mammals and their reptile ancestors. They are mammal-like in most respects, but still lay leathery-shelled eggs as snakes and lizards do.

Only two other kinds of primitive, egg-laying mammal survive in the world today. They are the short-beaked echidna, which lives in both Australia and New Guinea, and, most famously, the Australian duck-billed platypus. Egg-laying mammals like these are a special group known as monotremes, and they are of enormous interest to biologists because they confirm the evolutionary origin of mammals as deduced from the fossil record.

GIANTS OF THE FOREST

An enormous three-toed footprint, and a harsh cackling or booming sound are often the only clues to the presence of a cassowary. In most rain forests, the largest animal is a mammal, but in Australia and New Guinea, the real giant of the rain forest is a flightless bird.

Living deep in the rain forests, the cassowary is a shy bird of sturdy build and impressive stature. Standing the height of a human, it is the rain forest's equivalent of the emu that roams the open plains and grasslands of Australia.

In place of the emu's pale feathers, cassowaries have sleek black drapes of plumage. These dark, thick layers of feathers act as an effective heat trap, and the birds are only comfortable when shielded from the sun in the dense, shady rain forest. Since cassowaries do not fly, their flight feathers are reduced to curved, spiky quills, useful only for fighting and defence.

The bird's only show of colour lies on its featherless neck, where the naked skin

WORKING TOGETHER
A cassowary father guards his chicks (above) as they forage in the leaf litter. The lily-pilly (right) depends on cassowaries to disperse its seeds.

gleams in shades of red and blue, and where, in two of the three cassowary species, fleshy coloured wattles (folds of skin) dangle from the front of the throat. The head, in a paler shade, is capped by a bony helmet called a casque, which the birds use for pushing through foliage and for turning the soil when foraging.

Unusually for a bird, it is the male cassowary that incubates the eggs. His dedication to the task is immense: he neither eats nor drinks for the 50 day incubation period, and he never leaves the nest. When the young hatch, they are camouflaged with black and beige stripes, ready to accompany their father on foraging trips in the leaf litter. Cassowaries are usually fairly docile creatures, but the males may become very aggressive when protecting their young or defending their territory. Their enormous clawed feet can deliver a powerful defensive kick that is quite capable of disembowelling a human being.

SPREADING THE SEEDS

Although they also eat snails and insects, large fruits form the main part of the cassowary's diet. For certain rain-forest trees in Queensland and New Guinea, this makes the cassowary an indispensable ally. Research has shown that cassowaries have a very gentle digestive process that allows seeds to pass through unharmed. By eating fallen fruits, and moving on to another area before the seeds have time to pass through

BANANA-LOVING BAT *A black flying fox breaks off from a meal of bananas to give the leathery skin of its wings a careful cleaning.*

their intestine, these large, active animals spread the seeds far and wide, heightening their chances of sprouting in a suitable site and growing to reach maturity.

Some experts estimate that there are as few as 1000 wild adult cassowaries left in Australian forests today. Cassowaries prefer plants that produce particularly large plum-like fruits, such as the lily-pilly (*Acmena*), mountain gardenia (*Gardenia merekin*), satin-ash (*Syzygium* species), fig (*Ficus* species), and quandong (*Elaeocarpus* species). In the absence of monkeys and hoofed animals, there are few other creatures that can tackle fruits of this size and so spread the seeds.

Some researchers are anxious about the future of these particular rain-forest trees, should the population of cassowaries decline even further. Fortunately, however, the cassowaries are not entirely alone. There are a few other animals, such as the musky rat-kangaroo, the smallest and most primitive member of the kangaroo family, that also disperse these large fruits and seeds. The musky rat-kangaroo collects and buries

them in secret stores, which frequently get forgotten, allowing the abandoned seeds to germinate. Whether the rat-kangaroos are as effective at dispersing the seeds as the cassowaries remains to be proved.

Fruit-eating bats, such as the flying foxes, can also be important seed dispersers. These enormous bats, which owe their name to their long, fox or dog-like faces, spend the day hanging upside down in communal roosts. Much of the time they spend asleep, each bat dangling from a single foot and wrapped in the cocoon of its naked, membranous wings. On wakening, the bats preen and lick their fur. At dusk, they shriek and chatter, before pouring out of the roost to scour the forest for its fruits and nectar. The sky becomes dark with bats, many thousands of them from a single roosting site, each with a wingspan of nearly 4ft (1.2m).

Flying foxes navigate using their sensitive night vision, always alert for the rich scent of ripe fruit, for which they may travel up to 20 miles (32 km) in a single night. Where there are fruit plantations, flying foxes gorge themselves, multiply enormously and become pests, but in the rain forest they must sometimes work harder for a living. Greater flying foxes in New Guinea have been observed collecting fruit that had fallen into the sea and was floating on the surface a short way from the shore. Occasionally, the bats misjudged their swoop onto the fruit and fell into the water, whereupon they simply spread their wings and surfed in on the waves. Safely ashore, they struggled up the beach and climbed the nearest tree to relaunch themselves.

Bats are relatively choosy about their fruit diet, preferring some species of fruit to others. The banana fig is a particularly favoured delicacy for flying foxes. But what is good for the bat is not always good for the tree: some bats simply suck at the juicy flesh and spit out seeds as they eat, so that the seeds land immediately below the

parent tree, achieving virtually nothing in the way of dispersal. Animals of this kind ones that take the fruit without dispersing the seeds – need to be counterbalanced in nature by good seed-dispersers, so that some seeds do reach worthwhile sites.

THE BUSH THAT BITES

Many plants evolve ways of swinging the balance in order to make sure that good seed dispersers get the fruit and the rest are excluded. One of the most successful of such plants is the gympie or stinging bush (*Dendrocnide moroides*), common in the rain forests of Cape York, Australia. There cannot be many trees that are feared in the same way that poisonous snakes are, but the gympie has an equally terrifying reputation with local people, and is as carefully avoided.

Gympies are ferocious members of the stinging-nettle family, fast-growing shrubs that thrive in areas of disturbed rain forest, and reach heights of about 15 ft (4.6 m). Their heart-shaped leaves and seemingly inviting raspberry-like fruits are all defended by a well-developed weaponry that is

FORBIDDEN FRUIT *Poison-tipped hairs on gympie leaves give painful stings. Only birds protected by feathers and a tough skin can safely peck at the tasty berry.*

SEED DESTROYERS *Powerful hooked bills allow parrots, such as this electus parrot, to crush even the very hardest nuts and seeds.*

aimed specifically at mammals. Tiny hairs, tipped with poison, coat the leaves, stems and fruit of the gympie. Being made of silica, they are as sharp and brittle as splinters of broken glass. Once lodged in the skin, they stay there, causing an excruciating sting for which there is no effective remedy.

An encounter with a gympie can result in paroxysms of immediate pain, followed by an agonising skin inflammation that lasts for a number of weeks or even months. Dogs, horses and humans are all driven equally wild by the sting. Whenever the affected area comes into contact with water, the pain is renewed afresh.

But not all creatures are affected like this and some, notably the catbirds (so-named after their calls that sound like the mewing of a cat) and southern cassowaries, can peck happily at the fruits, oblivious to the stinging hairs. This immunity they owe to their coats of feathers and skin that is less sensitive than mammals' skins. In this way, the gympie reserves its fruits for the best dispersers, as well as protecting its leaves from browsing mammals.

In general, birds make very good seed dispersers. In New Guinea and its neighbouring islands, pigeons are particularly important; trees lure these plump fruit-eaters with a feast of succulent, coloured berries. The colours red and orange are especially attractive to species such as the wompoo pigeons, purple-crowned pigeons and nutmeg pigeons. All these birds must consume vast quantities of fruit to supply their needs, since it is not a particularly nutritious food

in its protein content, being mainly sugar, fibre and water.

Parrots and cockatoos cheat the system by cleaving the protective layer around the seed and eating the nutritious kernel within, a far better source of protein, vitamins and minerals than the fruit itself. This is a serious loss for the tree, depriving the seed of its chance of dispersal and growth.

COQUETRY AND COURTSHIP

Fruit is abundant in the rain forest. In such a bountiful environment, fruit-eating birds need not spend all their time foraging and they have plenty of energy to spare. In the course of evolution, this has led to elaborate and exotic forms of courtship, with the males expending huge amounts of time and energy on impressing a suitable mate. Among the fruit-eaters of the rain forests, the process known as sexual selection runs riot and achieves extraordinary results.

Sexual selection, the second major force driving evolutionary change after natural selection, is responsible for a number of the more beautiful or outlandish spectacles that exist in the living world. At its simplest level, sexual selection involves a female choosing males that are healthy and vigorous to father her offspring, ensuring that she combines her own genes with those of a successful partner. In

FANCIFUL FEATHERS

Spectacular tail streamers help the male greater bird of paradise to attract a female and persuade her to mate.

several species, the male demonstrates his vigour with a conspicuous body structure or patch of colour, such as the red comb and wattle of a cockerel.

Biologists believe that, by producing this colour or additional structure, the male is simply proving that he is in the best of health – a winner, in other words, who is worth backing. At the same time, however, the sexual advantage of this advertisement is weighed in the evolutionary balance, at every generation, by the costs involved in it. It may mean, for example, that the male needs more food and that it is therefore more vulnerable to predators through being more conspicuous.

Sometimes, when conditions are favourable, sexual selection runs away with itself and the ordinary checks on the male's display no longer operate. Then the effect of female choice is to amplify the males' advertisement with each passing generation.

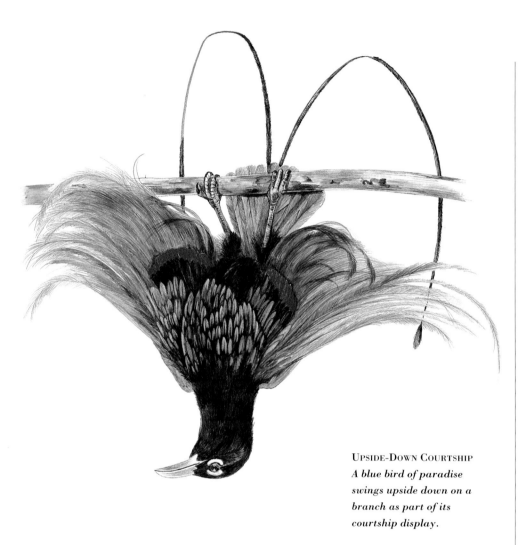

UPSIDE-DOWN COURTSHIP
A blue bird of paradise swings upside down on a branch as part of its courtship display.

emerge from a mass of wispy plumage around his hindquarters. Grasping his display perch with his feet, the male swings upside down to display his finery to full effect, swaying gently back and forth, while emitting a harsh, whirring call. The long tail feathers, meanwhile, form two impressive arches above the iridescent plumage, and conspicuous white patches almost completely obscure his eyes.

The smallest but perhaps most visually stunning of the entire group is the king bird of paradise (*Cicinnurus regius*). Males of this species are vivid crimson, with white bellies and fanlike tufts near the shoulders that are tipped with green. The tail is formed of two wire-like feathers, each of which opens out into a green rosette at its tip. The result is a creature so exotic that it looks almost unreal, rather as though an imaginative artist had painted a fictitious bird.

One bird of paradise has such incongruous head plumes that the first specimen brought to Europe was thought to be a fake. The King of Saxony bird of paradise (*Pteridophora alberti*) is just 7 in (18 cm) long, but it bears two 18 in (46 cm) streamers on the back of its head. These streamers look rather like the bunting that is used to decorate towns during festivals, each carrying a line of 30-40 miniature 'flags' that are a brilliant metallic blue on the outside and brown on the inside.

Since human beings arrived in these regions, the circumstances that favoured the evolution of these extraordinary birds have changed drastically. Once relatively safe from most forest predators, the birds of paradise have suffered at human hands thanks to their fantastic plumage. This has long been in demand for the ceremonial dress of New Guinean tribespeople; then, in the 19th century, it started to be exported to Europe in order to decorate expensive hats. Indeed, there was a time when some bird of paradise feathers were worth extraordinary sums of money.

Fortunately, adult males take five to ten years to mature. During that period, they have a dull plumage that protects them from the hunters. At any one time, there is a limit to the number of territories held by

Almost every female chooses a male who is just slightly more flamboyant and impressive than his neighbours, and as a consequence, it is his genes that are passed on to the next generation of birds.

Females who choose the less flamboyant males tend to produce less flamboyant sons who, in turn, have less luck with the females – the result being that the genes of these females gradually die out. The genes that determine female preferences are therefore being selected in tandem with the genes that determine male plumage. If there is no shortage of food, nor any great threat from predators to the survival of the males, then this process will reach to some quite illogical conclusions.

Over a number of generations, the self-perpetuating process can favour increasingly intricate and beautiful plumage, as well as increasingly complex displays. In New Guinea, both have reached a peak among

the birds of paradise, probably the most beautiful birds in the world.

Bizarre, iridescent and brilliantly coloured, birds of paradise are the undoubted highlight of New Guinea birdlife. Almost all live in the wet tropical forests, and many are restricted to tiny patches of mountainous terrain. A few have reached Australia, but most of the 43 species are exclusive to New Guinea and its offshore islands. Males are adorned with elaborate crests and plumes, or gorgeous fans and tassels, which they fluff out and flick in front of the female, so that a cascade of rustling, shimmering feathers catches the sun in her view.

One of the most exquisite displays is that of the rare blue bird of paradise (*Paradisaea rudolphi*) from the mountain forests of south-eastern New Guinea. The male has a black head and chest, and bright blue wings, but his most impressive adornments are two long, ribbon-like tail feathers that

mature, displaying males, and there is always a reserve of 'spare', immature males waiting for an opportunity to take over a territory. This factor seems to have saved most of the birds of paradise from extinction. If one male is removed, another fills its place. Since each male is able to fertilise many females, reproduction is not severely affected. Only the blue bird of paradise is in any immediate danger of extinction, and this seems to be more the fault of habitat destruction than hunting.

ARCHITECTS, ARTISTS AND COLLECTORS

Another group of fruit-eating birds, closely related to the birds of paradise, have also been strongly moulded by sexual selection, but in a different direction. The bowerbirds, a group of 18 species in Australia and New Guinea, range from the size of a starling to that of a crow. Although some are adorned with crests and bright colours, most

BUILT TO IMPRESS *Having built an elaborate thatched 'hut', the male Vogelkop gardener bowerbird plants mosses in his dancing ground.*

of the male bowerbirds are fairly drab and certainly far less spectacular than their bird of paradise cousins.

As if to compensate, the male bowerbirds lavish enormous amounts of time and attention on constructing elaborate arenas – simple platforms, pillars, walled avenues, or even roofed huts – just to attract females. Instead of luring a female with colourful and exotic plumage, male bowerbirds focus the female's attention on their works of art, decorated with an array of beautiful objects arranged to impress. In this bizarre way, male bowerbirds apparently avoid the energetic outlay of producing spectacular plumage each season, and also reduce the chance of attracting predators, at least when they are away from the bower while foraging for food.

Usually, it is the dullest species of bowerbird that create the most exotic bowers. Perhaps the most complex of all is the thatched 'hut', measuring some 8 ft (2.4 m) long and 4^1/$_2$ ft (1.4 m) high, that is constructed by the relatively drab Vogelkop gardener bowerbird (*Amblyornis inornatus*) of New Guinea. The MacGregor's gardener bowerbird (*Amblyornis magregoriae*) is more strikingly adorned, with an orange crest,

ADDED ATTRACTIONS *A male golden bowerbird usually decorates his towering building with lichens, mosses and coloured flowers.*

and builds a contrastingly simple maypole structure. This bird has been protected in parts of New Guinea by an ancient taboo. MacGregor's bowerbird is believed to assist local people in New Guinea in their choice of marriage partners – they therefore refrain from killing it.

Archbold's bowerbird (*Archboldia papuensis*) is a rare species from high in the mountain rain forests of New Guinea, where it was discovered in 1940. It uses tail feathers from the even rarer King of Saxony bird of paradise to decorate its bower.

In human terms, the male satin bowerbird (*Ptilonorhyncus violaceus*), which takes collecting to extremes, would definately be considered something of a kleptomaniac. Carefully and compulsively, he steals items and takes them back to his display area. For the satin bowerbird, blue is the favoured colour, although green and grey objects may also be present. In the past the main items were natural ones from the rain forest such as snail shells and

feathers, dead insects, bones, fruits and flowers. In recent times, the bowerbirds have become adaptable, adding clothes pegs, buttons, bottle tops, pens, children's toys and pieces of crockery to their ornaments. His lair or bower is an open-topped tunnel of vertically placed twigs, lined up along a north-south axis, which adjoins a display arena full of his loot. The bower

---

POISON BIRDS

The world's first poisonous bird was discovered in the rain forests of New Guinea in 1992. The bird, a type of pitohui (allied to the thrushes and flycatchers), has poisonous skin and feathers. The poison is a nerve poison related to that found in the skins of arrow-poison frogs, inhabitants of Central and South America.

---

walls are 'painted' a bluish colour with crushed berries and mud.

From July to January, the male tries to attract females into his bower. He picks up a particularly enticing object from his collection, and dances with it, spreading wings and tail. A female, if interested, enters the bower and allows him to mate. Males are often promiscuous, mating with many females, each of which constructs her own well-concealed nest elsewhere in which to raise the young.

Golden bowerbirds (*Prionodura newtoniana*) choose yellow, green or white decorations to enhance their elaborate bower. Lichens and seedpods adorn two pyramids of sticks, constructed around saplings which are joined by a low, horizontal perch. The entire bower may reach more than 6 ft (1.8 m) in height.

Male birds flit fussily about their bowers, adjusting their ornaments and flashing vivid yellow plumage. If a female is anywhere in the vicinity, the male bursts into a raucous, rattling song, often copying the calls of other rain-forest birds. His most elaborate display involves hovering above the bower, flicking his bright tail feathers to reveal the shimmering golden yellow of their undersides.

Young males are not able to build a sophisticated bower at once – it is a skill they have to acquire and that requires much practice. Around the forest there may be many half-finished bowers, abandoned by their apprentice craftsmen.

THE MOUND-BUILDERS

There is another construction engineer in the Australian rain forests. But this one has an altogether more practical use for his creation: it is an incubator for his mate's eggs that can be carefully maintained at the same temperature for months at a time. The bird is the male brush turkey (*Alectura lathami*) – a bird with dark brown or black plumage and a bald red head and neck, trimmed with a wrinkly yellow wattle. Normally this lies flat, appearing like a simple yellow choker, but when the male turkey is trying to impress or intimidate others, it

becomes a dangling fleshy ruff, reaching almost to the floor. At such times, the large, club-shaped tail is spread as a fan to reinforce his aggressive display.

In building their incubators, brush turkeys are instinctively making use of the heat that is generated naturally when plant matter decays: in effect, each male creates an enormous, very well-regulated compost heap. Construction takes many days, during which time the male scrapes and kicks leaf debris backwards onto a growing pile of litter and soil, first with one foot, then with the other. Eventually, the mound reaches about 5 ft (1.5 m) high and 13 ft (4 m) across. As the bacteria and fungi set to work decomposing the centre of the mound, it starts to warm up.

For the next six or seven months the male brush turkey maintains his mound at a stable 33°C (91°F), ventilating the middle

BRUSH TURKEY *A male brush turkey (left) stands on one foot and kicks leaf litter backwards with the other as he builds a huge incubation mound. A clutch of eggs lies in the warm heart of a mound (below). The female lays hers egg separately, at intervals, so that the chicks, too, emerge at intervals.*

RAIN FORESTS THAT SURVIVE

The Australian rain forest is confined to the north-eastern edge of the country, where an average 157 in (400 cm) of rain falls during the year, sometimes in torrential sheets, at other times as a drizzly mist. Much of the Australian rain forest has been felled, some in prehistoric times, some in the colonial era and some more recently, with increasing controversy over such destruction in the past few decades. North-eastern Australia has forest fragments totalling about 4000 sq miles (10 400 km²). They cloak the sides of mountains, carpet gullies, and arch over the streams that flow to the sea. In some places, lowland rain forests come down to the shore, merging into the stilt-rooted mangroves that hem parts of the coast.

New Guinea, favoured by a wetter climate, and steep inaccessible terrain, has retained a much greater proportion of its rain forest, which still covers some 270 000 sq miles (700 000 km²). Much is high and cloud-covered on the central mountain range, the trees drenched in ferns and mosses. New Guinea is something of an isolated rain-forest haven, cut off from the rest of the world by ocean. In its isolation, many of the original Australian immigrants have evolved and diversified, producing novel forms, similar to, and yet distinct from, their Australian counterparts.

QUEENSLAND RAIN FOREST
Australia's remaining tropical forests cover varied terrain from mountains to coastline.

when it gets too hot, or smothering it with another layer of insulating debris should it get too cool. To check the temperature, this master gardener digs an angled hole into his compost heap and then inserts his entire head and neck into it, testing the temperature and dampness inside with a thermometer-like tongue.

When the mound has reached a suitable temperature, the female can start to lay her eggs in it. She digs a hole about 2 ft (61 cm) deep and deposits a single egg at a time. She may produce between 25 and 50 eggs during a five-month season – a very strenuous exercise which is possible only if she is well-fed and healthy. After about 50 days of incubation the young hatch, each emerging separately as a result of the staggered egg-laying.

Hatching is no simple affair. Once it has broken free of the shell, a brush-turkey chick must dig its way out of the mound in a laborious marathon of scrabbling that can take as much as 48 hours. Moreover, when the chick finally makes its escape from the

rotting debris, there are no attentive parents to greet the exhausted creature – the male is much too busy tending the incubator while the female is laying more eggs. So the chick must instantly fend for itself, finding food, keeping warm, and staying alert for predators. Like many ground-dwelling birds, brush-turkey chicks hatch in an advanced state of development: although they are still coated in fluffy down, their wing feathers are fully formed, and they may fly within hours.

Brush turkeys are not the only mound-builders in the rain forest. Common scrub fowl (*Megapodius freycinet*) build mounds that are even larger than those of the brush turkey, but that are frequently shared by several pairs of birds. Smaller and less flamboyant than the turkey, common scrub fowl have a small crest instead of a yellow wattle, and lack the long tail. Most striking are their large, bright orange legs and feet. Large feet and sturdy legs are common to all mound-builders, which are known to science as megapodes, or 'large-footed ones'.

In New Guinea, scrub fowl sometimes exploit the egg mounds of brush turkeys, laying their eggs in an established mound. On the island of Simbo in the Solomon Islands they have found an even simpler way of avoiding all that hard work. They do not build mounds at all here, but make use of natural heat from volcanic activity underground, carefully choosing a spot where the temperature is just right.

RAIN-FOREST REFUGES

The rain forests of Australia and New Guinea glisten with the colour of birds: lorikeets, parrots, kingfishers, rainbow bee-eaters, cockatoos and sunbirds.

Vermillion, ochre and turquoise butterflies alight on the forest floor and flit through clearings. Geckos skitter up and down tree trunks and lizards stalk insect prey. Dragonflies skim the pools and streams, which are rich in fish, tadpoles and shrimps, and where mosquitoes flourish. Frogs inhabit the dampest parts of the forest, swelling their inflatable chests as

GREEN TREE FROGS *Feet tipped with sticky pads enable tree frogs to climb skilfully along branches and leaves. They are thus well suited to life in the forest canopy.*

night draws in to produce a chorus of croaks and chirrups. Near to the coasts, the rain forests may hide a few of the increasingly rare crocodiles. Freshwater species inhabit inland swamps, while estuarine species haunt the mangrove forests.

Although Australia shares much of its rain-forest wildlife with New Guinea and other adjacent islands, it has a great deal that is unique. Its remaining rain forest – amounting to just a small fraction of the area in New Guinea – is highly unusual, full

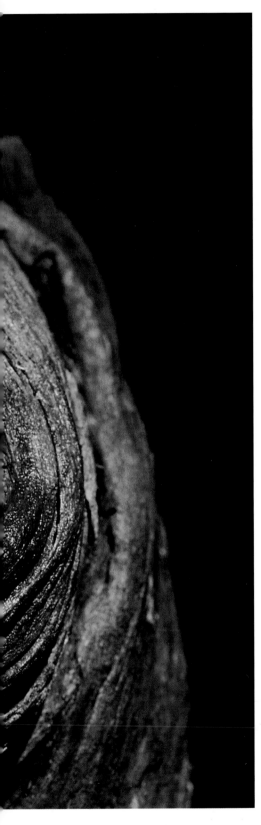

flowering trees, and the world was dominated by giant club mosses, huge tree ferns, tree-sized horsetails and conifers. Throughout the upheavals that were created by ice ages and volcanic activity, the arrival of human beings and fire, some of the mountainous parts of north-eastern Australia have retained their rain-forest cover, acting as refuges for rain-forest plants and animals threatened by fire, humans and the like elsewhere. Sites such as Bellenden Ker, Cape Tribulation and Mount Lewis have been refuges of this kind, leafy Noah's arks from which rain forest has regenerated in other areas whenever favourable conditions returned.

Despite the fact that Australian forests received other plants from Asia, such as the beautifully ornate orchids, the varied palms, and the gingers with their vivid red flowers, they have also retained many of their original, ancestral plants. Tree ferns still prosper in perpetually wet ravines and gorges. Enormous slow-growing kauri pines (*Agathis robusta*), closely related to the kind of coniferous tree that flourished across Australia 175 million years ago, continue to grow in the state of Queensland. Each of the largest living kauris may be well over 1000 years old. Hoop-pine (*Araucaria cunninghamu*) and klinki pine (*Araucaria hunsteinii*), relatives of the curious monkey puzzle (*Araucaria araucana*), still grow in Australia, as well as in New Guinea.

There are also the primitive tree-like cycads. Although these look something like palms (which are flowering plants) they are not, in fact, palms at all; instead, they are considered to be survivors of an evolutionary transition between conifers and flowering plants. They bear massive cones that are brilliantly coloured in some species.

Many ancient species of flowering plant linger on in Australia, including a particularly unusual vine-like magnolia called *Austrobaileya scandens* whose pollen is similar to fossilised pollen that is thought to be 120

ANCIENT SURVIVORS *These cycads are primitive tree-like plants that have remained virtually unchanged for some 200 million years.*

million years old. Biologists believe that this is the most ancient form of flowering plant still alive today.

The rain forests also shelter extremely primitive members of the plant families Myrtaceae and Proteaceae. These species are closely related to those that gave rise to the eucalypts, bottlebrushes, banksias and other characteristic Australian plants, the relative newcomers that now dominate so much of the continent. The ubiquitous eucalyptus forest is much younger than the rain forest and, as we now know, was derived from it.

Although the tropical rain forest is now reduced to tiny islands in a sea of cities and other vegetation, it still deserves respect and protection as the most ancient of all Australian habitats as well as the forerunner of most of the others that exist today. In recognition of this, thousands of acres of the Australian rain forest were declared a world heritage site in December 1988, meaning that their treasures should remain safe for many more generations to come.

of ancient kinds of plant, many of which are found nowhere else on Earth.

Parts of the Australian rain forest are so old that they date back to a time when flowering plants had not yet evolved, a time when there were no grasses, herbs, shrubs or

FOREST-LIVING IN SOUTH AND SOUTH-EAST ASIA

The Asian rain forests, some of the oldest in the world, are dominated by giant dipterocarp trees whose flowers can scent a whole forest. Flying lemurs swoop between the crowns of massive trees, and gibbons swing through the canopy below.

Suspended below the branch of a tree, it looks like a furry sack with a small squirrel-like head protruding at one end. Keeping a careful hold on the branch with long curved claws, this bizarre animal works its way along towards the trunk of the tree, resembling a strangely mobile blanket as it does so. Those same claws help it to negotiate its way onto the tree trunk, to hang there for a minute, and then to climb upwards in a series of lurching movements, the claws acting now as grappling hooks while the loose sack-like folds of fur flop against the bark.

In a matter of seconds, this clumsy, shapeless animal is transformed into something graceful and superbly adapted to its environment. The transformation occurs when the sharp claws loosen their grip on the tree and the animal launches itself sideways into mid-air, spreading its limbs out, as straight as tent poles, to stretch taut the skin that connects them.

The furry sack has become a furry kite, an astonishing metamorphosis. This magnificent gliding animal – known as a colugo – can travel as much as 450 ft (137 m) between trees while descending as little as about 40 ft (12 m).

The colugos (*Cynocephalus* species) live in Malaysia and the Philippines and have the alternative name of 'flying lemurs'. In fact, they are not true lemurs (large-eyed, tree-dwelling primates, mostly found in Madagascar), but a quite separate group of mammals. Nor do they fly, in any true sense; they are simply gliding from tree to tree. They cannot gain height while in the air, only swoop downwards. All altitude lost during gliding must later be recovered by laborious clambering up tree trunks. Despite this, the colugos swiftly cover great distances through the forests of Southeast Asia. They are the most accomplished gliding animals in the world, with far more extensive 'flying membranes' than other gliders including the flying frogs, snakes, lizards and so on. The colugos' membranes reach from limb to limb and from the neck to the outer fingers of each forelimb, with further sections of skin linking the fingers, so that they are webbed like the feet of a duck. Large, triangular flaps of skin also join the hind limbs to the long tail. Spread-eagled in flight, only a colugo's head and claws extend beyond its kite-like outline.

Colugos feed on leaves, buds and flowers, and occasionally a little fruit. Water is obtained by licking raindrops from leaves. During the day they hole up in hollow trees, emerging just before nightfall. They show many curious pieces of behaviour that are accommodations to their strange body form. When clambering along below a branch, they sometimes tuck the voluminous skin flaps in beneath their forelegs to prevent them catching on twigs. When passing urine

TAKEN FOR A RIDE *A young colugo is carried about on its mother's belly, wrapped in her wing-like folds of skin when she is at rest and clinging on tightly when she glides.*

or faeces, a colugo hangs from a branch by its forelegs like a trapeze artist, then splays its hindlegs and flexes its tail backwards to pull the gliding membrane out of the way. Colugos can scarcely move on the ground, so they never intentionally descend to earth.

FLYING FROGS AND SNAKES

The colugo is just one of the gliders found in the tropical rain forests of South-east Asia. There are many other animals in this region that use the same mode of travel, including the flying lizard (*Draco volans*) with mottled membranous 'wings' slung between its forelimbs and hindlimbs, the wings being held taut in the air by bony extensions of its ribs. These thin membranes vary from golden brown to luminous red in colour, a flash of brilliance that appears only when the lizard embarks on a glide and vanishes when the reptile lands on a nearby tree.

Similar glimpses of colour when airborne are also seen in some moths and grasshoppers in other parts of the world, and are thought to be useful in confusing predators. The startling colour the lizard reveals when gliding gives a potential predator something distinctive to pursue, but this disappears when the lizard lands, so that it no longer matches the predator's 'search image'. With luck the predator is so baffled by the change that it passes the lizard by. The male flying lizard also uses its colourful 'wings' for display purposes, when courting females.

Gliding animals have developed a variety of different body parts to make parachute-like surfaces. Perhaps the strangest are the so-called flying frogs, such as Wallace's flying frog of Malaysia and Borneo, equipped with extra-long toes linked by extensive webbing. By spreading its toes when airborne, the frog creates four small parachutes to slow its fall. Some flying frogs can flatten their whole body to give it yet more air resistance. The flying snake (*Chrysopelea pelias*) also uses this technique, sucking in its belly and flattening its body into a ribbon-like shape that floats gently downwards.

Giant flying squirrels (*Petaurista* species) swoop by night, some covering more than 330 ft (100 m) at a time on furry membranes stretched between their limbs. They steer

HIGH FLYER *A flying dragon lizard uses its tail as a kind of rudder to steer itself with, as it glides on its 'wings of skin' to a neighbouring tree.*

using their tails and limbs as rudders, and brake by shifting their body to a vertical position in the air. Alighting on a clear, vertical tree trunk, they scramble upwards to regain height for the next glide.

HEAVEN FOR GLIDERS

There are, in fact, more gliding animals in the tropical rain forests of South-east Asia than anywhere else on Earth, with the island of Borneo being especially rich in gliding species. Flying lemurs and the flying snake are unique to South-east Asia, as is the flying lizard, found only in the Philippines, Malaysia and Indonesia. Wallace's flying frog is also confined to this region, although other 'parachuting' frog species can be found elsewhere – the fringe-limbed tree frog of Central America, for example, has webbing between its toes to help it glide. A few gliders are found in other rain forests, such as the anomalures of Africa, but again they are outnumbered by the Asian gliders.

The reason for this difference can be found in the trees and other vegetation of the South-east Asian rain forests. In particular, dipterocarp trees – almost 500 species of them, all belonging to the family

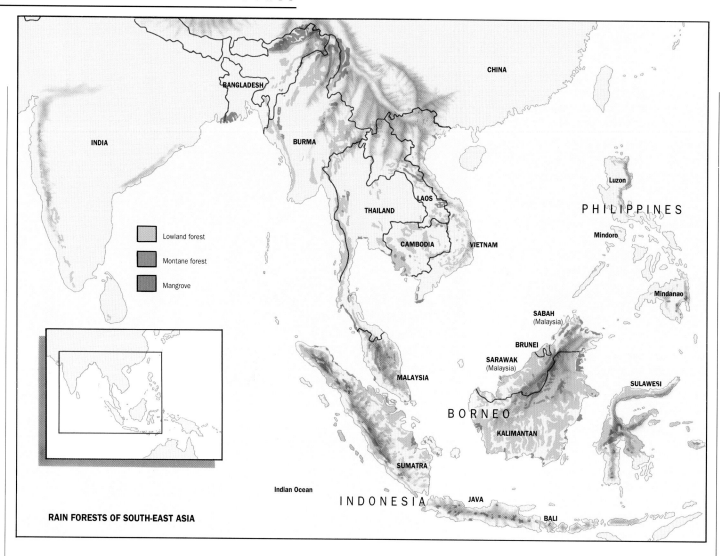

RAIN FORESTS OF SOUTH-EAST ASIA

SPLENDOUR OF THE ORIENT
Malaysia and Indonesia have
South-east Asia's largest
surviving rain forests. Smaller
forests are scattered from
western India to Vietnam.

Dipterocarpaceae – are characteristic of the region. They grow to enormous heights, with straight, unbranched trunks and compact crowns. Their great stature gives an especial-ly lofty and open feel to the rain forests of South-east Asia. Compared with the trees of rain forests elsewhere, dipterocarp forests have fewer lianas and other climbing plants slung between the high tree crowns.

Without a widespread network of links between the giant tree tops, non-flying ani-mals have been forced to evolve alternative strategies for getting from tree to tree. Des-cending to ground level and then climbing another tree is one possibility, but it is ex-pensive in energy and risky as well, because

there are predators lurking in the under-growth. Gliding is a viable alternative, for which the high and open conditions have turned out to be particularly suitable. Over evolutionary time, many South-east Asian animals have developed mechanisms that allow them to parachute from one tree to the next, unhampered by obstacles such as dense thickets of climbers and aided by the great height of the dipterocarps, which make ideal launch sites.

NOCTURNAL FLOWERING
Gliding animals are one phenomenon of the South-east Asian rain forests; another happens just once every five to eight years, when the canopy of the Malaysian rain forest is transformed.

As if in silent communication with one another, many thousands of tall trees burst simultaneously into flower, followed by thousands of others, then thousands more, all in rapid succession. Fallen petals, in

shades of cream and yellow, lie thick on the ground, sometimes over an area of several hundred square miles. In the evening, the scent of the flowers, opening high above in the canopy, filters down to the forest floor, a heavy, almost oppressive perfume. The extravaganza lasts for about three months in all. During that time, each tree may pro-duce up to 4 million individual flowers.

The event involves not just one tree species, but a number of different ones. However, they all belong to a single related group of dipterocarps that are known as the Philippine mahoganies (*Shorea* species). For many years, the phenomenal flowering of the Philippine mahoganies was a puzzle to biologists. To add to the mystery, there are several other groups of dipterocarp species that also engage in mass flowering.

The species within a particular diptero-carp group do not flower in precise unison. Instead, they apparently 'take it in turns' to flower, the species order always being the same. One species of tree starts the process and flowers for ten days, the second species begins flowering just before the first ends, a third one takes over just before the second species ends, and so on. This set pattern suggests some definite advantage to the mass flowering, and rules out the possibility that the trees simply flower together because they happen to be responding to the same environmental cue.

SOLVING THE PUZZLE

Why do they flower together but at fixed intervals? And how are they pollinated? The flowers are high in the canopy and cannot easily be seen because of the intervening layer of understorey trees. So for decades even the simple question of what pollinated the trees remained unanswerable.

During the 1970s, researchers working in Malaysia began to take a closer look at the Philippine mahoganies. They ascended into the canopy and homed in on the flowers of the giant trees by sitting in a special chair carried on a long, movable aluminium 'boom'. The boom was mounted securely on a large branch at the far end. In this precarious moving perch they kept watch on the flowers, day and night, waiting for animal visitors.

But rather than solving the mystery of the Philippine mahoganies' flowering, when they got up into the canopy the researchers found that it only deepened. It became evident that the blooms only opened an hour before nightfall, and that although they were heavily scented, they did not seem to produce nectar. They were not, therefore, attracting bats, moths or other likely nocturnal pollinators. Instead, under the cover of darkness, thousands of thrips flocked towards their perfume. Thrips are very small, slender insects with narrow feathery wings and a weak, meandering flight, so tiny that they could easily be dismissed as a fleck of dirt.

At first, the biologists thought very little about the thrips, but in the absence of other pollinators they began to take more notice of their activities. Each night the thrips clambered about the blooms, chewing at petals and pollen alike, and they did

indeed become coated with pollen in the process. Even so, these insignificant and un-dynamic creatures, with their feeble powers of flight, seemed implausible candidates for such a massive pollination task, carried out on giant trees scattered through the rain forest. They seemed to be little more than unwelcome visitors – tiny scroungers of the kind that are often found among flowers and fruit.

In time, however, it became clear that the thrips really were the key players in the pollination of Philippine mahoganies, although the details of the pollination process were decidedly unusual. Like all pollinators, thrips perform their vital task unintentionally, but in the case of the thrips the process seems to be particularly haphazard.

Having found a flower at nightfall, thrips stay put, feeding on the petals and the pollen. The flowers last only one night, and when they fall to the ground at dawn, they carry the tiny insects down with them. The adults usually flutter off the descending flowers, but the immature thrips stay with their flower until it reaches the forest floor. During the next day, these thrips mature and then fly weakly upwards towards the fresh crop of flowers that evening brings to the canopy.

POWER OF NUMBERS *The Philippine mahogany, among the largest of rain-forest trees, is pollinated by swarms of minute insects known as thrips.*

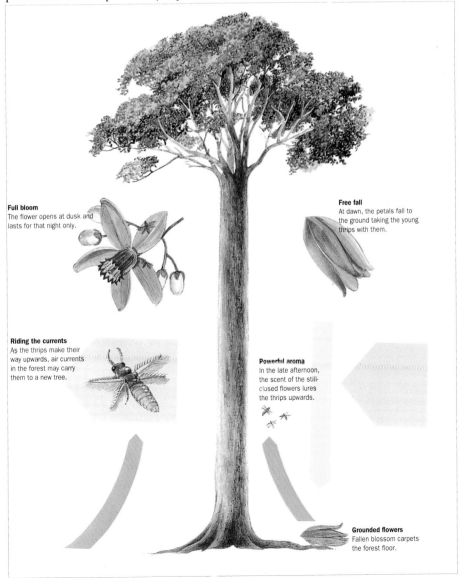

Full bloom
The flower opens at dusk and lasts for that night only.

Free fall
At dawn, the petals fall to the ground taking the young thrips with them.

Riding the currents
As the thrips make their way upwards, air currents in the forest may carry them to a new tree.

Powerful aroma
In the late afternoon, the scent of the still-closed flowers lures the thrips upwards.

Grounded flowers
Fallen blossom carpets the forest floor.

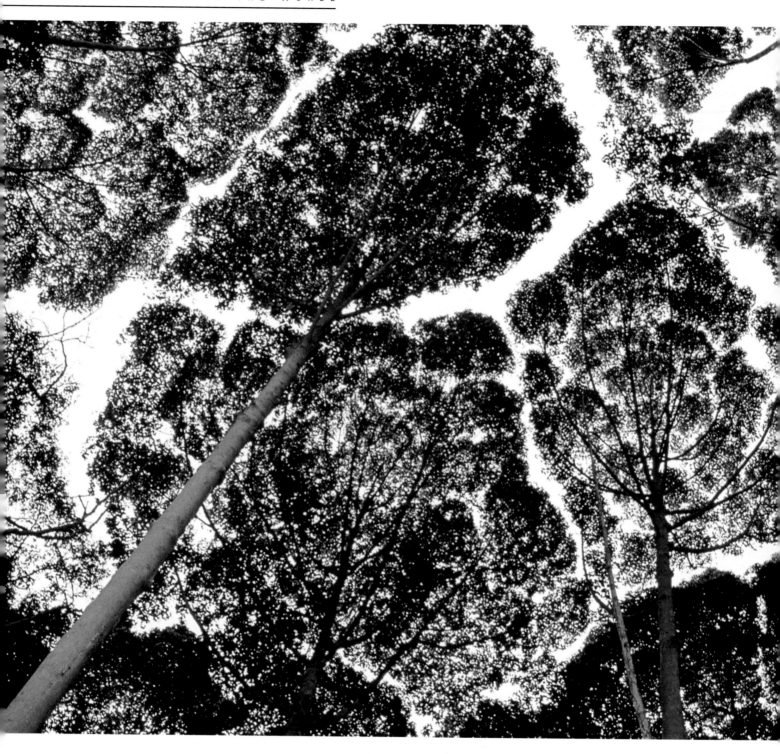

RAIN-FOREST CANOPY *Compact tree crowns stand a little apart from each other, a phenomenon known as 'crown shyness'.*

Once airborne, thrips are essentially passive, their flight being greatly aided and influenced by the air currents that flow through the forest. When the flowering of the Philippine mahoganies is in full swing, the little insects drift about in great clouds.

Rising up into the canopy and floating gently through it, the thrips can probably choose to quit the airstream and alight on flowers when they see them, but beyond that they have little control over their direction of flight.

As for the Philippine mahoganies, by late afternoon their flowers have not yet opened, but the scent is already very rich on the air, and the long slender female reproductive organs (known as stigmas) that

protrude from the closed flower make obvious landing sites for thrips. Once they have landed, they often groom themselves clean of the sticky pollen grains that they acquired the previous night. In this way, the pollen is delivered to its correct destination on the flower. With luck, this is the flower of another tree, because cross-fertilisation is preferable for the trees.

As darkness falls the flower opens, the thrips move down to chew on the petals, and become coated with pollen once again. The next day, the pollen of this flower will be delivered to the stigma of another flower – and so the process continues.

WHY THRIPS?

At first sight, thrips are a very poor choice as pollinators. Bees, butterflies, birds or bats can make direct purposeful flights from one tree that is in bloom to another of the same species, recognising the flowers and homing in on them in the certainty of a good meal. To make sure that the thrips deliver their pollen to another tree of the same species, all must flower at once, and they must flower prolifically.

Since the flight of the thrips is so haphazard, there is little chance of their discriminating between one dipterocarp species and another. To avoid crossing between species, or pollen being wasted on unsuitable flowers, each dipterocarp species needs to avoid flowering at the same time as other species in the group.

The real puzzle, then, is why groups of different dipterocarp species should flower in such a close-paced sequence. The answer to this lies in the infrequency of dipterocarp flowering (which is, in turn, due to the activities of seed-eating animals) and the curious life history of the thrip.

With a gap of up to eight years between flowerings, the dipterocarps cannot rely on a pollinator without other resources to fall back on. A variety of insects and birds could do the job, but they would require nectar as a reward, which is energy expensive. And nectar makes flowers a target for thieves such as flying lemurs and monkeys. The fact that dipterocarps flower infrequently and at odd intervals suggests that they are adapted to avoid the attentions of specialised seed robbers, and possibly flower thieves as well, by not providing a constant supply of food that would allow the numbers of these animal enemies to build up.

Thrips prove valuable to the dipterocarps because they can survive the intervals between flowering by chewing on the leaves or petals of other trees, or by sucking plant sap. These foods are less nourishing than the dipterocarp petals and the thrips survive

in relatively small numbers during the lean years between dipterocarp flowerings. But when food becomes plentiful, thrips can stage a population explosion at short notice.

They are impatient creatures when it comes to reproduction, galloping through their development from egg to mature adult in just eight days. The adults live for one to two weeks and each adult female lays about 30 eggs in her lifetime. As a result, 500 thrips can turn into 13 million thrips in the space of a month. By flowering in sequence, the dipterocarps encourage this spectacular growth in the thrips' numbers, producing a plague of the creatures that can service the vast proliferation of flowers.

At the same time, the dipterocarps cash in on the thrips' reproductive powers. Obviously, the first species to flower in each group has the leanest pickings, but it copes by producing, at the outset, a large number of flower buds that never open. These provide food for thrips and trigger off the outburst of reproductive activity.

Since the original research in Malaysia, biologists have investigated the other dipterocarp groups with mass sequential flowering. These too share a particular small insect as pollinator, either leafhoppers, bugs or tiny flies. The important thing about all these insects is that they are capable of reproducing explosively over a short period of time once the mass flowering begins. Flowering itself seems to be triggered by a period of drought, or by particularly cold night-time temperatures.

THE SEED BONANZA

A rain forest's canopy is not a flat, unbroken layer – it is undulating, with some trees projecting more than others. And above the canopy are the so-called emergents towering high above it. Many dipterocarps are among these, attaining heights

SWAMPED BY SEEDS After spinning down from towering heights, the winged seeds of dipterocarp trees accumulate on the forest floor.

of 200 ft (60 m) or more. In their elevated position, they can rely upon wind to disperse their seeds, something which is impossible for many rain-forest trees. These dry, winged seeds lack the tasty, coloured fruit that is associated with animal-dispersed seeds. Instead, they resemble those of

---

TREE MONOPOLIES

In peninsular Malaysia, dipterocarps often account for 57 per cent of the larger trees – those more than 8 ft (2.4 m) in diameter. In Sarawak the figure is 76 per cent, rising to 78-98 per cent in Sabah, and 100 per cent in the Philippines. Nowhere else in the world does a single tree family characterise a region of tropical rain forest in quite the same way. Of the 515 tree species in this family, just one lives in South America, and a few in Africa. The remainder, all rain-forest species, are found in South-east Asia.

---

sycamores or maples, helicoptering down from the lofty branches to land in their thousands on the forest floor.

Despite their 'wings', most of the seeds fall within 135 ft (41 m) of their parent, and as a result, many dipterocarp species grow together in small clumps. At most, their seeds travel about 1650 ft (500 m). Because of their limited powers of dispersal, some dipterocarp species are prevented from

HORNBILLS HELD HOSTAGE

For many hornbill species, imprisoning the female is a normal part of reproduction – a safety measure to secure the survival of the brood. Hornbills – notable for their large, distinctively shaped beaks – are found in Africa and throughout southern Asia, but most of the rain-forest species are found in Asia. Rain-forest hornbills mate for life and they like to nest in hollow trees, often enlarging existing woodpecker holes. Before the female lays her eggs, she begins to seal herself into the nest chamber, initially closing the entrance with wet mud from the outside, and later completing the barricade from within, using a mixture of her droppings and saliva. The male may help, bringing pellets of adhesive mud and sticky fruits. The natural plaster formed from these diverse ingredients sets very hard, and only a

tiny slit is left open. From now on, until the brood is fledged, the imprisoned female is totally dependent on her mate.

Safe from scavenging monkeys and predatory snakes, the female lays a clutch of eggs, between one and six. As she incubates them, the male brings regular deliveries of food, which he regurgitates and passes through the slit, a piece at a time. For her part, the female ejects any indigestible parts of the food remains, and defecates accurately through the tiny hole to her chamber. Scavenging insects help to maintain sanitary conditions within.

The female uses the solitude to moult. Her long tail feathers are the first to be lost – perhaps making her confined form less cumbersome to her. Gradually, all her other feathers are shed and replaced.

Incubation takes more than a month, and the young need another month or two to reach maturity. In some hornbill species, the mother stays with them, and when she finally emerges from confinement, she is flabby and unfit, so must build up strength again. In other species, the female breaks free of her prison before the chicks are fledged and helps her mate find food for the hungry youngsters. One breeding hornbill was seen to swallow 69 small fruits which were carried back to the nest for the young.

LOCKED IN *A male hornbill brings food to his mate, sealed into her nest in a hollow tree until the chicks are fledged.*

---

colonising new areas by a simple barrier such as a river, which could be easily crossed by a bird-dispersed species. On the island of Borneo, there are 57 dipterocarp species found in the Sarawak part of the island in the north-west that are not found in the Indonesian part, Kalimantan, separated from Sarawak by the Batang Lupar river.

Although their flowering times are slightly staggered, all the dipterocarp trees in one area manage to release their seeds at almost exactly the same time. This mass

BURST OF FLOWERS *As millions of dipterocarp flowers bloom, the forest is filled with a heavy scent.*

production is known as 'masting' – and is also seen among certain temperate trees, such as the beeches. The bounty attracts seed-eating animals such as weevils, pheasants, green pigeons, rats, squirrels and bearded pigs (*Sus barbatus*). But by 'flooding the market' with seeds, dipterocarps manage to satiate the appetites of these seed-eaters, and overwhelm them with excess, ensuring that at least some seeds survive the feast. The fact that the seeding occurs so infrequently and at irregular intervals thwarts the evolution of animals that specialise in eating dipterocarp seeds.

Other unrelated types of South-east Asian tree have evolved to produce fruit, nuts or pods at the same time as the dipterocarps, to take advantage of the protection against seed thieves provided by the glut. The overall effect on the wildlife of the rain forests is to limit the number of seed-eaters, particularly the songbirds, which are far fewer and less diverse than in American tropical rain forests, for example. The number of nectar-eating species is likewise restricted when compared with other rain-forest regions, because the dominant dipterocarps provide no nectar.

Upon falling to the ground, dipterocarp seeds germinate, almost immediately, producing a carpet of seedlings across the forest floor. Just as masting restricts the damage by seed-eaters, so this rapid germination may limit damage by herbivores, which cannot consume all the fresh shoots at once. The young dipterocarps survive for up to two years as small, stunted seedlings staying near the ground, but ultimately they die from lack of light unless a canopy gap opens above them. In cyclone-prone areas such as the Philippines, whole stands of dipterocarps may grow up in the wake of the destructive storms.

HORNBILLS AND BABBLERS

While gliders and dipterocarps are particular trademarks of South-east Asian rain forests, numerous other creatures contribute to their special character. Hornbills fly over the canopy searching for fruit, the flap of their wings producing loud 'swooshing' sounds. Iridescent green barbets, splashed with red, yellow or brown, pluck fruits, flowers and buds in the tree tops. Macaque monkeys congregate noisily in large groups, and acrobatic squirrels leap through the branches. Crowds of babbler songbirds – among the few that live in South-east Asia's rain forests – flit about the undergrowth, snatching at insects.

On the forest floor, wild pigs forage for fruit and nuts, while thrushes and bright, short-tailed birds called pittas pick over the leaf litter for insects, worms and snails. Occasionally, during the early morning, a male great argus pheasant (*Argusianus argus*) can be seen revealing his brilliance in a hilltop dance of dazzling golden plumage. Fanning his wing feathers, the pheasant reveals a spectacular array of 'eye' markings, rather like those on a peacock's tail, which are flaunted to impress a watching female. The pheasant gains its name from Argus, a giant of Greek mythology, who was said to have 100 eyes.

CREATURES OF THE NIGHT

Under the cover of darkness, many other animals emerge to feed. As dusk draws in, fruit-eating bats known as flying foxes flap past on their huge black wings. Cat-like civets emerge from their daytime resting places in hollow trees and burrows to ambush lizards, frogs, birds and small mammals. They are proficient climbers, using their curved claws to find purchase on the bark of trees.

The binturong (*Arctictis binturong*), one of a subgroup known as palm civets, has a dark coat and tufted ears. It is unusual among civets in having a muscular prehensile tail with which it grasps twigs and branches in the tree crowns. Binturongs are extremely versatile beasts. Besides foraging in the tree crowns, they can swim, dive and catch fish.

All civets produce musky scents from their genital glands, some of which are extremely powerful and persistent. The secretions are smeared on rocks, logs and vegetation, where they act as long-lasting 'signposts' marking territorial boundaries. Such signposts are effective even in the darkness of the forest night.

In the starlit tangle of canopy foliage, nocturnal lorises clamber slowly along branches. The slender loris (*Loris tardigradus*) lives in the rain forests of Sri Lanka and India, while the slow loris (*Nycticebus coucang*) extends from Bangladesh and Vietnam into Malaysia and Indonesia. Unlike their more active African relatives, the bush babies, lorises never leap and jump. Their movements are slow, deliberate and painstaking, so that they are almost undetectable in dense, shifting vegetation. Should danger threaten, they freeze, maintaining a statue-like immobility for a few hours if necessary.

Typically they catch insects, which they detect by smell in the darkness. Lorises can survive as hunters despite their lethargic pace because they are adapted to tackle toxic, irritant and unpleasant-smelling insects. Such creatures are usually conspicuous and easy to catch, making no effort to escape but relying on their sheer distastefulness to put predators off.

NIGHT STALKER *After waiting patiently in ambush, a slow loris suddenly lunges forward and grasps its insect victim in one of its powerful forepaws.*

The gloom of the forest floor hides plant-eating Malayan tapirs (*Tapirus indicus*), their striking black and white coloration providing surprisingly good camouflage in the dappled moonlight of the forest night. They browse on low vegetation, manipulating tender shoots with a flexible, fleshy snout derived from their upper lip. Tapirs are also fond of water plants: they wallow in rivers and may submerge themselves for several minutes to forage under water.

THE HUNTERS AND THE HUNTED

Night provides relative safety for small, defenceless animals that are particularly at risk from predators. Chevrotains, or Asiatic mouse deer, scamper through low passageways in the undergrowth on short, spindly legs. Individuals of the smallest species weigh only 4-5 lb (1.8-2.3 kg) and measure just 8 in (20 cm) from the ground to their shoulder. Chevrotains have white flecks or stripes on their brown coats to help camouflage them from the eyes of hunters in the twilight hours.

Stealth, patience and great agility in the trees mean that clouded leopards (*Neofelis nebulosa*) are among the most fearsome of Asian rain-forest hunters: they regularly take

HEAT DETECTORS *Around the reticulated python's mouth are heat-sensitive pits which allow it to locate warm-blooded prey, even in total darkness.*

CLOUDED LEOPARD *As well as stalking prey on the ground, this extremely athletic climber hunts by pouncing from the trees.*

chevrotains, but also hunt pigs, deer, porcupines, birds, monkeys and squirrels. They are extraordinary climbers, running up and down trunks with ease, and even dangling beneath branches. Much of their time is spent resting in the trees, but occasionally they leap down onto unwary prey below. The clouded leopard is patterned rather like a giraffe, with irregular, interlocking polygons, which are shaded to give a textured, three-dimensional camouflage. Although the leopard has few enemies other than man, the camouflage is valuable in keeping it hidden from potential prey.

Lurking in the crooks of trees or under fallen logs are other rain-forest dangers. Asia has a vast array of snakes, including the reticulated python (*Python reticulatus*), believed to be the longest snake in the world. Found from Thailand south to the Malay Archipelago and the Philippines, this giant has a maximum length of over 30 ft (9 m). Pythons find their prey using uniquely sensitive heat-detectors located in pits on their lips, enabling them to hunt accurately in total darkness.

Leeches also follow heat sources to find their warm-blooded targets. Traces of carbon dioxide – the gas we expel with every outward breath – provide them with a second clue to the presence of a potential prey. Leeches abound in South-east Asian rain forests, in the streams and damp undergrowth, but also on the wet leaves of the

shrub layer up to a height of at least 5 ft (1.5 m). From these vantage points, they can launch themselves onto passing mammals, such as tapirs or wild pigs, and they will also suck blood from human beings, making any excursion into these forests distinctly uncomfortable. The smaller species of leech will squirm through any available gap in boots or clothing to gorge themselves on blood.

A UNIQUE ASSEMBLAGE

Asia has several unique groups of animals, including the enigmatic tree shrews. Despite their name, they are not shrews, and they spend some or all of their time on the ground. These creatures, with their long bushy squirrel-like tails and pointed shrewlike snouts, are of interest to biologists. Their skeletons show a close similarity to fossils of early placental mammals, tiny nocturnal creatures that scuttled across the face of the Earth more than 100 million years ago, when dinosaurs were the dominant form of life.

Tree shrews, like most nocturnal mammals, mark their territory with characteristic scents. They have a scent gland in a rather odd position, on the underside of the body, and they scent-mark branches by sliding down them on their belly, their feet splayed out on either side.

Young tree shrews are treated with remarkable indifference by their mothers. Left in a separate nest, they are visited only once every two days, when they can suckle for 5-10 minutes. They are ready to go out into the world alone after a month, having received about 90 minutes of parental care since their birth.

Several primate groups are found only in Asia, including the small apes known as siamangs and gibbons. They are famous for their exceptionally long arms, their rapid swinging movement from branch to branch and their prolonged musical calls which take the form of duetting between male and female in some species. Gibbons feed mainly on fruit, plus some young leaves. They form monogamous pairs and only produce a youngster every two to three years. The gibbons' specialised way of getting around takes up to three years to master, so young gibbons are dependent on their parents for a long time.

Leaf-eating langurs, also known as leaf monkeys, are likewise restricted to South-east Asia. Tarsiers, tiny nocturnal primates weighing just 4 oz (115 g), are found only in the Philippines and Indonesia. They have prominent saucer-shaped eyes, close-set at the front of the head, and a long, naked tail. The head can be turned through almost 360°, rather like that of an owl, to give panoramic vision. Tarsiers make high-pitched bird-like calls, and leap acrobatically between upright branches, propelled by powerful kicks from their elongated hind legs.

Despite the meanness of the dipterocarps in providing food, the rain forests of South-east Asia are unusually rich in species. This is partly due to the continuous existence of parts of this rain forest over many millions of years, and the universal forces that tend to produce species diversity in rain forests. But there have been other factors at work, too. Much of South-east Asia is divided into islands, and the islands are often split by mountain ranges, ravines or rivers, providing a patchwork of varying habitats and fragmented

A BITE TO EAT *This species of tree shrew actually finds most of its food on the forest floor by rooting around with its long snout and claws.*

populations, all fertile grounds for the emergence of new species. The Philippines archipelago alone totals no fewer than 7100 separate islands.

When populations of animals or plants become isolated from others of their kind (by a barrier such as a mountain range, a river or a stretch of ocean) they gradually, as the generations pass, adapt to local conditions by the process of natural selection. Eventually, the isolated population may become so different from its original stock that even if they are brought together once again, in the case of animals, the two groups can no longer interbreed. Under these circumstances, the isolated population has become a completely different species.

A species that is found only in a particular part of the world is said to be 'endemic' to that area. While some animals and plants are endemic to Asia as a whole, many species are endemic just to a certain subregion or even to a single island. Their dependence on such a small range makes these species particularly susceptible to the various problems of habitat destruction, hunting or disease. Many of Asia's endemic species are threatened or seriously endangered, and some are balancing right on the brink of extinction.

RAIN-FOREST RARITIES

Clinging to existence in a national park on the Indonesian island of Java, the Javan rhinoceros (*Rhinoceros sondaicus*) is probably the rarest large mammal in the world. This grey, hairless rhino has a single horn at the tip of its nose. Unlike elephant tusks, which are made of ivory, rhino horn is formed of compressed hair. It is highly valued as a traditional oriental medicine and aphrodisiac, qualities that have led to the near-demise of rhinos at the hands of hunters.

Only about 50 individual rhinos remain in Java, with reports of between 10 and 15 more possibly surviving in Vietnam. Javan rhinos were once far more widespread, with different subspecies living as far afield as Sumatra, mainland South-east Asia and India. But like the silvery gibbon (*Hylobates moloch*), which has lost 98 per cent of its Javanese habitat through the activities of

loggers, the remaining rhinos have been squeezed into diminishing patches of forest.

The smaller, hairy, two-horned Sumatran rhino (*Dicerorhinus sumatrensis*) can still be found in mountain forests of South-east Asia, where it characteristically wallows in forest pools to keep cool. Like its Javan relative, the Sumatran rhino has been hunted for its horn, and only 1000 or so animals are thought to remain in the wild.

Beyond the range of the rhinoceroses, on the Indonesian island of Sulawesi (formerly Celebes), live the smallest of all wild cattle: the lowland and mountain anoas (*Anoa depressicornis* and *A. quarlesi*) which stand about 30 in (76 cm) high at the shoulder, hardly larger than a sheep. These endangered rain-forest creatures feed on low vegetation such as grasses, ferns, saplings, ginger and fallen fruit. The more heavily built tamaraw (*Bubalus mindorensis*), meanwhile, is restricted to Mindoro island in the Philippines. This dwarf buffalo is reputed by local people to be fearless and aggressive, but is now extremely rare.

The Philippine islands are also home to one of the world's most endangered birds,

RARE SIGHT *The monkey-eating eagle of the dwindling rain forests of the Philippines is in danger of extinction as its habitat shrinks.*

the Philippine or monkey-eating eagle (*Pithecophaga jefferyi*), a powerful bird of prey with a total population now estimated at 200. 'Monkey-eating' is a somewhat misleading name, since this magnificent eagle feeds mainly on colugos or flying lemurs, large birds and deer. Swooping down from the tree tops, it snatches its quarry with bare, outstretched talons. Each nesting pair lays just one egg a year.

MAN OF THE FOREST

The most famous of Asia's endangered endemics is the large, shaggy-haired rust-coloured orang-utan (*Pongo pygmaeus*). Orang-utans are restricted to lowland rain forests on the islands of Borneo and Sumatra, although fossil evidence indicates that they were once much more widespread.

The name orang-utan means 'man of the forest' in the Malay language, and these great apes show a striking intelligence, capacity for learning and, in captivity, an ability to use simple tools. However, they are less closely related to the human species than are the other great apes, the chimpanzees and gorillas.

Orang-utans' arms are much longer than their legs, almost reaching down to their feet when they stand upright. In the understorey of the dipterocarp forests and swamp forests, orang-utans move about carefully, using all four limbs to grip the branches. They can swing below a sturdy branch although they lack the considerable speed and grace of the gibbons. They also use trees as catapults to propel them from one to another – a form of locomotion that is uniquely theirs.

The principal food of orang-utans is fruit. They enjoy figs, rambutans (oval, red

PROJECT TIGER: PROTECTING DWINDLING POPULATIONS

Feared and revered throughout the centuries, tigers (*Panthera tigris*) have been both worshipped by humans for their power and strength, and hunted relentlessly, either as enemies or as trophies. They were once common in Asia, from the tropical rain forests and mangrove swamps, through the drier forests, into the northerly snow-covered conifer forests, grasslands and rocky country. Originally there were eight different subspecies, varying in coat pattern and geographical range. Of these, three are now feared extinct, and the remainder are severely endangered.

In the 1930s, there were 40 000 tigers in India. By 1972, a census indicated that there were just 1827. The decline was originally due to excessive hunting (one Maharaja is said to have killed 1157 tigers during his lifetime), but was later exacerbated by severe habitat destruction. In response, the Indian and World Wildlife Fund (now the World Wide Fund for Nature)

launched 'Project Tiger', initially creating 11 tiger reserves. The project was personally supported by the Indian Prime Minister of the time, Indira Gandhi, and met with

remarkable success. By 1990, there were more than 4000 tigers in India living in 18 reserves.

Despite the success of the project, there have been many problems, not least the conflicts arising between people and tigers. As human populations expand, tigers are inevitably forced into closer proximity with people. Injured tigers often look for easy prey, taking domestic cattle and sometimes even humans. Attacks on people are particularly common in the Sundarbans region – where in recent years, the number of people killed by tigers has exceeded the number of tigers shot by humans.

TIME FOR A COOL DOWN
Tigers are the largest of the big cats. During the hot season they often lie or stand in water to keep cool.

fruit with soft spines), durians (pleasant tasting, despite an extremely unpleasant odour), lychees and mangoes, but also supplement their diet with tender shoots,

SWINGING IN THE TREES *In general, orang-utans tend to be rather solitary animals, but the young often travel around in pairs as here.*

young leaves and nuts. Sometimes, too, they strip the bark off trees to scrape at its delicate inner lining, or steal birds' eggs and raid termite nests.

By night, orang-utans make a nest platform of folded leaves and bent saplings, and create 'umbrellas' of branches overhead to keep off the worst of the tropical rain. Females often share their nests with a single baby, which clings to its mother's fur.

Males sleep alone and by day, too, they are solitary creatures that become aggressively territorial in the presence of other males. Adult males can weigh up to about 220 lb (100 kg). They have broad faces that grow into baggy discs and enlarged throat pouches to amplify their calls.

THE LARGEST FLOWER IN THE WORLD

Like the orang-utans, the world's largest flower (*Rafflesia arnoldii*) is found only in the rain forests of Borneo and Sumatra. It is a rare and remarkable find. Measuring some 3 ft (1 m) or more across, *Rafflesia* appears to grow directly out of the leaf litter on the forest floor.

In fact, it is a parasite that sprouts from the roots of climbing plants, stealing a proportion of their water and food to supply its own needs. For this reason, *Rafflesia* needs no leaves of its own. Beginning life as a tiny seed about the size of a grain of salt, it arrives at the bark of a suitable host, having been brought there perhaps on the scrabbling paws of a squirrel or the trampling hooves of a deer. As it germinates, the seed sends thread-like extensions into its host. A year and a half later, a bud bursts through

FLOWERING GIANTS *The full splendour of* Rafflesia *can be seen for only a few days, before the flower begins to darken and shrivel away.*

the surface of the host root. It grows for nine months, swelling into a tightly furled orange-brown ball.

As it reaches maturity, five thick rust-red petals unfurl from the bud. At their centre is a warty sphere, with a broad, circular opening and a thick, overhanging rim. Hidden within are the sexual parts of the flower, the male anthers or female stamens, according to its sex, and dark red, scent-producing strands that exude an odour of rotten flesh. Carrion flies, deceived by the smell into investigating one *Rafflesia* after another, are the main pollinators of the enormous flowers.

The monstrous flowers remain open for just four days, before shrivelling up and darkening. After a few weeks, they have rotted away completely, leaving no obvious traces of their existence – although the unseen feeding threads of the *Rafflesia* plant remain alive within the host tree, building up their reserves to flower again. The withered female flowers leave behind thousands of seeds. Should one or two reach a suitable host, they begin the cycle again.

MONKEYS AND MANGROVES

Borneo is the third largest island in the world, and it still harbours enormous unspoiled tracts of rain forest. Besides their giant parasitic flowers and their orangutans, the rain forests of Borneo are also home to the curious-looking proboscis monkey (*Nasalis larvatus*), which is restricted to the mangrove swamps and riverine forests of this single island. The monkey's most prominent feature is the enlarged, pendulous nose of the adult male. Females, which are only half the size of the males, have small, upturned noses.

Proboscis monkeys feed on mangrove leaves in the inundated mangrove swamps that occur where the rain forest meets the coastline. They are excellent swimmers, diving into rivers from high branches and swimming underwater when necessary. Their feet are partly webbed to help them when swimming and when crossing the treacherously sticky mangrove mud.

Crab-eating or long-tailed macaques (*Macaca fascicularis*) also frequent mangrove swamps, but they are spread much more widely through South-east Asia than the proboscis monkey. These monkeys live mainly on fruit but they need extra protein, which they obtain by catching mangrove crabs, sitting patiently at a burrow until one emerges, then grabbing it with a lightning-fast reaction. Termites and small lizards are also used to supplement the macaques' diet.

Mangroves line the coastlines through much of Southeast Asia. Indeed, about one-fifth of the world's mangroves border Vietnam, Thailand, Malaysia, Sumatra, Java and Borneo. Sadly, they are suffering from human pressures, including damage from oil slicks, and large-scale conversion to rice paddies, fish ponds, and a number of industrial or tourist developments. During the Vietnam war, more than one-quarter of the original Vietnamese mangrove forest was killed by the mass application of herbicides.

THE SUNDARBANS

Today, the largest continuous stretch of mangroves in the world is the Sundarbans, an area covering about 2300 sq miles (6000 km^2) of north-eastern India and neighbouring Bangladesh. The curved roots of

MONKEY IN MOTION *Proboscis monkeys are good leapers and excellent swimmers, at home in the mangrove swamps and flooded forests of Borneo.*

the resident mangrove trees trap silt and debris as it passes back and forth with the tides. Mangroves provide natural coastal defences which protect the land, shielding it from the effects of storm waves that may exceed 13 ft (4 m) in height. The sheltered Sundarbans area is a haven for wildlife of all kinds. Clams, snails, oysters, lobsters, crabs, prawns and numerous fish make rich pickings for seabirds. Herons, storks and kingfishers hunt in the shallows.

At low tide, mudskippers (*Boleophthalmus* and *Periophthalmus* species) and climbing perch (*Anabas testudineus*) haul themselves across the mud on sturdy fins. These unusual fish not only obtain oxygen in the conventional way for fish, from water passing over their gills, but can also breathe air. This arrangement frees them from the constraints of permanent underwater life, and they live an almost amphibian existence on the border of land and sea. Their lifestyle

means that they are able to take advantage of terrestrial food, such as insects and spiders, in addition to marine offerings. But at the same time, it puts the fish at risk from land predators.

Fishing cats (*Felis viverrina*) wade and swim in search of fish and water birds, while hunting snakes slither over the silt and then drape themselves across the branches of mangroves. Other reptilian hunters, the endangered mugger (a kind of crocodile –

Crocodylus palustris) and the estuarine crocodile (*Crocodylus porosus*), lurk in the swamps awaiting larger prey.

The Sundarbans were also once home to the Javan rhinoceros, the swamp deer (*Cervus duvauceli*) and the wild water buffalo (*Bubalus bubalis*). Although all these species have long since disappeared from the area, other mammals, such as mongoose, wild boar and the spotted deer or chital (*Axis axis*), still flourish. The spotted deer feed on mangrove leaves and grasses. As they browse in the swamps, they fall prey to crocodiles, and are chased by powerful Indian tigers, for which the area of the Sundarbans is one of the last strongholds.

Tigers, which can cover an astonishing 33 ft (10 m) in a single leap, prey in addition upon wild pigs, monkeys, cattle, fish, crocodiles and lizards.

Tigers also roam the rain forests of the Western Ghats and Nilgiri hills on India's west coast. These western hill forests are important sites for the endangered gaur

---

LIFE'S VARIETY IN THE RAIN-FOREST CAVES OF SARAWAK

Deep in the rain forest of Sarawak, on the island of Borneo, are some of the world's largest limestone caverns. They house a bizarre collection of animals. Some make their living from the forest outside, while others remain constantly in the caves, surviving by eating the other animals and their droppings. These represent an important food source, imported by animals such as bats that forage elsewhere and roost in the caves. Their droppings accumulate in a thick and pungent layer on the cave floor.

Among the most curious of the cave inhabitants are little birds called

FOREST CAVE *Many rain-forest animals shelter in Sarawak's Great Deer Cave, one of the largest caves in the world.*

cave swiftlets (*Collocalia* species). Several million of them may breed in one cave, building their nests on sheer rock faces. Some species incorporate feathers, lichens or plant fibres into their nests. But two species of cave swiftlet make nests from nothing more than their own gluey saliva which sets into a solid rubbery material. The nest is painstakingly built up, layer by layer, into a cup-shaped bracket affixed to the cave wall.

These nests are highly valued as a delicacy in China and Hong Kong, where they are used to produce 'bird's-nest soup'. Collecting and exporting them has become a multimillion dollar industry in the areas where they breed – mainly coastal caves in limestone areas with regions of rain forest

immediately inland from them, providing feeding grounds for the swiftlets. Nest collectors take enormous risks, ascending spindly bamboo ladders or makeshift vine ropes to heights of more than 300 ft (91 m) in order to reach the nests. Below, the accumulated guano is a treacherous quagmire.

Swiftlets share their caves with several kinds of bat. By day, the swiftlets leave the cave to forage for insects while the bats roost. By night, the situation reverses, and as the swiftlets return to roost, the bats flood out into the forest. Those swiftlets that live in the deepest parts of the cave have evolved a clicking echolocation mechanism, similar to that of bats, which they use as a substitute for vision. They are able to find their way through pitch-black passageways and

GLUED TO THE WALL
A colony of white-bellied swiftlets make their nests on the side of a limestone cave.

convoluted chambers, back to their own nest and nestling.

The swiftlets are preyed on by remarkable cave-dwelling snakes that can scale the walls and dangle from stalactites. They pick nestlings from their precarious nests and even catch adults in flight. For any chick that falls to the floor, there is a veritable army of creatures ready to snap it up – giant crickets, hunting shrews and scavenging crabs.

Sometimes, rain-forest animals will venture into the caves to steal the pickings. Sambar deer and bearded pigs come to munch at the guano – probably to rectify a nutritional deficiency.

CRAWLING WITH LIFE *The cave's floor is a source of food for many creatures, including this scavenging cave centipede.*

(*Bos gaurus*), wild cattle with thick horns, large heads and sturdy humpbacked bodies. They mainly eat grass, feeding as small herds in forest clearings and other open areas, withdrawing into the forest itself to shelter from the noonday heat.

The forests shelter a number of species that are endemic to the region, including the goat-like Nilgiri tahr (*Hemitragus hylocrius*), the Nilgiri langur (*Presbytis johnii*) and the extremely rare lion-tailed macaque (*Macaca silenus*). Lion-tailed macaques have a ruff of pale fur surrounding their faces, and a lion-like tip to their tail – hence their name. There are now probably fewer than

FISH OUT OF WATER *Two mudskippers search for food in the exposed mud of a mangrove swamp, a restless zone where sea and rain forest meet.*

200 of them left in the wild. Although their range overlaps with that of the Nilgiri langur, the two primates do not compete with each other for food. The langurs feed mainly on leaves, while the lion-tailed macaques prefer fruit.

WELL-KEPT SECRETS

In recent years, the Asian rain forests have revealed several unexpected surprises. In 1981, the rare giant bee of Indonesia was rediscovered, nearly a century after it was first described by the Victorian naturalist Alfred Russel Wallace. In the interim, no other specimens had been collected, and the bee was presumed extinct. Female giant bees, which are at least three times the size of a honey bee, build their nests inside the existing nests of tree termites.

In 1982, zoologists working in Thailand found a group of kouprey (*Bos sauveli*), the largest and most primitive of the wild cattle. The kouprey, which was unknown to science until 1937, was thought to have been exterminated by warfare in Cambodia and Vietnam.

Although rediscoveries are highly significant, the finding of a completely new large mammal is even more exciting. In 1992, scientists in Vietnam discovered the Vu Quang ox (*Pseudoryx nghetinhensis*), a wholly new genus and mammal species that is superficially similar to the Arabian oryx, a straight-horned antelope. Their initial finds

MAGNIFICENT MONKEY *The lion-tailed macaque, easily identified by its thick mane of pale fur, is now one of the world's rarest monkeys.*

were dead specimens, but very recently, a young female was caught alive in the forest.

This discovery was quickly followed by another. From the examination of trophies in the homes of Vietnamese hunters, biologists established that a previously unknown kind of deer was living in the same area as the Vu Quang ox. The skulls were similar to those of a muntjac deer (tiny deer, originally from southern Asia but now established in parts of Europe, standing no more than 2 ft – 61 cm – at the shoulder), but they were larger, and their antlers were longer than those of any other muntjac.

For a while, the living animals remained elusive. Then, in 1994, the first living giant muntjac was discovered – not in Vietnam, but just across the border in neighbouring

NEW DISCOVERY *In the pristine montane forests of northern Vietnam, a hitherto unknown mammal, the Vu Quang ox, was recently discovered.*

Laos. Two biologists, visiting a local logging company to arrange a helicopter ride, were astonished to find an adult male giant muntjac in a small enclosure at the company headquarters. The creature, at about 88 lb (40 kg) weighing twice as much as a common muntjac, fitted perfectly with the description pieced together from the skulls. It has a scientific name, *Megamuntiacus vuquangensis*, and has recently been glimpsed in the wild, surviving among the shadowy vegetation of its native rain forests as its ancestors have done for thousands of years.

OUT OF AFRICA AND MADAGASCAR

Forest elephants clear a road through the undergrowth and ghost-like okapis vanish into the maze of dappled sunlight. High in the forested mountains at Africa's heart, mountain gorillas feast on clumps of bamboo that grow among the trees.

The naturalist and explorer Cuthbert Christie, writing in the 1920s, gave an account of a mysterious inhabitant of the rain forests of Central Africa: 'Probably no animal is so shy or so ghost-like in its movements through the forest. It is, I should think, the most difficult of all beasts to catch even a sight of in its dim and far-off solitudes.' The animal was the okapi, which had been discovered by Europeans only at the turn of the 19th and 20th centuries.

The first suggestion of this animal's existence came from the 19th-century explorer Sir Henry Morton Stanley, who reported rumours of a donkey-like animal living in the remote north-eastern part of the Congo Basin. Stanley never saw one but had heard that the Pygmy peoples living in the region, whose knowledge of the rain forest was paramount, captured it for food.

In 1899, Sir Harry Johnston, the British governor of Uganda, helped to rescue eight Pygmies who had been kidnapped by a showman and were being taken to Paris to appear in an exhibition. The Pygmies stayed for a while at Johnston's house in Entebbe, a strange establishment where a chimpanzee, two baboons, parrots and eagles all lived alongside the human inhabitants, and a baby elephant was allowed into the house for tea, helping itself to jam sandwiches. Beside the front door was a large snake pit which Johnston found useful in deterring 'the more boring class of visitors'.

Johnston was an accomplished naturalist, interested in almost everything about Africa, including the mysterious 'donkey' reported by Stanley, and he questioned the Pygmies about it while they were with him. 'They at once understood what I meant,' reported Johnston, 'and pointing to a zebra skin and a live mule, they informed me that the creature in question, which was called okapi, was like a mule with zebra stripes on it.'

FINDING THE OKAPI

In 1900, while escorting the Pygmies back to their home in the rain forest – a safari on which, as usual, he took his pet monkeys with him, perched on the heads of the porters – Johnston tried to find the okapi. At that stage, he thought it might be an aberrant species of zebra which lived in the forest.

During his trek through the forest, he encountered troops of black colobus monkeys (*Colobus angolensis* or *Colobus guereza*), a dainty blue duiker (*Cephalophus monticola*) and several long-legged elephant shrews (*Petrodromus*). He saw touracos and narina trogons (*Apaloderma marina*), and heard the weird, unearthly screams of the tree hyraxes (*Dendrohyrax doresalis*) – but of the okapi there was not a glimpse. 'When the natives showed the tracks of a cloven-footed animal like the eland, and told us these were the

EERIE FOREST VOICES *Diminutive tree hyraxes live in the Central African rain forests, where they make terrifying screaming cries out of all proportion to their size.*

ELUSIVE OKAPIS *Wild okapis are very difficult to find, and usually only fleeting glimpses of them are seen in the forest. These two are captive animals.*

footprints of the okapi, I disbelieved them, and imagined that we were merely following a forest eland. I declared impatiently that I wanted something more like the spoor of a donkey.'

Johnston was wrong about the prints, as he himself discovered a few months later. Although he never observed a live okapi, he was sent a skin and two skulls by the Pygmies after his return to Entebbe. The crucial cloven hooves were missing, but this did not matter, for Johnston knew enough about anatomy to see at once that the animal was neither horse nor eland. Its distinctive teeth clearly showed that it was a relative of the giraffe.

Johnston was amazed by the discovery. As a direct descendant of the short-necked browsing animals which had evolved into the lofty giraffe, the okapi was a fascinating zoological discovery, almost a 'missing link'. It aroused enormous interest throughout the world, accompanied by intense excitement at the idea that a large mammal of a completely unknown kind had remained concealed in the forest for so long.

UNSEEN BROWSERS

Okapis are still hard to locate and almost impossible to observe while going about their everyday life. They have raised wariness to an art form and vanish into the forest thickets at the first sign, sound or scent of anything the slightest bit unusual. The large shell-like ears pick up the slightest sound. The creature's colouring, apparently so bold, with a luscious chestnut pelt on the back and pure white stripes across the buttocks and hind legs, proves excellent camouflage in the visually complex world of the rain forest.

Even when a naturalist happens to encounter an okapi in the forest, the animal can be remarkably close and yet escape notice, as it stands motionless, waiting for its moment to escape. The white areas seem like part of the kaleidoscope of sunlit vegetation and blind the eyes to the red-brown shades of the rest of the coat. The visible fragments of white break up the outline and are unrecognisable as a part of any living animal until the okapi suddenly snorts and bolts away, its neck held out straight in front, the staccato beat of its hooves fading into the forest.

Other than this snort, okapis make no sound, for their vocal cords, like those of the giraffe, are very poorly developed. How the two sexes communicate and locate each other for mating is unknown, but scent marking may play an important role.

RADIO TRACKING

Recent research has used the Pygmies' technique of trapping okapis. This captures them, alive and unharmed, in pits disguised with a covering of thin branches and large leaves – it is the same method that produced Johnston's history-making specimens. It is a hazardous occupation, because the pits are more likely to capture leopards than okapis, or there may be an angry forest buffalo within. Both of these are dangerous and difficult to release.

Captured okapis are carefully fitted with collars carrying radio transmitters while still in the pit, and then released. Radio transmitters issue a radio-wave signal that cannot be detected by any animal and does no harm to the okapi, but the signal is picked up by special receivers carried by the researchers. Each transmitter emits its own characteristic signal allowing individual okapis to be tracked through the forest. Despite this technical assistance, the researchers still find it remarkably difficult actually to observe their quarry. The okapi

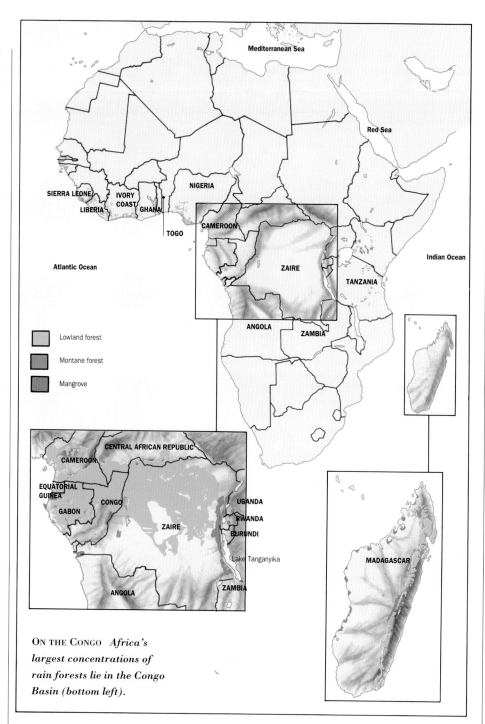

ON THE CONGO *Africa's largest concentrations of rain forests lie in the Congo Basin (bottom left).*

may stand perfectly still for up to an hour if it suspects that it is being watched – during which time the researcher turns off the receiver to economise on batteries – then it moves off in absolute silence, leaving the researcher behind, still thinking the animal is close by.

Very occasionally naturalists are lucky enough to see a wild okapi feeding, relaxed and unaware that it is being watched. It

hooks down the leaves of small understorey trees using its very long, black prehensile tongue which can wrap itself around a tender young shoot and pull it within range of the teeth. The okapi eats nothing but leaves and feeds on 100 or more different species of tree and shrub, choosing the youngest leaves whenever possible.

Whatever else the okapi does in its life, it does it with the utmost discretion – as a

result, nothing is known about its courtship behaviour, its encounters with rivals or with predators, or how it gives birth or rears its young. Almost a century after it was found, the okapi is still an enigma.

GIANT FOREST HOG

Another sensational find came not long after that of the okapi, in 1904 – it was the discovery of the giant forest hog. It too inhabits lowland rain forests, but it has a considerably wider range, extending west as far as Liberia and south to northern Tanzania, venturing out of the rain forest and into the wooded savannahs in some areas. Quite how this wild pig remained unknown to European naturalists for so long is something of a puzzle, for it does not share the okapi's quiet and secretive ways. It is noisy in its feeding and when scraping out wallows in gravelly riverbeds. During the rutting season the female makes surprisingly loud and discordant cries.

Despite its name, the giant forest hog is something of a sham, for although it is the largest of the wild pigs it grows no more than about 3½ ft (1.1 m) tall at the shoulder, and certainly does not reach the size of

NOISES IN THE UNDERGROWTH
The giant forest hog has a rich vocal repertoire, ranging from squeaks and chirrups to loud bellowing grunts.

a rhinoceros as was rumoured in the early 1900s. An impression of bulk is created by the long, rough black hairs which stand on end whenever the animal is alarmed. The hairs on the neck and the back of the head reach 6-7 in (15-18 cm) and add greatly to the hog's stature, the illusion being especially effective in the shadows of the rain forest as the giant hog ferociously challenges an intruder. Males have been known to charge without provocation.

THE SECRETIVE FOREST

Even today, there are remarkable finds to be made in the African rain forests. During the 1980s a population of western lowland gorillas was found in the south-eastern part of Nigeria, an area where they had been thought to be extinct for 30 years. Three hundred gorillas are now estimated to live in this area, their presence kept secret by their strict avoidance of human contact. Eastern lowland gorillas have been rediscovered in western Zaire, while a totally new species of primate, the suntailed guenon (*Cercopithecus solatus*), was found in central Gabon in recent years.

Much of the Congo Basin is still difficult to explore, a maze of tangled vegetation and impenetrable swamps, where maps turn out to be wildly inaccurate and the most hardy explorers are defeated by the intense heat, suffocating humidity, malaria, tsetse flies and sweat bees.

NEWLY FOUND *Until recently the suntailed guenon of Gabon, a relative of the vervet monkeys, was quite unknown to biologists.*

The Congo bay owl is known only from one or two dead specimens that have been found, while the lives of animals such as the clawless Congo otter, with its delicate hands – a little like those of humans and equipped with tiny 'nails' rather than claws – remain a mystery. This otter seems to live around torrential mountain streams deep within the rain forest, but its odd paws, with minimal webbing unlike those of other otters, raise the suspicion that it gathers food on land rather than in the water. The evidence available suggests that it eats frogs and eggs.

Equally elusive is the aquatic genet. This creature has never been seen alive by any naturalist, and is known only from animals that have been shot or trapped in a small area of dense rain forest in north-eastern Zaire. It has a slim chestnut-coloured body, rather like that of a weasel, with a surprisingly long and bushy black tail. In evolutionary terms, the aquatic genet has moved in the opposite direction to the clawless otter, for it is a fish-eater descended from land-based predators.

TALL TALES

It seems that the African rain forests still have hiding places that have survived the steady incursion of humankind. Indeed, there are those who believe that dinosaurs of the kind known as sauropods – long-necked, lumbering, semi-aquatic beasts –

survive in remote lakes and rivers. Many local stories tell of such animals, called n'yamala in Gabon, where they are said to inhabit large riverside caves, and as mokole-mbembe in the Congo where sightings have been repeatedly claimed in Lake Tele. There is no real evidence to support these myths, and some of the more recent 'sightings' have subsequently been admitted as fabrications. The likelihood of dinosaurs having survived anywhere on Earth is remote indeed, yet the stories seem to have a perennial appeal, and they regularly inspire modern-day adventurers to penetrate the rain forests.

The remarkable ability of the African rain forest to conceal its various inhabitants is related to its particular structure, which differs from that of rain forests elsewhere on the globe. Although in places the canopy trees meet overhead and screen out the light, creating an unbroken ceiling of green, there are large parts of the African forest which have a more broken canopy. Here, the outermost leaves and twigs of the tallest trees do not touch each other, so more light reaches the forest floor than in many other rain forests.

The influx of light encourages the growth of shrubs and understorey trees, so

that the vegetation is sometimes very dense at ground level, providing ample cover in which large animals such as the okapi and the giant forest hog can conceal themselves.

SHAPING THE FOREST

In some swampy parts of the Ituri forest of the Congo, where the okapi lives, there is a plant that is known as phrynia (*Sarcophrynium arnoldianum*) with large oval leaves up to 2 ft

ON THE MARCH *Led by an elderly female, a group of forest elephants bulldoze their way through the thick jungle undergrowth.*

(61 cm) long and 1 ft (30 cm) wide, carried on thick stalks that shoot straight up from the ground, 4-5 ft (1.2-1.5 m) long. Phrynia clumps may cover several acres and hidden within them during the day are the chief architects of the African rain forest: forest elephants. Without them the African forests would be very different.

Elephants are like living bulldozers. They push their way through the undergrowth with their heads down, forcing a passage with the forehead and the upper trunk. The tip of the trunk comes in useful to grasp branches and lift them out of the way or push them down to the ground where they can be crushed underfoot. They also move thick-stemmed lianas aside with their trunks.

The elephants' regular nocturnal movements through the forest create pathways, 2-3 ft (60-90 cm) wide, trodden down so hard by their feet that plants have difficulty regrowing in the soil. Some may be hundreds of years old, for the path is trampled down far below the level of the surrounding ground. Branching off at intervals from these 'elephant highways' are smaller paths, less regularly used.

When feeding, elephants pull down branches with their trunks, then strip them of leaves. They rip at the bark of certain trees with their sharply pointed tusks, until there is a detached piece large enough to be seized with the tip of the trunk. Pulling on this, they remove a strip of bark which they then chew. Fruit-bearing trees are occasionally felled to obtain the fruits, the

roots first being exposed and severed by the tusks, then the tree forced over by shoving with the forehead. Other trees, however, actually benefit from the elephants' liking for their fruits because the fallen fruits are picked up from the ground and their seeds are dispersed, enjoying an excellent start in life by germinating in a rich pile of elephant dung. The elephants' pattern of food preferences – the bark ripped from one tree, the young leaves stripped from another, the saplings of a third species destroyed wholesale, while the seeds of a fourth are usefully dispersed – has no doubt helped to determine the particular mix of trees in the African rain forests for thousands of years.

OPEN PLAN

The open canopy of the African rain forest owes much to the activities of the forest elephant. Where clearings are created by elephants on the march, or congregating at traditional meeting 'stations', the earth is trodden too hard to regrow plant cover, so there are tracts of open ground. Elsewhere, elephant browsing keeps the canopy open by preventing the saplings of canopy trees from ever growing to their full height. Shrubs, saplings and understorey trees spring up but are just as quickly chewed back, maintaining a constant level of sparse plant cover at these lower levels.

A third activity that affects the forest structure is digging with the tusks for salt-rich soil, which is prized by forest elephants for much-needed minerals. Once areas have been dug over and abandoned, they regrow a dense covering of understorey plants, a real 'jungle' which provides two vital resources for antelopes, forest buffalo, okapis and other forest animals: fresh young leaves and dense protective cover. The elephants themselves also like to hide in these leafy coverts by day, if there are no phrynia clumps available. After more than a century of intensive ivory hunting, forest elephants are extremely shy of human contact.

One bird that likes the open conditions created by elephant movement is the white-breasted guinea fowl (*Agelastes meleagrides*) found only in West Africa. This ground-feeding species picks up insects and seeds

LIVING WITH ELEPHANTS
White-breasted guinea fowls
find their food on ground
where the vegetation has been
trampled down by elephants.

from the forest floor, moving quickly about on the trodden earth of the elephant trails and stations. With the steady disappearance of the forest elephants from West Africa, combined with extensive deforestation, the white-breasted guinea fowl is now declining in numbers.

Forest elephants are smaller than the familiar African elephant of the savannah, the largest adult males standing only about 9 ft (2.7 m) at the shoulder rather than 13 ft (4 m). The ears are differently shaped, but in general the animals are very similar, and most experts consider them to be the same species, *Loxodonta africana*, although they place them in different subspecies. One of the most noticeable differences, other than size, is the skin. That of the forest elephant is dark in colour, almost black, and far more supple than the hard grey skin of the bush elephant. This difference may simply be due to the moist conditions in which the rain-forest elephants live.

FOREST ANCESTORS

The fossil record shows that the plains of Africa, between about 3 million and 20 000 years ago, were inhabited by a different species of large elephant, related to the Indian elephant *Elephas*. Before that, a direct ancestor of the modern African elephant, known as *Loxodonta adaurora*, was widespread, but seems to have been displaced by

Elephas. There is no trace of *Loxodonta* in the fossil record for over 2 million years, so how and where did these animals survive?

The answer is that they were sheltering in the rain forests, where the catastrophic impact of the ice ages was minimised. They survived without trace there because fossils are rarely formed in rain forests, decomposition of bone being rapid.

Then the last Ice Age wiped out the plains-dwelling *Elephas*, leaving a vacant stage onto which the forest-dwelling *Loxodonta* could step at the close of the Ice Age, about 10 000 years ago. Forest elephants were probably as small then as they are today, but in the open conditions of the savannah they evolved into the large and majestic African bush elephants.

PYGMY HIPPOS

The evolution of the massive lake-dwelling hippopotamus echoes that of the bush elephant, since it, too, evolved from a smaller forest-dwelling form. A close approximation of that ancestor can be found in the pygmy hippo, a rotund and rubbery, pig-like

creature that still survives in the rain forests of West Africa. In this case, however, the two are distinct species.

The differences between the pygmy hippo and its larger and more famous relative offer a fascinating insight into the haphazard routes by which evolution sometimes proceeds. Pygmy hippos – weighing a relatively modest 500 lb (225 kg), compared with up to 4.5 tonnes for lake-dwelling hippos – feed on grass in the forests, together with a few roots, leafy shoots and fallen fruit. They may hide in watery places when danger threatens, and tend to live near streams, but are much less aquatic than the lake-dwelling hippo. Their eyes are not positioned on top of the skull to permit them to submerge almost completely, for example.

Both species have a thin skin that is not properly waterproof. They produce an oily secretion that lubricates the skin, as well as providing a more waterproof outer layer and protecting against infection.

WATER BABY *Pygmy hippos*
prefer to mate in the water,
and six to seven months later
the female gives birth to a
single young one.

Worldwide climatic changes about 10 million years ago produced shrinking forests and spreading grasslands, and this probably fostered the expansion of the ancestral hippos out of the dense rain forest. They would first have moved into areas of woodland on the edge of the forest, where their favourite food – grass – was becoming more abundant. But the dry conditions were far from suitable, and they became nocturnal feeders, avoiding the harsh glare of daylight by returning to the rain forest.

Lakes and rivers provided the key to the next step in their evolution, for the newly evolving hippos could shelter in them during the hours of daylight and so detach themselves further from the protective damp blanket of the forest. Slowly, very slowly, the hippos became less dependent on forests, more aquatic, larger and more fearsome – for there were new predators in this habitat, both on land and in the water, which were difficult to hide from. In time, the gargantuan hippo of today evolved, a remarkably successful animal in numbers, but one that cannot expand to areas without lakes or deep rivers. In a sense, it is still tied to its forest-dwelling past.

AFRICAN GLIDERS

Where canopy trees meet and form a continuous layer of branches and leaves, small animals can travel long distances through the tree tops, switchbacking from tree to tree. The drawback of the African rain forests, from a tree-dweller's point of view, is the interrupted canopy – its frequent breaks inhibit movement through the higher reaches of forest.

Gliding is one solution, but the African trees do not have that magnificent unbranching height seen among the dipterocarps, which makes gliding so attractive a solution to life in South-east Asian forests. The African gliders are fewer in number and do not reach the sizes attained by the colugos and giant flying squirrels of Asia. All the same, they are of particular interest because they belong to a group of rodents, known as anomalures, that is unique to the African rain forests.

The name suggests an anomalous creature, and the anomalures do, indeed, live up to that name, looking something like a cross between a squirrel and a mouse, but in fact being neither. These odd little animals split off from other rodents about 50 million years ago and have several features that are all their own, including two rods of cartilage like the spokes of an umbrella sticking out from the body on either side, just behind the forelimb. These give added support and manouevrability to the gliding 'membranes' that connect the forelimb and hindlimb on each side.

The underside of the tail is also peculiar, with a row of pointed scales that project downwards towards the tail-tip and act like the spikes on an athlete's shoes, gripping the bark if the anomalure presses its tail against a tree trunk. This extra grip is valuable when the animal lands after a glide, as well as helping the anomalure to climb upwards so that it can regain height for the next takeoff. The alternative name for anomalures, scaly-tailed squirrels, reflects this odd feature.

FLIGHT PATH *West Africa's anomalures can glide long distances from tree to tree. They are equipped with stiffened membranous 'wings'.*

The smallest of all these gliding animals are the pygmy anomalures or 'flying mice' (*Idiurus*), about the size of a house mouse but more chunky in build. They have a long plumed tail that looks like a slightly tattered feather as it floats out behind the tiny glider, planing down from tree to tree. These animals are extraordinarily skilful when they are airborne. They launch themselves effortlessly, then swoop off towards another tree, travelling as much as 150ft (45m) with little or no loss of height. They can bank steeply to avoid obstacles, twist in mid-air, go into impressive downward spirals, or double back on themselves to perform magnificent S-shaped glides.

Alighting on a tree, the pygmy anomalures then scuttle about in mouse-like fashion, disappearing into crevices if they have located a hollow tree that is suitable as a

daytime shelter. They roost communally, sometimes in large numbers, 100 or more huddled together inside the same tree in a huge, heaving mass of soft fur.

The other anomalures, while larger, are just as graceful in flight. The largest species, known as Lord Derby's anomalure, is able to make a glide of at least 330 ft (100 m) and possibly more than twice that distance. They flick their bodies upright as they approach the target tree, in typical anomalure style, so that the claws and spiny tail can hook into the bark. In this species, the body grows up to 16 in (40 cm) long, and the tail as long again. By contrast, the pygmy anomalure is never more than about 3¾ in (9.5 cm) long, although its tail may grow to 5 in (12.5 cm).

All anomalures live in the densest areas of the African rain forest, and they are very difficult to study. There are only six 'flying' species in all, plus a seventh species that is flightless (*Zenkerella*), having no trace of a

gliding 'membrane'. It is extremely rare, and nothing is known about its way of life. Did this non-gliding form evolve from the gliders? Or is it a direct descendant of some ancestral anomalure which did not glide? Yet again, this is a secret that the rain forest so far refuses to reveal.

THE CLOWN OF THE FOREST

The mandrill's face looks as if it has been created with a circus clown's make-up. It has the typical elongated dog-like head of a baboon, but a scarlet stripe runs down the centre of the muzzle and widens out into a blob around the nostrils. On either side of this red band are curving stripes of pale blue with purplish furrows between them. This vividly coloured naked skin covers a strangely shaped muzzle, with curved ridges of expanded bone that underlie the blue stripes.

The purpose of these clown-like colours is far from lighthearted – they are there for

FACE VALUE *The distinctive face of the male mandrill probably serves as a constant reminder of his dominant status within the group.*

aggressive display. Only adult males sport the full set of colour markings: females and young lack the central red stripe, and have smaller blue facial ridges. This discrepancy between the sexes is a clear indication that the colours form part of social signalling, expressing maleness and dominance.

The vibrant colours of the mandrill's face are unlike the faces of most other baboons and are usually explained as an adaptation to rain-forest life. Baboons living on the open plains signal to each other with a ritualised yawn in which the head is tossed back and the mouth opened wide to display the massive canine teeth. In this way, the males in a troop assess each other's strength and aggression, and the leading male asserts his supremacy over the younger males and the females, which helps maintain the social structure and cohesion of the troop.

For most of each day, these open-country baboons are in constant visual contact, and they do not repeat the aggressive yawn frequently, except following a temporary separation of some members of the troop. This suggests that the status quo must be reinforced after separation.

Speculation about the mandrill's gaudy face has focused on the fact that the rain forests are cluttered with shrubs, lianas and tree trunks, so that members of a mandrill troop constantly lose sight of one another. If the aggressive yawn display had to be repeated each time the animals had been visually separated, then a huge amount of time and energy would be expended on this activity. Mandrills tend simply to 'snarl' – raising the skin at the sides of the muzzle to display their long canine teeth – rather than bothering with the full yawn.

Some biologists have interpreted the blue ridges lying on each side of the muzzle as a permanent display that mimics the wrinkled skin produced by a snarl. This false scowl created by the colourful muzzle is clearly visible through the trees, and it becomes increasingly prominent with age, advertising the status of the male. As for the red stripe, it could be a visual boast about the size of a male mandrill, showing exactly how long his muzzle is.

THE BLACK-FACED DRILL

There is, however, one problem with this explanation. North of the River Sanaga in Cameroon lives a different species, related to the mandrill but quite distinct from it, known as the drill. It, too, inhabits lowland rain forest, and while it also has some bony ridges on its muzzle, akin to those of the mandrill, the skin that covers the face is entirely black. No one can be sure if this undermines the explanation offered for the colourful visage of the mandrill, because little is known about how drills assert and maintain dominance within the troop.

One noticeable feature that the drill and the mandrill share is a large area of bare colourful skin on the rump. In both species it is blue, edged with pinkish red, a bright circular target that probably acts as a signpost to be followed through dense forest when the monkeys are travelling as a group. However, the colours brighten, particularly the red colour, when the animals are excited, owing to increased blood flow. This suggests that the signals may have a more complex function than simply showing the way through the forest.

CLIMBING HIGH

The drill and mandrill both feed on the ground, climbing up into trees only to sleep, unlike the other monkeys found in the African rain forests, which feed in the trees, taking leaves, flowers, fruit, nuts, insects, lizards and other foods.

Monkeys abound in the forests of this continent, from leaf-eating colobus monkeys (*Colobus* and *Procolobus*) to the more omnivorous mangabeys (*Cercocebus*), the drab talapoin (*Miopithecus*) to the colourful diana monkey, and its relatives, such as the red-bellied monkeys and red-tailed monkeys (*Cercopithecus*). Also plentiful are the monkeys' smaller and more primitive relatives, the pottos and bush babies, which hunt in the shrub or understorey layers for insects

and other small prey. Again, the elephant-made structure of the forest may explain this abundance of primates (monkeys, apes and their relatives), because the broken canopy favours animals that are expert climbers, and do not need to travel from tree top to tree top by the direct canopy route.

The golden potto (*Arctocebus calabarensis*) is a small, slow-moving predator that feeds on the foul-tasting, toxic insects others cannot eat, overcoming their poisons or irritant chemicals. These distasteful foods are rejected by predators that can afford to find more palatable prey, and studies with captive animals show that even golden pottos – also known as angwantibos – will choose less noxious food items if these are offered to them. When feeding in the wild, golden pottos try to make their diet less unpleasant, by scraping off irritant hairs from caterpillars, for example. After feeding, they quickly wipe clean their nose and mouth.

Pottos (*Perodicticus potto*) are slow climbers, like the golden pottos to which they are distantly related, moving through the branches of the shrub and understorey layers with great deliberation. Pottos range through a variety of forest types, and their diet varies accordingly, but those living in the rain forest mainly eat fruit, supplementing this diet with a few insects and some tree gums, excavated from tree trunks in a manner similar to that used by the pygmy marmosets of South America. Occasionally, small birds and bats are caught while sleeping; these provide a much-needed source of additional protein.

SURVIVING THE NIGHT

Young pottos have a strange upbringing. For the first few days after birth, the young one is carried around clinging to its mother's fur. But this hampers the adult in her search for food, so the regime is quickly changed to one where the female leaves her offspring suspended from a branch when darkness falls. It hangs there, alone, silent

EATING BARK AND LEAVES *Bark, fruit and insects all form part of the black and white colobus monkey's diet, along with the leaves of the forest trees.*

LEISURELY CLIMBER A golden potto clings to a West African rain-forest branch. Golden pottos use hands and feet to climb at a steady pace around their habitat.

and very still in the forest night, entirely unprotected should a predator stumble upon it. Fortunately, few discover the helpless infant. Just before dawn, the mother returns and carries it to the nest where they pass the day, asleep together. Clearly the nest is too easily detected by small nocturnal predators for the mother to risk leaving her young one there unguarded. The solitary nights continue for three to four months, after which the young potto follows its mother as she feeds, climbing onto her back for the occasional ride when it is tired.

Bush babies are far more energetic creatures than the leisurely pottos, leaping impressive distances to cross gaps between understorey trees. The tiny needle-clawed bush baby (*Euoticus*) can leap across a gap of up to 26 ft (8 m), 50 times its own body length. It loses some height on a jump of this length, but it can leap 8 ft (2.4 m) in a straight horizontal jump.

By jumping and clambering through the forest, needle-clawed bush babies manage to avoid descending to ground level except on rare occasions. The main food of these tiny, huge-eyed animals is tree gum, which they collect nocturnally, using 500-1000 different feeding stations in a single night and taking just a small amount of gum from each place. Other foods include fruit and small insects.

LARGE AND SMALL

There are both dwarfs and giants in the African rain forests. The royal antelope (*Neotragus pygmaeus*) is the smallest antelope in the world, standing no more than 12 in (30 cm) at the shoulder, although its hindquarters arch above the shoulder blades like those of a rabbit or hare. The powerful hare-like hindlegs allow it to leap away rapidly into the undergrowth if disturbed, darting and twisting as it makes its escape. Its African name means 'king of the hares' – hence 'royal' antelope.

This delicate miniature feeds mainly on a variety of fallen fruit, leaves and flowers that it finds on the forest floor. It weighs about 8 lb (3.6 kg), scarcely more than the goliath frog, one of the forest giants and the largest frog in the world, capable of attaining a total length of 32 in (81 cm). This amphibian lives in large dank pools within the forest, but forages in the undergrowth for food, mainly insects, though sometimes taking mice and other small rodents as well.

THE GREAT APE

Some monkeys and apes also achieve massive proportions in the African rain forest. The mandrill is the largest of the monkeys, measuring some 20 in (51 cm) high at the

---

SPICY LEAVES THE GORILLAS LOVE

Gingers are superbly adapted rain-forest plants, found throughout the tropics, but thriving in remarkable variety in the forests of the northern Congo Basin. The world's tallest ginger grows here, *Afromomum giganteum*, whose fronds can measure a full 20 ft (6 m) from the point where the stalk sprouts from the ground to the tip of the leaf.

The lifestyle of forest gingers is an interesting one, for they rely on gaps opening up in the forest canopy when a large old tree is felled by storm winds. The horizontal underground stems of gingers, called rhizomes, have lain quietly in the ground for years, but respond enthusiastically to the sudden increase in light, sprouting dozens of fresh young fronds, followed by flowers and fruit. In the few months that are available before the new

branches and leaves of trees fill the gap and shade the area once again, a ginger plant can both set seed and develop new rhizomes that enlarge its tenure of the forest floor.

Ginger rhizomes (the 'root ginger' of the cultivated variety) contain chemicals which give them their hot, spicy taste. These are undoubtedly present to deter small gnawing rodents, or rooting animals such as forest hogs, who dislike the burning sensation of pure ginger juice in the mouth. Fungi and bacteria, which could rot the rhizomes, are also prevented from growing by the same cocktail of chemicals. It is these chemicals that allow gingers to survive in their dormant state in the moist hot soil of the rain forest.

The stems of gingers also contain some of the same spicy ingredients, and the leaves are laced with smaller amounts. Apparently, they

are not hot enough to deter gorillas, however, for the fronds of the giant ginger are the favourite food of lowland gorillas.

THE LEFTOVERS Split stems and white pith at a feeding site are the relics of a lowland gorilla's giant ginger feast.

MASTERS OF DISGUISE

Encapsulated by fleshy lids, each of the chameleon's bulging eyeballs swivels independently of the other to help the creature to locate prey. The chameleon grips tightly to branches with pincer-like toes, and its well-camouflaged body becomes motionless as its eyes roll forwards to converge on a resting butterfly. It stays there for a moment, absolutely motionless. Then suddenly a tongue as long as its body shoots forward with pin-point accuracy. The butterfly has no time to react. It is instantly encapsulated by the tongue's gluey flesh and sticky saliva, then delivered to the chameleon's waiting mouth.

Chameleons live in a variety of forested and wooded habitats, and rain forests are one of their most important refuges. Many live in Africa, while Madagascar is home to two-thirds of the world's chameleon species. These stealthy creatures prey on numerous different insects, compensating for their own slow and deliberate movements with the lightning-fast action of the tongue, which is pushed out by a combination of muscle action and hydraulic force (using body fluids to pump the tongue up).

Most chameleons are tree-living, but on the forest floor of the Central African rain forests lives the tiny brown chameleon known only as *Brookesia spectrum*. Like other chameleons, it has a body that is deep but slender, looking substantial when seen from the side, but very slim when viewed head-on. This tiny inhabitant of the forest floor, measuring no more than 3 in (7.5 cm) long,

THREATENING BEHAVIOUR
A Milano chameleon puts on an aggressive display as it attempts to defend its territory against an intruder.

is a mottled brown, with two dark brown diagonal stripes that look like the veins of a leaf. When it stays still it exactly matches the dead leaves among which it lives, a near-perfect protection from predators.

The tail of *Brookesia spectrum* is not needed for gripping branches when climbing, so it is not a long, coiled, muscular, whip-like appendage as in other chameleons. Instead, the tail is flattened like the body and tapers to a point, so that it resembles the end of the 'leaf'. The legs of this chameleon are tiny matchstick affairs, since it no longer needs powerful limbs for climbing.

This species of chameleon has no need to change its colour, since its forest-floor habitat is a uniform brown, but other chameleons are famous for their rapid colour changes which provide camouflage in the shifting light conditions of the forest. Courtship displays are also enlivened by ripples of colour, and there are belligerent pigment changes when challenging rival males. A chameleon may also darken in colour to absorb more warmth from sunlight, during the chilly hour after daybreak.

The changes are produced by moving out a dark brownish pigment, known as melanin, from reservoirs deep in the skin. If these pigments are absent from the surface layers, the chameleon's skin colour is yellow, owing to yellow cells and oil droplets at the surface. Layers of cells that underlie the yellow cells, known as guanophores, are colourless normally but reflect blue light when there is melanin just behind them. So partial outward movement of melanin produces a blue backdrop to the normal yellow tint, and the overall effect is green. Subtle variations of green are possible, from yellowish to bluish.

Further movement of melanin brings it closer still to the surface and gives the chameleon a brownish-yellow skin. These

changes do not take place uniformly and chameleons are often patchily coloured with different shades, a pattern that gives extra camouflage. The movement of the dark pigment is controlled by nerve impulses from the brain, and colour changes can be achieved in a matter of minutes.

A chameleon's camouflage helps it to steal up on prey, and it also provides vital protection against potential predators. The ultra-slow movements, sometimes no faster than the movement of the hands of a clock, likewise aid concealment. Another defensive tactic comes into play at night, if a chameleon is approached by a predator, such as a snake. It releases its grip on its branch in an instant, and tumbles down through the foliage, out of reach.

HANGING ON *A baby Jackson's chameleon clings to its parent's back. As with all chameleons, the parent has feet that are divided into two equal halves, allowing it to grip the branch like a vice.*

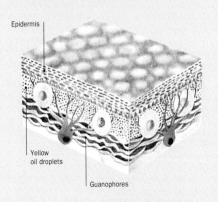

Epidermis

Yellow oil droplets

Guanophores

Partial melanin movement

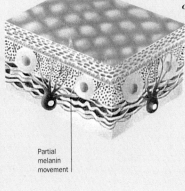

Complete melanin movement

Melanophores

INSTANT CAMOUFLAGE
Movement of the pigment melanin lies behind the chameleon's changes of colour. With the melanin confined to the melanophores, yellow oil droplets beneath the epidermis give the skin its colour (below). Partial movement of melanin towards the skin surface gives a green colour (below left and above left), while further movement gives the creature a brown colour (left and above right).

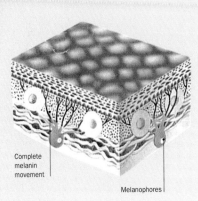

shoulder and weighing up to 120 lb (54 kg). But it is easily outclassed, for sheer bulk, by the gorilla, largest of the apes.

There are three subspecies of gorilla, two living in lowland rain forests, the third and largest – the mountain gorilla – in the chill and misty cloud forests that cloak the volcanic mountains along the borders of Rwanda, Burundi and Zaire. A separate small group of mountain gorillas lives in Uganda's 'impenetrable forest', a patch of dense and forbidding jungle that has so far resisted human encroachment. To withstand the hostile climate of their home, where hailstorms are not unknown, the mountain gorillas have very long dense fur, far thicker than that of lowland gorillas. Their larger size may also be an adaptation to the cold.

Mountain gorillas, like the lowland gorillas, live in small family groups led by a large male known as the 'silverback'. This name describes the development of a saddle-shaped area of white hair across the middle of the back, a change in coloration that appears on all males over ten years old. The silverback defends the group against attack by potential enemies – mainly human beings – and establishes his rights to lead the group when challenged by lone males. Much is at stake, for the group may contain several females of breeding age, all of whom mate only with the silverback. Young males and young females both leave the group of their own accord, once they are mature, and join forces with other lone gorillas or small newly formed groups. Young female gorillas may move on from the first male of their choice, after being impressed by a larger or stronger male.

All these social contests are carried out with a maximum of threat and bluff, and a minimum of real violence. The same is true when silverbacks defend their groups, standing upright and beating their chests with their fists to produce a resonant booming sound, tearing down branches for dramatic effect, and charging the opponent with terrifying speed and momentum if all else fails. Actual injuries are rare, and the real-life gorilla bears little relation to the violent 'King Kong' image of the cinema.

Gorillas are actually very gentle animals, eating a simple diet of leaves in the case of the mountain gorilla, while lowland gorillas take both leaves and fruit. They eat no meat, unlike chimpanzees, and they often seem to be benignly curious about small passing

HAPPY FAMILIES *If left to themselves in the wild, mountain gorillas tend to form very stable groups, each protected by a large male silverback.*

animals, such as chameleons: several massive gorillas were once observed grouped around a small chameleon, staring at it with intense concentration as it nervously moved past.

MADAGASCAR: THE EXTRAORDINARY ISLAND

As the evening sun vanishes behind the forest canopy, a bundle of dense red-brown fur, lodged in the fork of a large tree, begins to stir. After a day spent sleeping in a tree-top refuge, this, the largest of Madagascar's native predators, awakens to begin its nocturnal search for prey. The long slender form – measuring up to 57 in (145 cm) from nose to tail tip – moves swiftly up tree trunks, making an occasional leap from branch to branch. With no birds, reptiles or other suitable prey to be found, the agile climber turns its attention to the forest floor. Forelimbs flexed in front, with tail and hindlegs wrapped around a narrow trunk, the hunter gently descends head-first to the ground.

Equally at home here, it is alert for any rustle or movement in the undergrowth. One swift pounce and a roosting bird is suddenly imprisoned by the powerful claws; a well-aimed bite brings a quick kill and early breakfast. Its way of moving and feeding, its size and cat-like features, led early naturalists to believe that it was related to the leopards and other big cats. Closer study of its anatomy led to the discovery that the fossa (*Cryptoprocta ferox*) is actually an outsized member of the civet-mongoose family.

CAT-LIKE CARNIVORE *The fossa is an excellent climber and stealthy hunter, living in the thickest parts of Madagascar's forests.*

Other, more typical members of the family – small, weasel-shaped animals – also live in the same forests, including the salano (*Salanoia concolor*), the fanalouc (*Eupleres goudoti*) and the fanaloka (*Fossa fossa*). It was from animals similar to these that the fossa itself evolved in the isolation of Madagascar, cut off from the rest of the world by sea.

Owing to this isolation, there were no large cats to become top predators in the Madagascan rain forest. The fossa has filled the gap, developing its impressive size and strength from small and slender beginnings, its ancestors gradually growing larger over millions of generations. The fossa is unique. Found only in the forests of Madagascar, and hunted by man, its rarity is now a cause for concern.

ISLAND PRIMATES

From alarming hoots and eerie wails, to soft choruses of hums and grunts, the voices of the lemurs are often heard in the rain forests of Madagascar. Many of the lemurs are nocturnal and their name, derived from Latin, means 'luminous-eyed ghosts'. These

UPRIGHT TREE-DWELLERS *The eyes of a pair of indris gleam from the shadows. Indris stay upright as they scramble from tree to tree, using their arms to cling on.*

unusual animals, found only on Madagascar, represent an ancient stock, relatives of the ancestors of monkeys and apes.

Lemurs are smaller-brained than the monkeys and are generally more primitive, which is why they are thought to have died out elsewhere in the world – they were unable to compete with monkeys that filled a similar niche. It is only on Madagascar, an island the monkeys never reached, that lemurs have survived. Their nearest living relatives outside the island are the bush babies, pottos and lorises, small nocturnal animals that survive alongside monkeys by occupying a completely different niche and not competing with them.

Lemurs once flourished on Madagascar, but with the arrival of human beings over 1000 years ago, at least 14 species became extinct. These included *Megaladapis*, an animal the size of an orang-utan, but with the bodily proportions of a koala. Many remains of this giant species – which probably became extinct about 500 years ago – were discovered alongside cooking pots. Among present-day, large-bodied lemurs are the

THE MOTH THAT JUST HAD TO EXIST

Orange *Tambourissa* fruit spangled with black seeds, red shades of Begonia, and over a thousand species of orchid, such as the leopard-spotted, green-yellow flowers of *Cymbidiella rhodochilla* – all these bring a kaleidoscope of colours to the rain forests of Madagascar. Even at night, the undergrowth sparkles with the luminous white flowers of the comet orchid (*Angraeceum sesquipedale*).

On examining the unusually long spur of this plant, which extends to 14 in (36 cm), the eminent Victorian naturalist Alfred Russel Wallace deduced that an insect with a similarly long tongue must be the flower's pollinator. His logic was impeccable, for the flower's nectary was located at the base of the spur, and it produced sugary nectar on which an insect might well feed.

Incredulous at the idea that an insect with such a preposterous tongue might exist, few entomologists took Wallace seriously. However, many years later, a large sphinx moth was discovered with a proboscis that could indeed unroll to reach the orchid's nectary. It has an impressive wingspan of 6 in (15 cm). The sphinx moth was named *Xanthopan morgoni praedicta* in honour of Wallace's prediction. The discovery that a moth pollinates this orchid explains its luminous glow, which serves to guide the rare, nocturnal insect towards its flowers.

PREDICTED PARTNERS *With its elongated tongue, Wallace's moth (right) can sip nectar from the dangling spurs of the comet orchid (far right).*

monkey-sized indri (*Indri indri*) and the diadem sifaka (*Propithecus diadema*). Both species are active by day and spend most of their time in the trees, moving beneath the canopy by leaping from trunk to trunk. The indri, the largest living lemur, is up to 28 in (71 cm) tall and can weigh 22 lb (10 kg). Its leaps can cover as much as 33 ft (10 m).

THE CURIOUS AYE-AYE

Huge bat-shaped ears, bulging eyes, spindly fingers with one extra-long digit on each hand, a big bushy squirrel-like tail and protruding front teeth – few animals look as bizarre as the aye-aye (*Daubentonia madagascariensis*). This solitary nocturnal animal is another primitive species of primate, although it does not belong to the lemur family. A truly extraordinary animal, the aye-aye is the only living member of its family. Like the lemurs, it is confined to Madagascar, where it feeds on wood-boring insects in rain-forest trees.

Using its large, sensitive ears the aye-aye carefully listens for any sounds beneath the bark of a dead branch – sounds that reveal the presence of its prey. Then it excavates the wood by gnawing with its sharp front

teeth and scrabbling with its fingers, using the extra-long middle finger to probe deep into crevices and pull out any insect grubs. These same fingers also help it to scrape out the juicy pulp from shelled fruits, providing the aye-aye with another important source of food.

With a liking for coconuts, an important crop for Madagascan villagers, and the unfortunate status of being a bad omen, the aye-aye often used to be killed on sight by local people. The aye-aye has managed to survive centuries of such persecution, only to encounter a newer threat that it cannot evade: the current destruction of the rain forests on Madagascar. If the forests go, the aye-aye goes with them, together with the rain-forest lemurs, the fossa and many other unique animals.

HOLD ON TIGHT *Long, spindly digits with curved and claw-like nails help the aye-aye to excavate beetle grubs from rotten wood.*

Rain-forest destruction is particularly acute on Madagascar, and the rapid loss of habitat is alarming indeed because there is so little of it left. The same is true of much of West Africa, whereas for Central Africa the wholesale destruction of the forest is only just beginning. Experts believe that measures are urgently needed to save these remaining rain forests of Africa, with their precious and fascinating wildlife.

RAIN-FOREST SURVIVAL 3

DEAD WOOD *Trees felled in the Amazonian rain forest await the saw mill.*

TROPICAL RAIN FORESTS ARE AMONG THE WORLD'S MOST COMPLEX AND SPECIES-RICH COMMUNITIES. COVERING LESS THAN ONE-TENTH OF THE EARTH'S SURFACE, THEY NONETHELESS SUPPORT MORE THAN HALF OF ALL LIVING SPECIES — SCIENTISTS WORKING IN AN AREA OF 3/4 SQ MILE (2 KM^2) IN THE AMAZONIAN RAIN FOREST FOUND THAT IT CONTAINED NO FEWER THAN 300 DIFFERENT SPECIES OF TREE ALONE. WITHIN THE RAIN FORESTS, THE LIVES OF COUNTLESS PLANTS AND ANIMALS ARE LINKED IN A BIOLOGICAL WEB OF INTRICATE RELATIONSHIPS. HOWEVER, WITH EXPANDING HUMAN POPULATIONS AND RAPID ADVANCES IN TECHNOLOGY, THE FUTURE OF THESE FRAGILE ECOSYSTEMS IS UNDER THREAT.

KATYDID *Just one of the rain forest's countless inhabitants.*

THE FUTURE OF THE FORESTS

Throughout the tropics, rain forests are rapidly disappearing.

Scientists are concerned that species which managed to

survive even in the depleted forests of the ice ages, more than

10 000 years ago, are being pushed to the brink of extinction.

Writing in 1914, the visionary mission doctor and theologian Albert Schweitzer recorded some of the problems involved in commercial logging in Gabon on the west coast of Africa:

'Several men must toil hard for days before the axe can finish its work, and even then the tree does not always fall. It is tangled into a single mass with its neighbours by powerful creepers, and only when these have been cut through does it come, with them, to the ground . . . The next work is to clear the track by which these mighty logs, weighing sometimes as much as three tons,

are to be rolled into the nearest piece of water. Then begins a contest with the roots which have been left in the ground, and the huge tree tops which are lying upon it, and not infrequently the mighty trunk has embedded itself three feet [0.9 m] in the soil. But in time the track is got fairly ready, the portions which run through swamp being filled up with wood.

'The pieces – spoken of as "billets" – are rolled onto the track, thirty men with rhythmical shouts, pushing and shoving at each one and turning it slowly over and over on its axis . . . The thirty men in an afternoon's work seldom move one of the "billets" more than eighty to ninety yards [73 to 82 m].

'And time presses! All the timber must be got to the pond to be ready for the high water at the end of November and beginning of December, since it is only just then that the pond is in connection with the rivers. Any timber that misses this connection remains in the forest, and is reduced to such a condition by the parasitic wood insects that it is not worth buying.'

Schweitzer went on to describe the equally difficult process of getting the timber to the coast, the logs being floated downstream in huge rafts. The journey, which was full of potential setbacks, took at least 14 days and frequently ended in the loss of the logs. Small wonder that little of the Central African forest was felled, despite intense activity by French logging companies throughout the colonial era.

Much has changed since Schweitzer's time. Today, chainsaws do the work of axes, and do it in a fraction of the time.

FOREST CONVOY *Modern transport in the form of powerful trucks makes light work of carrying huge logs from a forest in central Borneo.*

Logs can be hauled from the forest by massively powerful vehicles equipped with caterpillar treads. Even so, circumstances have conspired to keep the Congo Basin as one of the largest unscarred tracts of rain forest in the world. For a long time, the unconquerable problem, in this swampy terrain, was access.

Now even that last obstacle is gone. The river is no longer the only highway to the sea. In 1992, the Trans-Gabonese railway was completed, creating a 400 mile (650 km) rail link between Libreville on the coast and Franceville in the far south-east of the country, cutting through the very forests described by Schweitzer. It provides a relatively easy means of moving logs from the inland forests to the coast, making large-scale logging in this area commercially feasible for the first time.

Access roads are being built to link the railway with distant areas of rain forest. The forests that shelter red-crowned parrots, black-headed orioles and other colourful birds such as the yellow-cheeked trogons, that are a refuge for mandrills (large West African baboons), lowland gorillas and a dozen different species of monkey, are under serious threat.

ATTACK ON THE FORESTS

Throughout the tropics, much the same story can be told about the rain forests. Advances in technology, along with new roads and railways, have opened up terrain that was once impenetrable and therefore safe from any large-scale commercial exploitation. Expanding human populations, needing fresh land, have moved into the forests,

FOREST HIGHWAY *The building of many new roads has opened up vast tracts of the world's rain forests to land developers and logging companies.*

either voluntarily or by government decree. The fact that the land is often quite unsuitable for agriculture has not prevented this invasion. The trade in timbers coming from the rain forests – commonly described as 'tropical hardwoods' and including mahogany and teak – is fuelled by demand from affluent parts of the world, notably Europe, North America and Japan. Overall, exports of tropical timbers to industrialised nations has risen sixteenfold since 1950 and has laid huge areas of tropical rain forest to waste. Everywhere the forests are under attack as never before, and the pace of destruction is accelerating.

The present rate of deforestation is estimated at 1.3 acres (0.5 ha) per second, which adds up to an astonishing 65 000 sq miles (170 000 km^2) of tropical rain forest per year – an area slightly smaller than the state of Oklahoma or twice the size of Austria. Much of that land will never regenerate the same magnificent forest it supported before, even if left undisturbed, because the thin soils that underlie many rain forests tend to be severely damaged by the felling of the trees. Once the tree cover is removed, there is often widespread erosion and loss of nutrients. Environmental experts calculate that unless the current rate of destruction slows

MARCH OF TECHNOLOGY *The chainsaw and other advances in technology have helped to accelerate the rate of deforestation around the globe.*

down, there will be no tropical rain forest left in 40 years' time.

Given the massive biodiversity in the tropical rain forest, this destruction has frightening implications. It is estimated that, worldwide, 20 000 species become extinct each year, most of them going into oblivion without ever having been described or named. In other words, a species dies out every half an hour.

LIVING IN THE FOREST

For thousands of years, human beings have benefited from the rain forests without destroying them. Most areas of tropical rain forest, apart from the chill and misty cloud forests, support human life and have long

been inhabited. There are two basic ways of surviving in the forest, as a hunter-gatherer or as a shifting cultivator. Both lifestyles have been practised for thousands of years, and, in their traditional form, do no long-term damage. The human inhabitants of the rain forests have long since become a part of the forest ecosystem.

Hunter-gatherers, such as the Semang and Penan of Malaysia, and the Pygmies of the Congo Basin, live entirely on wild foods, such as nuts, roots, fruit, honey, fish and meat. They need to range through large

areas of forest to survive in this way, and they have an intimate knowledge of the forest. Men do most of the hunting and women most of the gathering, both using a variety of ingenious methods to collect food, such as dipping their arrows in deadly poisons made from plants or from toxic tree frogs. In this way a small arrow, shot from the ground up into the canopy, can kill quite large prey. To collect honey, a Pygmy will smoke wild bees from their nests by lighting a small smoky fire of green leaves in the base of a hollow tree. Once the bees have been

FOREST MEAT *Rain-forest people rely on wild animals for meat. This Malaysian hunter holds a blowpipe, used for firing poison darts.*

evicted, the Pygmy climbs up the tree, using a safety harness of rope made from lianas.

Shifting cultivators, such as the Iban of Sarawak and the Yanomami of Amazonia, clear a small area of forest to grow crops, staying there for two or three years. They then relocate the village and clear a new

NO ORCHIDS, NO BEES, NO NUTS

Brazil nuts are among the most prized products of the Amazonian rain forests. Attempts have been made to grow brazil-nut trees in plantations, but these failed – the trees flowered, but no nuts formed. When biologists investigated the problem, they found that the bees which pollinate the flowers, known as euglossine bees, were lacking. These bees depend on the perfume of

certain orchids for successful courtship, and the orchids grow only in the rain forest itself. Without the complex web of relationships with other plants and animals, the brazil-nut tree was barren.

Brazil nuts sold commercially are still collected from the forest, or from trees in clearings – the brazil-nut trees are protected from felling by law. Other forest nuts and fruits may

also have commercial value, and be a source of income if exported. One study of an area of rain forest in Peru found that the value of the edible items that could be collected and sold was several times the value of the timber if harvested sustainably. However, problems of distribution and marketing have to be solved.

Tapping wild rubber trees is another form of economic activity

NUTTY FRUIT *A cut through the thick seed coat reveals many Brazil nuts within.*

that is important in Amazonia, and which utilises the forest without destroying it. From the 1960s onwards, the traditional rubber tappers found themselves in conflict with those clearing the forest for cattle ranching, an activity with very poor results on rain-forest soils but one which was encouraged by tax incentives. When the rubber tappers made a more concerted attempt to change government policy regarding the forests, their leader, Chico Mendes, was murdered. However, since his death, in 1988, the tax incentives for clearing forest and introducing cattle ranching have been abolished in Brazil.

TREE TAPPING *Latex oozes from the slanting cuts made across a wild rubber tree.*

FARMING THE FORESTS *An area of Malaysian rain forest has been cleared for an oil-palm plantation (above), while part of Amazonia blazes in the annual 'burning season' when huge tracts of rain forest are destroyed (left).*

patch of forest. Keeping on the move is essential because the fertility of the soil declines quickly, and weeds become increasingly troublesome.

The forest heals over the clearing with remarkable speed, as long as the felled area is small. Because the forest looms all around such a small plot, the soil is to some extent protected from erosion, and the trees can quickly repopulate it with seeds. A tangled jungle springs up very soon after the plot is abandoned, and in time this can develop into mature forest.

At the outset, shifting cultivators harvest anything useful from a plot before it is cleared; then they fell some of the trees and hack out the undergrowth. Finally, once the dead vegetation has dried out a little, they set fire to the plot. This creates a layer of ash containing mineral nutrients from the trees, such as potassium and phosphorus. The ash enriches the thin soil, at least temporarily. The larger fallen tree trunks are often left in place; this helps to reduce soil erosion.

Shifting cultivators need a large area of forest in which to operate, because they cannot return to the same area too frequently. However, they can coexist indefinitely with the forest and its wildlife, given enough space. Indeed, theirs is almost the only form of agriculture that is viable on the least fertile rain-forest soils. As well as growing crops, shifting cultivators collect some wild foods, and most rely on hunting to supply them with meat.

THE HUMAN INVASION

Some forest soils are sufficiently fertile to allow more settled agriculture, as in parts of West Africa. Where this is true, significant areas of forest were permanently cleared centuries ago, and larger settlements have developed. Indeed, any areas of the world that still have huge tracts of uncleared forest – as in much of Amazonia, the Guyanas, Central Africa, Borneo and New Guinea – can be assumed to have relatively infertile, unproductive soil, on which long-term settled agriculture has always proved impossible. Thus attempts to move landless farmers into the forest are doomed to failure.

Attempts of this kind have been made in Indonesia, where overcrowding of the inhabited islands, notably Java and Bali, is a serious problem leading to the degradation of the environment on those islands. A long-standing 'transmigration programme', which began in a small way almost a century ago, was stepped up in the early 1980s: some 6 million people have been moved from their native islands to new settlements on Sumatra, Irian Jaya (the western part of New Guinea), Kalimantan and other less populated islands. The forest has been destroyed for these settlements, but the soil is often too poor to support the people, and they have frequently exchanged difficult living conditions for even worse ones. The migrants, forest, wildlife and indigenous people of the forests are all suffering as a result.

In Brazil, people have been moved into the forest for slightly different reasons – not

BARREN SOIL *As population pressure increases, cleared land is being overworked, giving the rain forests little chance to regenerate.*

so much in their case because of overcrowding, but because there is widespread rural poverty due to unequal distribution of land. Landless people have been encouraged by the government to move into the Amazon Basin. At one point, the formerly uninhabited region of Rondônia, on Brazil's western border with Bolivia, had 5000 people moving in every month and suffered one of the highest rates of deforestation in Amazonia. Again, the land is poor, and yields are low.

The migrants may attempt to practise shifting agriculture, along the lines of traditional forest farmers, but they often lack the skills and knowledge necessary, and clear the forest much more extensively, creating open

tracts of land on which the trees cannot later regenerate so easily. With such a large number of people trying to scrape a living from an area of forest, the cleared plots are not allowed enough time to recover their fertility before being cleared once again.

Where migrants move into areas that already have indigenous shifting cultivators, the traditional inhabitants find themselves confined to smaller areas. This forces them

REARING THE WORLD'S LARGEST BUTTERFLY

Hidden in small areas of rain forest towards the south-eastern corner of Papua New Guinea is the world's largest and perhaps most spectacular butterfly: the Queen Alexandra's birdwing (*Ornithoptera alexandrae*). Males have beautiful iridescent turquoise-green wings with dark markings and a yellow body. The females are far less colourful, but they attain the greatest dimensions: the largest female on record had a wingspan of just over 11 in (28 cm) – the size of a small bird.

Queen Alexandra's birdwing butterfly is not only the largest and heaviest butterfly in the world, but also one of the rarest. Its populations have suffered in the past from overzealous collectors, to whom each butterfly could ultimately be worth more than its weight in gold. Since

these butterflies fly quickly and spend their time high above the ground, usually between 50 and 100 ft (15 and 30 m), they are very hard to catch, and were originally brought down with sprays of dust or water from a shotgun. Today the butterfly is a protected species, and any collector must have a special licence.

Farming of the birdwings is now encouraged, and is a highly successful enterprise, supplying collectors without depleting wild stocks, while ensuring an income for local people. Villagers in Papua New Guinea plant small gardens of the plants that the birdwing butterflies prefer, and then rear some eggs in captivity, producing fresh, undamaged butterflies that command high prices. The villagers have been taught to release some of the butterflies they

rear, so that wild stocks are maintained. This scheme is a way of protecting both the butterflies and the forest, by making them of greater economic value.

QUEEN ALEXANDRA'S BIRDWING *The high value placed on this exquisite butterfly by collectors has helped to conserve rain forests in Papua New Guinea.*

NO HIDING PLACE *The future looks bleak for the Müller's gibbon as more and more of its habitat in the rain forests of South-east Asia is destroyed.*

than the amount that has been recommended as sustainable, in purely forestry terms, by the International Tropical Timber Organisation. It is even more out of step with the rates that would provide adequate living space for the forest animals and native people.

In October 1994 a new policy was brought in 'to ensure a sufficient supply of logs'. This opened up over 15 000 sq miles (40 000 km²) of 'tribal lands' to loggers, abolishing the rights of traditional forest-dwellers to use these forests for hunting, gathering or shifting cultivation, rights that had been officially recognised since the 1950s.

'We are now like fish in the pool of a drying-out riverbed,' observes Mutang Tuo, a hunter-gatherer of the Sarawak forests. 'If the logging does not stop immediately, we Penans will not survive. We suffer from hunger because, with our forests, the companies are also destroying our sago-palms, wild fruit trees and plantains. And they cause a depletion of our fish and game and all that we need in our daily lives.'

Logging is the main cause of rain-forest destruction throughout South-east Asia. The tragedy is that the forests are being destroyed for short-term profits, with no thought to the future. 'Tree-mining' is an apt description of the activity. In Thailand, all the worthwhile forests have been logged out in the past two decades, and the country is now forced to import timber. Soil erosion and the pollution of rivers with silt have left many villages with no source of clean drinking water.

As forests disappear in South-east Asia, loggers are beginning to turn their sights to Central Africa and Amazonia as a new source of supply. Currently, while highly valuable

to return to the same forest plots and clear them more often. They too suffer lowered soil fertility and poorer yields. A system of forest agriculture that has worked well for thousands of years is breaking down under pressure of human numbers.

CUT AND RUN

Shortly after dawn in the forests of Sarawak, the calls of the Müller's gibbon begin. The female produces a poignant song of rising notes, a cascade of sounds that ends in a rich bubbling finale. Her mate, meanwhile, issues long hoots at intervals, a haunting sound that echoes through the forests. Together they inform other gibbons anywhere in the vicinity that this is their territory, that they are a pair who have mated for life, and that they will welcome no intrusions by others of their kind.

As the gibbons end their calling and begin searching for food, another sound is heard. It is the distant drone of chainsaws, gnawing into 300-year-old dipterocarp trees. A few miles away, an area of forest is being felled. The loggers are supposedly practising selective felling, in which only the most

valuable timber trees are removed, and the forest is left to regenerate. But as the mighty dipterocarps fall, they bring other trees down with them. And as the giant hauling machinery moves in to remove the logs, it demolishes large numbers of smaller trees, and fatally damages others. For every timber tree felled, at least another five are killed. In the worst circumstances, another 25 trees may be destroyed. The soil is churned up by the machinery and the way opened for erosion by the deluge of tropical rain that will soon follow.

The drone continues, interspersed occasionally by the crashing of a felled tree. The gibbons shy away from the noise, and go deeper into the unfelled reaches of the forest. But this forest is shrinking every day, and while the gibbons are not aware of it yet, the loggers are moving steadily in from every direction. One day there will be nowhere left to escape to.

More than two-thirds of all tropical hardwoods sold worldwide come from Sarawak, one of the states of Malaysia and part of the island of Borneo. The current production rate is estimated to be 70 per cent more woods such as mahogany are logged in Amazonia – often illicitly, on tribal lands – there is not yet the wholesale plunder seen in parts of South-east Asia.

ANOTHER APPROACH

Environmental experts believe that logging could be done in a more careful and responsible way, with less damage to the forests, and with respect for the indigenous people, preserving much of the forest for the next generation. One project that shows the feasibility of such an approach is now being tried out in Papua New Guinea. The project depends on mobile sawmills, known as 'wokabout somil' in Pidgin English, which are sold to local communities of forest people, so that they can fell individual trees and process the timber themselves, without the involvement of large commercial logging companies.

The timber can be prepared in the forest and exported along rivers or existing dirt tracks. It is a central element of the project that no new roads are made into the forests, 'because they bring destruction in their wake'. The conservation organisation running this project ensures that villagers know how to harvest timber sustainably, by not taking too much timber from one area of forest, and how to avoid soil erosion by not felling near waterways or on steep slopes.

The potential benefits to the villagers are enormous, and about 600 portable sawmills have so far been sold in Papua New Guinea. This project has inspired similar attempts at sustainable forestry elsewhere in the South Pacific, including Fiji, Vanuatu and the Solomon Islands.

Tropical hardwoods are valued for their durability. To survive in the hot and humid conditions of the rain forests, tree trunks must be well protected from insects and fungi. The wood of rain-forest trees is richly laced with active substances that deter pests and make the timber resistant to the elements. Teak, for example, can be made into garden furniture that survives rain and sun.

Yet much of the timber now being felled is not used for these special purposes. A great deal is made into plywood, and sold to customers in the West who have no idea that they are purchasing tropical hardwoods. On Japanese building sites, plywood made from tropical hardwoods is used for moulding poured concrete. Each piece is used just once, and then thrown away, a sad fate for a tree that took hundreds of years to grow and which once provided a home for hornbills, gibbons, fruit pigeons and thousands of smaller animals in its ample branches. Sapele and meranti, both from South-east Asia, are widely used for doors and windows when woods such as pine will

last equally well since they are all nowadays treated with preservatives.

The reason that tropical hardwoods are used so widely is simply that they are cheap – and they are cheap because the forests are being 'mined'. No new trees are being planted, and there is no long-term care of the trees as there is in the forests of northern Europe and America. Otherwise it would not make economic sense to import plywood to Europe from Malaysia, when plywood can equally well be manufactured from Scandinavian birch trees.

THE LUNGS OF THE WORLD

The destruction of the tropical rain forests affects us all, not just the inhabitants of the forests. For the forests are still so huge that they alter the very climate of the planet. A great deal of the rain that falls over the forest evaporates soon afterwards, forms clouds and falls again, an oscillating layer of steamy vapour that sits over the tropics like a moist blanket, protecting them from the full force of the sun. As more and more of the forest vanishes, the tropics are expected to grow hotter and the desert areas to spread. No doubt, there will be effects on climate beyond the tropics, for all the different regions of the world are linked by the flow of wind and water about the globe. Exactly what the worldwide effects might be are difficult to predict accurately.

The warming of the tropics may be accelerated by the increasing levels of carbon dioxide in the air – the well publicised 'greenhouse effect', whereby carbon dioxide, released by the burning of coal, oil, petrol and gas, traps heat from the sun and makes the planet hotter. Destruction of the rain forests could augment the greenhouse effect, because the burning of rain forests also releases huge amounts of carbon dioxide into the air, liberating carbon atoms that were once locked up in the wood and leaves of massive trees. Although, during

WASTED WOOD *Tropical hardwoods are processed into plywood in a Brazilian logging yard. The cheap plywood will then be sold abroad.*

KEYSTONE SPECIES — KEEPING THE FOREST ALIVE

A strangler fig in fruit attracts animals in noisy hordes – gibbons, monkeys, parrots, pigeons, hornbills and many other fruit-loving birds, as well as thousands of insects. Strangler figs are often fruiting when few other trees or bushes offer much to eat, and this makes them especially valuable. They keep the fruit-eaters going in what might otherwise be lean times.

This makes strangler figs a crucial

part of the rain forest, species without which many others could not survive. If the figs go, then so do many fruit-eaters, and their demise may affect other species of tree and shrub which depend on these animals for seed-dispersal. With the disappearance of other plant species, further animals may become extinct, if they have specific needs that are fulfilled only by those plants. The knock-on effects could be considerable, given the complex interdependence of rain-forest life.

Strangler figs, and other crucial plants and animals, are known as 'keystone species'. One of the problems with any form of timber extraction, however carefully managed, is that it may take out keystone species, and so unravel the fabric of rain-forest life. In South-east Asia, for example, the strangler figs most often grow on large dipterocarp trees – the very trees that yield most timber. Even selective logging may have devastating effects on wildlife, unless such interactions are understood by the logging companies, and allowance made for them when extracting timber. More understanding of forest life is essential in ensuring that rain forests survive, not as 'ghost forests', devoid of most of their original animal life, but as real living forests.

STRANGLER FIG *When fruiting, this strangler fig provides a rich feast for many creatures.*

the regrowth of jungle vegetation, some of this carbon dioxide is reabsorbed, the compensation is only partial because the new vegetation lacks the great height and mass of the original forest.

Changes in the Earth's climate are nothing new. For most of its history, Earth has been warmer than it is now. It has also experienced at least seven major 'ice ages', when global temperatures fell dramatically, and up to 40 per cent of the Earth's surface became a wintry wasteland.

Within any one ice age, the climate was not uniformly cold. There were some warmer periods, known as interglacials, when the ice covering the polar regions retreated, interspersed with colder glacials when the area of ice expanded. These changes have occurred – and will continue to occur – on a cyclical basis, influenced by changes in Earth's orbit around the Sun. There have been at least 20 glacial periods in the last 2.5 million years, the last ending about 10000 years ago.

Although the tropics did not freeze in the last glacial, their climate and vegetation were substantially altered. Regions that are now tropical rain forest received far less rain, and became fragmented rain-forest pockets in a wider expanse of savannah. Parts of what is now the Amazon rain forest were verging on desert. When the climate changed again, the rain forests recolonised the land around their scattered refuges, and regained much of their former area.

DISAPPEARING FORESTS *These Kayapo Indians of Amazonia, like many other rain-forest peoples, face the destruction of their whole way of life (right). Every day vast tracts of the world's rain forest are being wiped out (below).*

If rain forests have recovered from a vast reduction in area before, it is tempting to believe that they can do it again, this time not from devastation wrought by climatic

changes, but by human beings. However, the time taken to recover from these prehistoric calamities was measured in millions of years, not in human lifespans. More importantly, the current speed of destruction is far more rapid than anything the Earth has known before. Natural climatic changes took many thousands of years to come about, giving the plants and animals time in which to adapt to changing conditions, time to evolve ways of living outside the forest and so survive until the forest returned. Life is adaptable, but it needs time to adapt.

Environmental experts believe that the present pace of destruction allows no time; that we are pushing the rain-forest animals and plants to the brink of extinction. They stress that it is up to us to provide the tropical rain forest with a breathing space, a chance to recuperate, in order that the richness of rain-forest life may continue for generations to come.

THE ETERNAL CYCLE OF FOREST LIFE

From pollinators and seed-dispersers, to predators and parasites, the rain forests are rich with the interwoven life cycles of plants and animals. Death and decay are closely followed by birth and growth making sure little goes to waste.

Battle commences. Assessing its giant opponent, the tiny crab rears up and plunges its sharp-tipped claws through the creature's tough outer integument or casing, like a miniature knight lancing the hide of a dragon. The creature thrashes its long segmented body and lunges at the crab with venomous jaws. The crab, smaller and more agile, dodges the writhing beast, and continues its attack, driven by an instinct that overrides natural caution. With gripping pincers, the crab lacerates and punctures its enemy, until, mortally wounded, the giant centipede crawls away.

Exhausted, the little crab returns to its sentry duty, alert for further threats. The crab is a female, and her ruthless aggression is fuelled by the overriding urge to protect her young. The immature crabs nestle in a pool of clear water, surrounded on all sides by towering walls of green. But their nursery is not a seaweed-lined rock pool, nor is it even close to the sea shore. For the ancestors of this remarkable crab (*Metopaulias depressus*) abandoned the sea long ago, having found a unique niche – far from the salt and tides of the ocean, and about 65 ft (20 m) above the ground. The crab's home is a reservoir of rainwater enclosed by the smooth curve of a bromeliad's leaves, high in the canopy of the rain forest of Jamaica.

Such an unconventional habitat presents many novel challenges, including a range of predators that would never be encountered by crabs living in the sea. In this case, the bromeliad crab's opponent is a carnivorous tropical centipede, with a poisonous bite and a body some eight times as long as the crab's shell.

LOCKED IN COMBAT *High in the branches of a Jamaican rain forest, a bromeliad crab is outsized but far from vanquished by a poisonous centipede.*

DAY AND NIGHT IN THE RAIN FOREST

With the spinning of the Earth on its axis, the cycle of night and day is imposed upon the other cycles of tropical rain-forest life. Because most of the rain forests are close to the Equator, night and day are of approximately equal length throughout the year. While darkness signals a time to sleep and rest for many animals, for others it is an opportunity to become active and search for food. As dusk falls, drab moths replace colourful nectar-seeking butterflies. Birds find a roost for the night and bats take over in the night sky. Insect and bird-

pollinated flowers close or fall to the ground, while those pollinated by bats or moths unfurl their petals. Even mosquito species change shifts: the malarial *Anopheles* mosquitoes bite only by night, whereas other species are active in daylight hours.

The great majority of rain-forest mammals, such as mice, antelope and tapirs, are nocturnal, or active in the twilight hours around dawn and dusk. Monkeys seem to be the exception. While nearly three-quarters of the lemurs, lorises and tarsiers are nocturnal, there is only one kind of nocturnal monkey: the owl monkey

(*Aotus*) of Central and South America, also called the night monkey or douroucoulis. Monkeys foraging by day have a good view of food, mates, potential predators and competitors. Weighed against this, they also run a greater risk of being spotted by predators, and of suffering heat stress in the midday sun. For the owl monkey with its large eyes and excellent night vision, there are certain advantages to a night-time existence. It is better concealed from predators, has fewer direct monkey or bird competitors, and can track down insects and small mammals that are hidden by day. It may also benefit from a greatly improved sense of smell in the cool, moist night air.

As the day shift takes over from the night shift, predators have learned to take advantage of the rush-hour traffic. Outside the entrances to the caves of Sarawak bat-hawks await the rush of flying

SMELLS IN THE DARK *At night the flowers of the New World calabash tree give off a cheesy odour, a smell that bats love.*

IN THE SAFETY OF THE NIGHT
As the sun sets over a rain forest in the Americas, an owl monkey awakes to begin its nocturnal search for food.

prey at dawn and dusk. Bats flooding out of the caves in the evening may fall prey to the bat-hawk, and so may birds returning to roost. Smaller, non-flying creatures use the trunks of trees as highways to and from the canopy. Predators such as scorpions, tree frogs, geckos and spiders stand in wait for the morning and evening commuters.

Although the centipede would not attempt to eat a healthy adult crab, it has a taste for the young ones, which represent an easy meal, a sitting target. Spiders also come to take their chances with the baby crabs, but they too risk being crushed between the mother's powerful pincers. Even hungry lizards are deterred by the mother's aggressive displays, backing off and choosing to find food elsewhere.

In order to guard her young effectively, the female bromeliad crab keeps them all in one place, something that would be much more difficult in the ocean environment, where crab larvae usually drift on the currents and have to fend for themselves.

She selects a pool at the base of one of the larger bromeliad leaves. To make the tiny pond more suitable for her infants, the crab meticulously removes all floating and sunken debris, dragging away leaves, twigs and bark – if left, their gradual decomposition over the following days and weeks would use up some of the precious oxygen in the water. The only litter to be tolerated, indeed actively accumulated, is a little heap of empty snail shells. Their chalky content – calcium carbonate – neutralises the slight acidity in the water, improves the water quality for the larvae, and provides extra calcium which they need to strengthen their own armour casing.

Any prior residents that might pose a threat to the young are also hauled out and disposed of. Predatory damselfly nymphs, which live under water, breathing through gills at the tip of their abdomen, are a particular threat. They are fierce predators, grasping prey with a flick of their powerful hook-like jaws.

FAMILY LIFE

For the previous ten or twelve weeks, the female crab has been carrying a clutch of fertilised eggs around with her, attached to the underside of her abdomen. As she nears the completion of the bromeliad-pool nursery, some of the eggs begin to hatch, and the tiny swimming larvae are released into their new home. Crab larvae pass through a series of moults as they grow, changing in form until they resemble perfect miniatures of their parent. In the bromeliad crab, development to the adult form is complete in just ten days, but the young adults are still extremely vulnerable at this stage.

Food is scarce in the diminutive pond, and they are unable to forage for themselves. Their mother hunts for millipedes and snails in the surrounding area of the plant, and delivers a constant supply of prey to speed the growth of her brood. She tends and defends them for eight weeks until they reach a size when they are no longer at such risk from predation or dehydration. By investing time and energy in parental care, the mother crab ensures the survival of her own genes, which are carried by the soft, defenceless bodies of her young.

Even when the young crabs are capable of fending for themselves, they seem reluctant to leave their home bromeliad. As their mother goes on to raise her next brood, young from the previous breeding season remain close to her. One bromeliad plant may contain two or three broods of siblings: there may be anything between 10 and 60 young crabs of varying sizes in a single plant. With the exception of the bees, wasps and termites, it is very unusual for invertebrate animals (those without backbones) to live together in family groups. No other crab has yet been found to do so.

Living in family groups is not the only trait that makes the bromeliad crab unique. None of its sea-dwelling cousins prepare a nest for their young, nor provide them with food. Like the bromeliad crab, most female sea crabs carry their fertilised eggs on the underside of their abdomen until they hatch, but almost all of them abandon their larvae to the ocean currents immediately afterwards. One or two species may continue to carry their brood for a short while, but the young are soon left to disperse and forage for themselves.

If other crabs can safely abandon their offspring to their fate, why then has the bromeliad crab evolved to be such a dedicated mother? There is little doubt that its

unique behaviour is in some way connected to its unusual habitat. In many ways, the bromeliad pool is actually a harsher habitat than the sea, changing rapidly in temperature, and lacking the prolific floating plankton on which marine-crab larvae depend. Nor can the bromeliad pool hold many young, so that the normal reproductive strategy of crabs – to lay eggs prolifically and trust that some survive – is unworkable here.

The combined threats of physical hardship, starvation and predation have shaped the behaviour of the crab over evolutionary time. In effect, the adoption of a rain-forest habitat has forced the crab down evolutionary avenues which its marine relatives have never needed to explore, opening up new possibilities and widening its range of behaviour. The result is a crab which cares for its young and lives socially with its kin – behaviour more usually associated with birds or mammals than crustaceans.

Biologically, it seems that almost anything is possible in the rain forest. Here, in perhaps the richest environment on the planet, natural selection has produced a range of survival strategies so elegant and novel that they often defy the imagination. The lives of

rain-forest animals and plants have become linked in a biological web of enormous intricacy, each in some way dependent on another for the continuation of its genes.

POLLINATION PARTNERSHIPS

One of the most extraordinary rain-forest relationships involves the figs (*Ficus* species) and their tiny insect pollinators, the fig wasps (family Agaonidae). Figs are among the most successful and diverse plant families in the tropics, varying hugely in form, with some species growing into tall trees, others remaining as shrubs, others twining their way through the forest as vines, and a few living as epiphytes, perched on the branches of the canopy. Figs are common in all major rain-forest regions, but are most abundant in South-east Asia. Worldwide, there are more than 900 recognised species, and, remarkably, each seems to have its own corresponding species of pollinating wasp.

HIDDEN BOUQUETS *Each young fig hides a cluster of flowers. Once pollinated, the fruits ripen, providing abundant food for passing animals.*

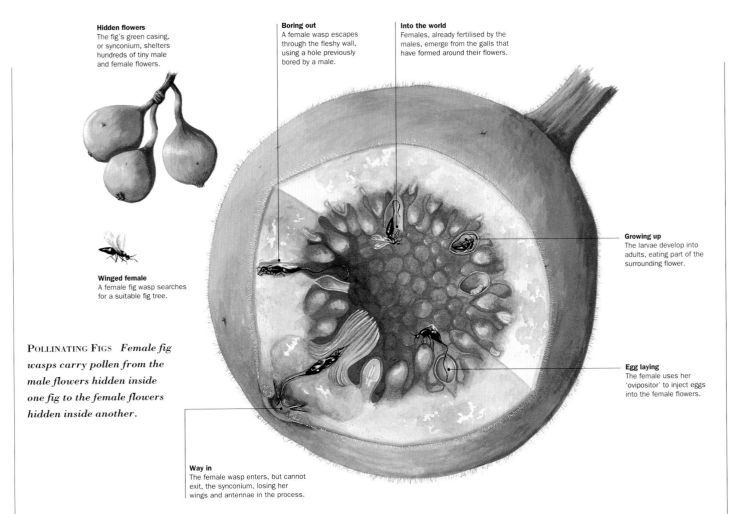

Hidden flowers
The fig's green casing, or synconium, shelters hundreds of tiny male and female flowers.

Boring out
A female wasp escapes through the fleshy wall, using a hole previously bored by a male.

Into the world
Females, already fertilised by the males, emerge from the galls that have formed around their flowers.

Winged female
A female fig wasp searches for a suitable fig tree.

Growing up
The larvae develop into adults, eating part of the surrounding flower.

POLLINATING FIGS *Female fig wasps carry pollen from the male flowers hidden inside one fig to the female flowers hidden inside another.*

Egg laying
The female uses her 'ovipositor' to inject eggs into the female flowers.

Way in
The female wasp enters, but cannot exit, the synconium, losing her wings and antennae in the process.

Instead of displaying their flowers in advertisement, as many other tropical plants do, figs hide them inside what looks like a rather uninviting green gourd. It is actually the casing of an unripe fig, known as a 'synconium'. Hundreds of brown flowers are clustered inside this protective casing, carpeting its inner walls. Female flowers and male flowers nestle alongside one another. Since they are enclosed from the outside world, it might well be assumed that insects play no role in pollinations, and that the male flowers pollinate the female flowers in private, shunning assistance from outside. In practice, this kind of 'inbreeding' is genetically undesirable for the fig, and is rendered impossible because male flowers mature after the female ones. To breed successfully, the figs rely upon the tiny fig wasps.

A female wasp, born inside a fig, and carrying pollen from her birth place, flies off in search of a place to lay her eggs. She is lured to another fig tree by wafts of a specific chemical attractant that is only released by trees when their fig flowers are at exactly the right stage of development. Finding a fig, the wasp forces entry into the synconium through a tiny entrance concealed by scales. It is a suicidal act, a one-way ticket. As she battles her way into the fig, a female's wings are torn from her body, and her antennae are irreparably damaged. Fungal spores, bacteria and dirt that might contaminate the fig are probably also stripped away. The vital pollen, however, is tucked into special pockets in her abdomen, and so survives the ordeal. Sometimes several females manage to force their way into the same fig. Occasionally a latecomer becomes wedged in the tiny entrance hole and dies there.

Once she is inside the fig, a female wasp is barred from leaving by backward-pointing projections around the entrance hole. Wounded and exhausted, she clambers across the walls of the synconium, seeking female flowers to serve as nurseries for her young. Probing the flowers with her needle-like ovipositor, she attempts to insert eggs right into their ovaries. Some of the flowers have shallow ovaries, ideal sites for egg-laying, while others have ovaries that are too deep to reach. The latter are abandoned in favour of more accessible flowers.

As she goes, the wasp uses her front legs to remove pollen from the special abdominal pouches and to brush it across the stigmas, simultaneously fertilising flowers in which eggs have been laid and those in which there are no eggs. It is a remarkably methodical process, in marked contrast to the haphazard delivery performed by most insect pollinators, which seem quite oblivious to their pollen load.

By delivering pollen to the flowers in which her valuable eggs are deposited, a female ensures that seeds start to develop, on which her young can later feed. In doing so, she unwittingly pollinates those deep-ovaried flowers that contain no wasp eggs. It is these that go on to form fertile seeds, and make the wasp's incursion worth while for the fig. Any figs that are not pollinated are

THE TREES THAT TIME FORGOT

The complex living pieces of the rain-forest jigsaw do not always fit together perfectly. Evolution is a continuing process that never reaches an end point. Animals and plants are constantly evolving to keep abreast of changing conditions. Sometimes, parts of rain-forest systems may be out of balance, still 'catching up' with changes that have taken place – perhaps many generations ago.

Examples can be found among the fruiting trees of Central American forests. Many trees here produce an excess of large-seeded fruits which fall to the ground and rot. For the tree, this seems a wasteful process. Why does this happen? The clue comes from African forests, where similar fruits are picked up from the forest floor and eaten by animals such as elephants.

In the Corcovado Reserve of Costa Rica, for example, the stinking toe or Guapinol tree, *Hymanaea courbaril*, produces oval fruits, about 5 in (12.5 cm) long, with a hard reddish-brown outer casing when ripe. Inside,

the seeds are surrounded by a sweet floury pulp. Some are broken open by agoutis, which tend to destroy rather than disperse the seeds, but others just lie and rot.

Scientists believe that when fruits such as these evolved, their seeds must have been dispersed by some now-extinct large herbivores. Fossil evidence adds weight to this theory. For alongside fossils of monkeys, tapirs and peccaries there are the remains of large herbivorous animals such as giant ground sloths and huge elephant-like gomphotheres. While the sloths are thought to have preferred a leafy diet, the gomphotheres probably ate large fruits and dispersed their seeds. Roughly 10 000 years ago, many of these large Central American herbivores became extinct. The effect would have been equivalent to

WASTED BY THE WAYSIDE *The seeded fruits of the cannonball tree collect and rot beneath its branches – examples of fruit that evolution left behind.*

removing the elephants, rhinoceroses and bush pigs from the African forests of today.

What remains are tree species which evolved through interactions with the gomphotheres and their predecessors, but have not yet had

enough time to adapt to their absence. Calculations show that trees with life spans of 100-500 years are unlikely to have passed through sufficient generations since the time of the extinctions to evolve new reproductive strategies.

'aborted' by the tree, falling to the ground, hard and immature.

After injecting her eggs into the flowers, a female wasp dies, entombed in the very fig that is to nourish her offspring. The larvae, meanwhile, eat their way to maturity in the flower, devouring a small portion of their own crib as they grow. Flowers with wasps inside are rendered sterile by their presence, since a gall forms around the larva, and the seed is eaten as it forms. The devoured seeds – between 20 per cent and 80 per cent of the total in a single fig – are the 'price' that the fig pays for its pollination service.

Somehow, the presence of wasps in a fig delays its ripening, ensuring that the insects

SHROUDED IN MIST *In the water cycles of the tropics, the rain forests, such as this one in Borneo, play a crucial role, holding moisture like a sponge.*

are not accidentally consumed by hungry fruit-eating animals before they have a chance to hatch. Males emerge first, wingless but determined. Immediately, they set to work cutting their way into flowers inhabited by females, and mating with them through the incision, before they have a chance to emerge. If only one female entered the synconium originally, then there will be inbreeding among brother and sister wasps, but if several laid their eggs in the same fruit, there will be some outcrossing.

It is the males that enable the females to escape the confines of the figs and as one male is not strong enough to break through the fig wall, they must cooperate in this enterprise. The males collectively excavate an escape tunnel through the wall of the fruit, and then die, their mission complete. Meanwhile, females gather pollen from the male flowers, which are now mature, packing it into the special pouches on their bodies.

They fly off with it, seeking another fig tree of the same species in which to deposit the next generation of eggs, and to continue their life cycle.

Once the fig wasps have emerged, fig fruits turn from green to purple, ripening and softening. They either fall to the ground or are plucked by animals. Figs are major fruit trees in the rain forest, providing food for a wide range of fruit-eaters, some of which oblige by dispersing the fig seeds. So by ensuring the continuity of their own genes, the fig wasps also inadvertently ensure the continuation of the fig and the fruit-eaters that depend upon it.

DEADLY INVADERS

Even in the apparently impenetrable fortress of the hard green unripe fig, developing fig wasps are not entirely safe. Other kinds of wasp encroach upon the fig wasp life cycle in order to carry out their own.

One parasitic wasp with an immensely long ovipositor is able to inject its own eggs into the fruit and uncannily locate the developing fig-wasp larvae within. By laying its eggs adjacent to the larvae, a parasitic wasp ensures that its own young have a source of food: the flesh of a developing fig wasp.

Some parasitic wasps look exactly like fig wasps, and gain access by the same privileged route – through the narrow scale-covered entrance. But they carry no pollen, and are of no benefit to the fig. The parasites leave the fig through the exit hole cut by the surviving male fig wasps. In fulfilling their own cycles of life, the parasitic wasps become another factor in this complex part of the rain-forest equation.

A NECESSARY EVIL

Parasites are normally detrimental to their host, taking a proportion of its food supply, debilitating or even killing it. Yet very occasionally, the intrusion of a parasite into an animal's life cycle can bring unexpected benefits. Chestnut-headed oropendola birds (*Psarocolius wagleri*), found from southern Mexico to western Equador, suffer from two kinds of parasitism. One is by an insect, which feeds directly on its host, and the other is by a bird, which behaves rather like

HANGING HIGH *The oropendolas of the Americas, such as the chestnut-headed oropendola (below), build their nests on the tips of branches (right). Although out of reach of most predators, the nestlings are still at risk to birds such as toucans.*

a cuckoo, laying its egg in the oropendola nest and diverting the foster parents' time and energy from their own chicks. While the insect parasite has no benefits whatsoever, the parasitic bird can, under some circumstances, be something of a bonus.

In appearance, oropendola birds are rather like small crows, only slightly more colourful. Although their bodies are mainly black, the tail feathers are yellow, and the head is chestnut, with a large and cream-coloured beak. Males are much larger than females, and there are fewer of them. At the nesting colonies, females outnumber males

by five to one, and males mate promiscuously with many females in the group.

Nests are crafted by the females alone. By weaving together fine grasses and other leaves, the females create long pouches of soft basketware which cradle the young in a swaying vertical sling. There are often 30 or 40 nests in any one tree, and sometimes as many as 100. The nests dangle like drab Christmas stockings from the branches, making the trees look, from a distance, as though they are laden with large, elongated fruits. Each nest has a small opening at the top. Being strategically located at the tips of

branches, the nests are out of the reach of many predators. The eggs and chicks are still vulnerable to flying creatures such as toucans and bats, or agile tree-climbers like opossums and snakes. But by far the worst enemy comes in a much smaller and more insidious guise. It is the tiny parasitic botfly.

Adult botflies (*Philornis* species) lay their eggs on the skin of an oropendola nestling. When the grubs hatch, they feed on the flesh beneath the skin. Individually, botflies do not kill chicks and one or two botfly grubs will merely irritate a nestling and slow its development. But more than ten of them together will almost certainly be fatal.

Unable to catch or deter all the thousands of botflies that gather near their nesting site, oropendola birds have found other ways to minimise botfly attacks. Trees that are home to colonies of stinging wasps or stingless, biting bees called trigonids, are usually free of botflies and the oropendolas make their nests there. Bees and wasps are fearsome defenders of their nests, turning on any insect that might pose a threat to the colony. Botflies do not threaten bees and wasps in any way, but nonetheless they are treated as enemies by the ferocious swarms. It is possible that botflies have a similar chemical smell or wingbeat to insects

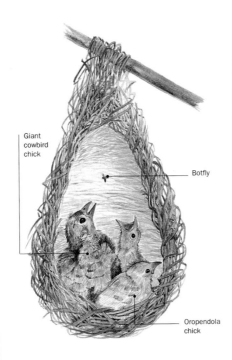

Giant cowbird chick

Botfly

Oropendola chick

TROPICAL LONDON

Forty-five million years ago tropical conditions extended much farther north of the Equator than they do today. Fossil evidence suggests that tropical rain-forest plants grew in parts of North America, Greenland and Europe. There was tropical rain forest covering London, and mangrove swamps around parts of the British coast. Tropical animals including lizards, tapirs and flying lemurs lived on Ellesmere Island in the Canadian Arctic.

that do parasitise bee and wasp nests, which inspires this animosity.

Oropendola birds are not fully immune to attacks from bees and wasps, but they are better able to tolerate their stings and bites than many other birds. After a period of

adjustment, the bees bother the oropendolas less. Biologists believe that the bees become accustomed to the birds' scent and come to accept them as just another part of the surroundings.

Not all nesting oropendola colonies are accompanied by resident bees or wasps: swarms are unpredictable, and often move on to another site. Those birds that are unprotected from botflies have one last line of defence – and a very unusual and circuitous one at that. By accepting the eggs of a cuckoo-like brood parasite, known as the giant cowbird (*Scaphidura oryzivora*), the parent birds effectively make the best of a bad situation. Although the larger parasitic chick will consume much of the food destined for the oropendola nestlings, denying them a good start in life, the cowbird chick also improves the survival chances of the brood by combatting the botflies.

VIGILANTE CHICK

The larger cowbird chick grows faster and is stronger than its adopted siblings. It is better able to defend itself against botflies, and extends its services to the oropendola chicks, greedily snapping up the grubs as they hatch, and even picking them from beneath the skin of the other chicks. In doing so it reduces their death rate by 90 per cent, a massive benefit to the oropendolas.

CUCKOO-STYLE CHICK *A giant cowbird chick (on the left) nestles in with oropendolas. The cowbird actually helps its smaller nest-mates by gobbling up botflies.*

Research has shown that, in oropendola colonies without bees and wasps, cowbirds are quite blatant about their brood parasitism. The oropendola foster parents make no effort to stop them, or to remove the egg. However, in colonies where bees or wasps are present, oropendolas are unwilling to accept the giant cowbirds' intrusions. Cowbirds parasitising these nests are much more careful, slipping in unnoticed. If their chick is detected as a fraud, it is ejected by the oropendolas, who have the protection they need from the bees or wasps.

This complex web linking the life cycles of cowbirds, oropendolas, botflies, bees and wasps is just one of the many-stranded interactions taking place in the rain forest. Countless animal and plant life cycles are woven into an intricate tapestry of codependency. Like the relationships between figs and fig wasps, these are the result of many generations of evolutionary trial and error.

WATER WHEELS

Cycles are an integral part of life at all scales in the rain forest. Perhaps the most evident is the cycling of water which falls first as raindrops, seeping though foliage and soil, only to ascend again as ethereal mists when the tropical sun warms the forest. Water evaporates from every damp surface, steaming off wet vegetation, rising from the surface of bromeliad pools, and escaping through the pores of leaves. Plants must draw water into their roots from the surrounding soil to replace the enormous quantities being evaporated through the leaves above.

Nearly 50 per cent of the rain falling over the Amazon Basin is returned to the atmosphere via the forest plants. As it ascends, the evaporated water cools and condenses into larger droplets, forming clouds, and eventually falling once again as rain. In the Amazon region, clouds are blown from east to west across the vast expanse of trees,

DRIPPING LEAVES *A waxy surface (far left) and pointed 'drip tips' (left) are two ways to make sure that excess water does not build up and damage rain-forest leaves.*

and water molecules that originated in the Atlantic Ocean are cycled slowly across the entire basin.

Not all rainwater evaporates from the site where it lands. Some is destined to sink deep into the ground below the reach of the plant roots, or to meander towards the sea in a maze of river tributaries. During the year's wettest months in the Amazon, rivers swell and burst their banks, inundating areas of forest for months at a time, then draining away again, leaving tree trunks clad with slimy algal growths and freshwater sponges. The distinction between river water and ground water is blurred, and both become part of a much slower water cycle that operates over months, years or centuries.

Water, of course, is not the only substance in constant flux. There is the endless cycle of birth and death, of growth and decay. Indeed, every single atom within an animal or plant is ultimately involved in a much larger cycle of its own. As plants unfurl, grow and shed their leaves, and as animals eat, grow, breathe and moult, chemical elements are cycled between their bodies and the surroundings.

When, eventually, plants and animals die and decompose, the essential chemical

nutrients making up their bodies are recycled. They are inadvertently returned to the environment from whence they came thanks to the activities of various fungi and

bacteria, all of which are intent on their own growth and reproduction. In the rain forest, the processes of decay are speeded up because of the warm, moist conditions.

CONSTANTLY FLOWING *With at least 4in (10cm) of rain falling each month, there is little chance of rain-forest rivers and streams running dry.*

After seven months in a Cameroon rain forest, nothing remains of an elephant carcass apart from its teeth, and small fragments of its skull. After two years, the bones are gone and even the teeth have almost decayed to nothing. Such remarkably efficient recycling means that rain forests are poor areas for the formation of fossils, because animal remains usually decompose long before they can be buried by sediment and so turned to stone.

THE ELEMENT OF LIFE

Carbon is the main chemical element in all living things, the common 'building block': molecules made from chains of linked carbon atoms are used in the construction of every cell in every animal and plant. Carbon occurs naturally in mineral form as graphite and diamond. It is present in the chalky casings of coral reefs, in seashells and limestone rock, and in coal and oil deposits. It is also found in small amounts in the atmosphere, as a colourless gas. This gas, called carbon dioxide, forms just a trace (0.03 per cent) of the air around us, where it is far outweighed by oxygen and nitrogen.

Despite the fact that there is so little carbon dioxide in the air, all the carbon atoms now present in living plants must have once passed through this gas phase, for it is only as a gas that carbon can enter plants and thus become part of the rain-forest world. It does so by a chance encounter with the leaf of a plant.

CAPTURING CARBON

Like most plant leaves, that of the cerillo tree (*Casearia corymbosa*), growing in the Central American rain forest, is riddled with pores on its underside. These pores are gateways, and a carbon dioxide molecule passes through one of them to drift inside, wafted by weak air currents along a series of channels and passageways, passing between loosely packed plant cells. The surfaces of these cells are damp, and the carbon dioxide molecule adheres to one, dissolving in the water on its surface. From there it is tugged through a membrane, and onward, through fluid and past sus-

pended chambers and compartments until it is absorbed by a chloroplast, a thick disc-shaped object, full of delicate membranes, piled on top of one another and packed with green pigment.

As a ray of tropical sunlight filters down through the canopy, it hits the leaf, striking the green pigments in the chloroplast, and triggering a whole series of reactions. Energy from the sunlight splits water into its constituent atoms of hydrogen and oxygen. The carbon dioxide molecule is whisked up, joined with energy-enriched hydrogen and other molecular fragments until, eventually, its carbon atom is linked to five others in a chain. It has now become part of a sugar molecule, an energy-rich food source.

The cerillo tree can use this sugar molecule in a number of ways. It may be broken down to release energy for immediate use, or diverted for the production of vital fats and proteins, or linked up with other sugars to make cellulose for strengthening cell walls. Confined inside its sugar molecule, a carbon atom might also be destined to help to sweeten a swelling fruit, or to fuel new growth at an extending root tip or a developing leaf bud.

This particular sugar molecule slides unhindered through the sap of the leaf veins and then travels through the tree's internal piping to a developing seed at the very tip of the branch. There, the sugar is split apart and recombined with other parts to make a protein, which is stored in the seed's kernel.

ENTERING THE FOOD CHAIN

The sweet red fleshy fruit surrounding the cerillo seed splits open when ripe. A parrot arrives to eat the fruit but it drops the seed, which falls to the ground among thousands of others. Before it has a chance to germinate and make use of its protein store, the seed is discovered by a weevil, which bores through the seed coat, and munches at the nutritious kernel within. The protein containing the carbon atom is consumed.

Inside the weevil's digestive tract, the protein is broken into tiny fragments. Having passed through the wall of the gut, these fragments are reassembled, and the carbon molecule becomes incorporated into a new protein in the body of the weevil. Three days later, the weevil is devoured by a small green *Anolis* lizard, that sits at the base of a shrub, scanning the leaf litter for the movements of

CARBON CYCLE *Darting among the rain-forest leaves, the weevil-eating* Anolis *lizard plays a small but vital part in the recycling of carbon.*

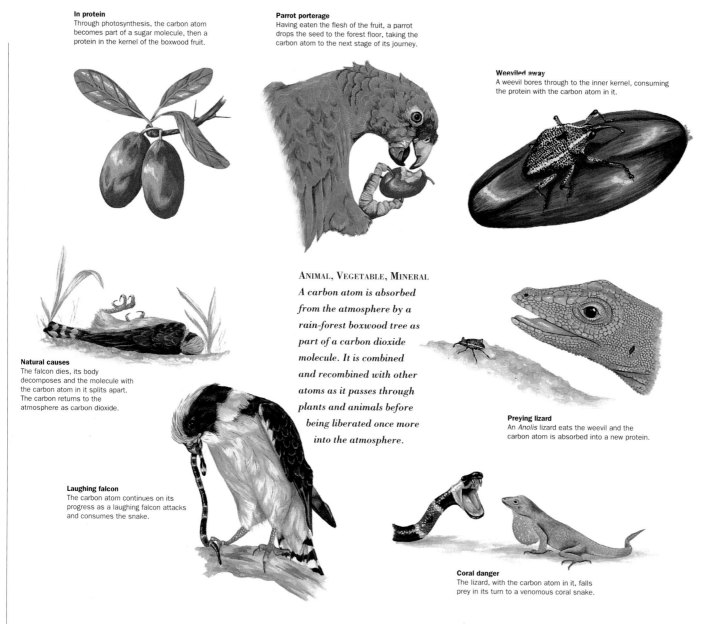

In protein
Through photosynthesis, the carbon atom becomes part of a sugar molecule, then a protein in the kernel of the boxwood fruit.

Parrot porterage
Having eaten the flesh of the fruit, a parrot drops the seed to the forest floor, taking the carbon atom to the next stage of its journey.

Weeviled away
A weevil bores through to the inner kernel, consuming the protein with the carbon atom in it.

ANIMAL, VEGETABLE, MINERAL
A carbon atom is absorbed from the atmosphere by a rain-forest boxwood tree as part of a carbon dioxide molecule. It is combined and recombined with other atoms as it passes through plants and animals before being liberated once more into the atmosphere.

Natural causes
The falcon dies, its body decomposes and the molecule with the carbon atom in it splits apart. The carbon returns to the atmosphere as carbon dioxide.

Laughing falcon
The carbon atom continues on its progress as a laughing falcon attacks and consumes the snake.

Preying lizard
An *Anolis* lizard eats the weevil and the carbon atom is absorbed into a new protein.

Coral danger
The lizard, with the carbon atom in it, falls prey in its turn to a venomous coral snake.

crickets, cockroaches and other small arthropods. Before long, the lizard, in its turn, falls prey to a coral snake (*Micrurus* species). Coral snakes, banded with yellow, red and black markings, are extremely venomous. They grasp their prey between their teeth and inject venom into their victims through hollow fangs. The lizard stands no chance of escape, and is swallowed head first.

Months later, as the coral snake basks in a forest clearing, it is spotted by a laughing falcon (*Herpetotheres cachinnans*) from its tree-top perch. The snake's vivid colours warn off most predators but the laughing falcon is not deterred by even the most venomous snakes. It drops silently onto the serpent,

biting off the head in a deft and instantaneous kill, and devours it piece by piece.

The carbon atom, which passed from the atmosphere into a plant, and thence from a seed, to a weevil, a lizard and a snake, finally enters the falcon, one of the top rain-forest predators. When the falcon dies next season, its carcass falls to the ground and starts to rot. As the bird decomposes, fungi and bacteria consume the soft parts of its body and break down the molecules.

They split apart the molecule in which the carbon atom sits, breaking the bonds that tie it to its neighbours, and releasing the energy that originally came from the sun. Nutrients are liberated, back to the soil,

LIVING FORESTS *Tangled vegetation hints at the amazing complexities of rain-forest life.*

where new life will spring from death. The atom of carbon returns to the atmosphere as carbon dioxide, bound tightly to two new oxygen atoms.

The carbon dioxide molecule floats slowly about, carried by an air current towards the canopy. For weeks it is part of the atmosphere, floating, falling, rising. Until one day it happens to drift into the pore of a leaf again. A new cycle has begun, in which the same carbon atom once more becomes part of the vibrant life of the rain forest.

PICTURE CREDITS

T = top; B = bottom; C = centre;
L = left; R = right

3 Michael & Patricia Fogden. 6 Tom Stack & Associates/Kevin Schafer & Martha Hill, BL; Survival Anglia/Dieter & Mary Plage, BR. 7 Luiz Claudio Marigo. 8 Tom Stack & Associates/Inga Spence. 9 Michael & Patricia Fogden, TC; Gerry Ellis Nature Photography, BL; Natural Science Photos/Carol Farneti Foster, CR. 10 OSF/Richard Packwood. 11 The Wildlife Collection/Martin Harvey. 12-13 Tom Stack & Associates/Chip & Jill Isenhart. 14 Ardea London Ltd/François Gohier, BL; Gerry Ellis Nature Photography, TR. 15 Zefa Pictures/Minden/Frans Lanting, TL; OSF/Kjell Sandved, BR. 16 Gerald Cubitt. 17 OSF/G.I. Bernard. 18 Luiz Claudio Marigo, TR; NHPA/Martin Wendler, BL. 19 Siena Artworks Limited, London. 20 Premaphotos Wildlife/K.G. Preston-Mafham, TR; Gerald Cubitt, BL. 21 Gerald Cubitt. 22 NHPA/Haroldo Palo Jr, BR; Planet Earth Pictures/John Lythgoe, BL. 23 Michael & Patricia Fogden, TR; DRK Photo/Stephen J. Krasemann, BR. 24 Michael & Patricia Fogden. 25 Bruce Coleman Ltd/Marie Read, TR; Bruce Coleman Ltd/Carol Hughes, TC; Still Pictures/Bios/Alain Compost, BL. 26 Jacana/Jean-Paul Hervy, TL; Gerald Cubitt, BR. 27 NHPA/Peter Johnson. 28-29 South American Pictures/ Marion Morrison. 30 Planet Earth Pictures/Brian Kenney, B; Luiz Claudio Marigo, TR. 31 DRK Photo/Michael Fogden, TR; Premaphotos Wildlife/K.G. Preston-Mafham, BR. 32 Michael & Patricia Fogden. 33 Gerald Cubitt, TR; Siena Artworks Limited, London, BR. 34-35 Siena Artworks Limited, London. 36 Jacana/Ferrero & Labat. 37 Planet Earth Pictures/André Bărtschi, TL; Luiz Claudio Marigo, CR; Gerald Cubitt, BC. 38 Planet Earth Pictures/Carol Farneti Foster. 39 OSF/G.I. Bernard, TL; DRK Photo/Larry Ulrich, TR. 40 Gerald Cubitt, TL; OSF/Breck P. Kent, TC; NHPA/Stephen Dalton, BR. 41 Luiz Claudio Marigo, BC; Gerald Cubitt, TR; Jacana/Varin & Visage, TL. 42 Planet Earth Pictures/André Bărtschi, BL; Planet Earth Pictures/John Lythgoe, BR. 43 South American Pictures/Tony Morrison, TL; Luiz Claudio Marigo, BR. 44 Michael & Patricia Fogden, TL; Still Pictures/Alan Watson, BL; Biofotos/Brian Rogers, CR. 45 Luiz Claudio Marigo, TC; DRK Photo/Stephen J. Krasemann, TR; Ardea London Ltd/Jean-Paul Ferrero, BL. 46 NHPA/Roger Tidman, BL; Gerald Cubitt, BR. 47 Michael & Patricia Fogden, TL; NHPA/Dr Ivan Polunin,

TC; Bruce Coleman Ltd/Alain Compost, BR. 48 Planet Earth Pictures/André Bărtschi. 49 NHPA/G.I. Bernard, TL, TR; Ardea London Ltd/J.S. Dunning, BR. 50 Premaphotos Wildlife/K.G. Preston-Mafham. 51 Luiz Claudio Marigo, TL; NHPA/Haroldo Palo Jr, BR. 52 Still Pictures/Bios/Genevieve Renson, BL; Bruce Coleman Ltd/Dr John Mackinnon, TR. 53 Luiz Claudio Marigo, TC; Survival Anglia/Dr F. Köster, BR. 54 Michael & Patricia Fogden. 55 Premaphotos Wildlife/K.G. Preston-Mafham, TR, BL. 56 Luiz Claudio Marigo. 57 Premaphotos Wildlife/K.G. Preston-Mafham. 58 Bruce Coleman Ltd/Olivier Langrand, BL; Bruce Coleman Ltd/Peter Ward, TR. 59 Survival Anglia/Nick Gordon. 60 Ardea London Ltd/Hans & Judy Beste, TR; Michael & Patricia Fogden, BC. 61 Premaphotos Wildlife/K.G. Preston-Mafham, BL, TR. 62-63 Planet Earth Pictures/André Bărtschi. 63 Bruce Coleman Ltd/Michael Fogden, BR. 64 Planet Earth Pictures/David Tipling, BL; Bruce Coleman Ltd/John Cancalosi, T. 65 Luiz Claudio Marigo, BR; Gerald Cubitt, TL. 66 NHPA/G.I. Bernard, BL; NHPA/James Carmichael Jr, BR. 67 Siena Artworks Limited, London. 68 South American Pictures/Tony Morrison. 69 Planet Earth Pictures/Richard Coomber, TR; Siena Artworks Limited, London, CR. 70 NHPA/George Gainsburgh. 71 NHPA/James Carmichael Jr, BL; Siena Artworks Limited, London, TR. 72 OSF/Photo Researchers/Ulrike Welsch, BL; DRK Photo/Michael Fogden, TR. 73 Siena Artworks Limited, London. 74 Bruce Coleman Ltd/Luiz Claudio Marigo, TC; Ardea London Ltd/Andrea Florence, BR. 75 OSF/Photo Researchers/Tom McHugh. 76 Ardea London Ltd/Andrea Florence, TL; Doug Wechsler, BR. 77 Planet Earth Pictures/André Bărtschi. 78 OSF/Photo Researchers/Gilbert S. Grant. 79 Ardea London Ltd/P. Morris, BL; Premaphotos Wildlife/K.G. Preston-Mafham, TR; OSF/Photo Researchers/Gregory G. Dimijian, TR. 80 Siena Artworks Limited, London. 81 DRK Photo/Michael Fogden. 82 NHPA/Stephen Dalton, TL; Gerry Ellis Nature Photography, BR. 83 Michael & Patricia Fogden, TR; Siena Artworks Limited, London, BL. 84 Planet Earth Pictures/Norbert Wu, TL; Michael & Patricia Fogden, TC; Luiz Claudio Marigo, BR. 85 Luiz Claudio Marigo. 86 Still Pictures/Bios/Klein & Hubert. 87 Siena Artworks Limited, London. 88 Siena Artworks Limited, London. 89 Biofotos/C. Andrew Henley, TR; Bruce Coleman Ltd/Alain Compost, BL. 90 Still

Pictures/Bios/J. J. Alcalay, BR; NHPA/A.N.T./C. & S. Pollitt, TR. 91 Bruce Coleman Ltd/C.B. & D.W. Frith, TR; OSF/Lloyd Nielsen, CR. 92 Ardea London Ltd/Hans & Judy Beste, TL; Siena Artworks Limited, London, BR. 93 Bruce Coleman Ltd/Alain Compost, TL; OSF/Hans Reinhard, BR. 94 Siena Artworks Limited, London. 95 Bruce Coleman Ltd/Dr John Mackinnon, BL; Bruce Coleman Ltd/C.B. & D.W. Frith, TR. 96 Ardea London Ltd/Hans & Judy Beste, C; Siena Artworks Limited, London, BR. 97 Bruce Coleman Ltd/Fritz Prenzel. 98-99 OSF/Kathie Atkinson. 99 Gerald Cubitt, TR. 100 OSF/P. & W. Ward. 101 Auscape International/Jean-Paul Ferrero. 102 Siena Artworks Limited, London. 103 Siena Artworks Limited, London. 104 Zefa Pictures/Minden/Mark Moffett. 105 Gerald Cubitt. 106 OSF/Richard Davies, BL; Siena Artworks Limited, London, TR. 107 Still Pictures/Bios/Alain Compost. 108 NHPA/Karl Switak, BC; Bruce Coleman Ltd/Erwin & Peggy Bauer, TL. 109 Bruce Coleman Ltd/Rod Williams. 110 Still Pictures/WWF/R. Kennedy. 111 OSF/Konrad Wothe, BL; Still Pictures/WWF/Martin Harvey, TC. 112 Bruce Coleman Ltd/Gunther Ziesler, TL. 112-113 Auscape International/Jean-Paul Ferrero. 114 Ardea London Ltd/Jean-Paul Ferrero, CR; Planet Earth Pictures/Philip Chapman, BR; Gerald Cubitt, BL. 115 Gerald Cubitt, TL; Still Pictures/ WWF/David Hulse, CR; Bruce Coleman Ltd/Erwin & Peggy Bauer, BL. 116 Gerry Ellis Nature Photography. 117 FLPA/J. Zimmermann. 118 Siena Artworks Limited, London. 119 Siena Artworks Limited, London, TR; FLPA/F. Hartmann, BL. 120-121 DRK Photo/Peter Veit. 122 Siena Artworks Limited, London, TL; NHPA/Gerard Lacz, BR. 123 Siena Artworks Limited, London. 124 The Wildlife Collection/John Giustina. 125 Gerry Ellis Nature Photography. 126 Dr Simon K. Bearder. 127 Dr E. Rogers, ICAPB, The University of Edinburgh. 128 Natural Science Photos/C. Dani & I. Jeske. 129 The Wildlife Collection/Ken Dietcher, TR, TC, BL; Siena Artworks Limited, London, BR. 130 Ardea London Ltd/D. Parer & E. Parer-Cook. 131 Bruce Coleman Ltd/Olivier Langrand, BL; Premaphotos Wildlife/K.G. Preston-Mafham, TR. 132 Siena Artworks Limited, London, TC; Bruce Coleman Ltd/Konrad Wothe, TR; Natural Science Photos/C. Dani & I. Jeske, BR. 133 Gerry Ellis Nature Photography, BR; Still Pictures/Mark Edwards, TL. 134 The Wildlife Collection/Martin Harvey. 135 OSF/Rob Cousins, TL; Bruce Coleman Ltd/Luiz Claudio

Marigo, BR. 136 Still Pictures/Edward Parker, BL; Planet Earth Pictures/André Bărtschi, CR. 137 Gerald Cubitt. 138 Still Pictures/Andre Maslennikov, T; The Environmental Picture Library/Herbert Girardet, TC. 139 Planet Earth Pictures/Richard Matthews, TR; Worldwide Butterflies/Robert Goodden, BR. 140 The Wildlife Collection/Tim Laman. 141 Still Pictures/George Monbiot. 142 Gerald Cubitt. 143 The Environmental Picture Library/Herbert Girardet, TC; Bruce Coleman Ltd/Alain Compost, B. 144 Dr Rudolf Diesel, University of Bielefeld. 145 Premaphotos Wildlife/K.G. Preston-Mafham, CL; Tom Stack & Associates/Gary Milburn, TR. 146 Bruce Coleman Ltd/Gerald Cubitt. 147 Siena Artworks Limited, London. 148 The Wildlife Collection/Martin Harvey. 149 Planet Earth Pictures/Andrew Mounter. 150 OSF/Photo Researchers/Tom McHugh, BL; The Wildlife Collection/Jack Swenson, BR. 151 Siena Artworks Limited, London. 152 Gerry Ellis Nature Photography, TL; Premaphotos Wildlife/K.G. Preston-Mafham, TC; Bruce Coleman Ltd/Michael Freeman, BR. 153 Still Pictures/Bios/Michel Gunther. 154 Siena Artworks Limited, London. 155 OSF/Photo Researchers/Karl Weidmann.

FRONT COVER: OSF/G.I. Bernard; Tom Stack & Associates/Roy Toft, C.

77-004-3